BLUE
YONDER

BLUE

KENTUCKY: THE UNITED STATE OF BASKETBALL

Lonnie Wheeler

YONDER

ORANGE FRAZER PRESS

Wilmington, Ohio

ISBN: 1-882203-20-8
Copyright 1998 by Orange Frazer Press

Orange Frazer Press, Inc.
Box 214, 37h West Main Street
Wilmington, Ohio 45177

Library of Congress Cataloging-in-Publication Data
Wheeler, Lonnie.
  Blue Yonder : Kentucky, the united state of basketball/Lonnie Wheeler.
    p.   cm.
  Includes index
  ISBN 1-882203-20-8
    1. University of Kentucky--Basketball--History.   I. Title.
  GV885.43.U53W54   1998
  769.323'63'0976947.-DC21   98-11539
                                                     CIP

Printed in Canada

Cover: Drew Cronenwett, Al Hidalgo, and Dan Mueller, Graphica

*To Abby, Clark, and Emily, because the last time
I dedicated one to them, it got switched into another book
and mine ended up being to somebody named Hilary.*

Acknowledgements This book benefited terrifically from the kindness and cooperation of numerous individuals, most of them connected by their appreciation of Kentucky basketball. The author would like to offer public thanks for the contributions of Dave Baker, Donna Cassady, John Clay, Ralph Hacker, Bryon Jordan, Diane Massie, David Norris, Wayne Onkst, Bill Partin, Jon Scott, Jerry Tipton, Bob Zink; Dr. Charles Hay, curator of the Eastern Kentucky University archives; Jeffrey Suchanek of the University of Kentucky's Special Collections archive, whose oral history tapes were of immeasurable value; Brooks Downing and the staff at the University of Kentucky's Sports Information Department; Derek Anderson, Bill Keightley, Shelby Linville, Kyle Macy, Bill Mike Runyon, Jason and Charity Ryan, George Williams; George Grider and the wonderful gentlemen of The Coffee Club; the gracious souls of Cat Chat; Ron Garrison and Mike Johnson of the *Lexington Herald-Leader*, whose vivid photographs tell a story of their own; Bob, Beth, and J.R. VanHoose for their considerable indulgence; Chris Dodd for her professionalism; Dr. Jeffrey Burch and H.B. Elkins for the use of their expertise; Clark Wheeler for his companionship; Martie Wheeler for her sacrifice; David Black for his loyalty; and Marcy Hawley and John Baskin for their substantial faith.

Contents

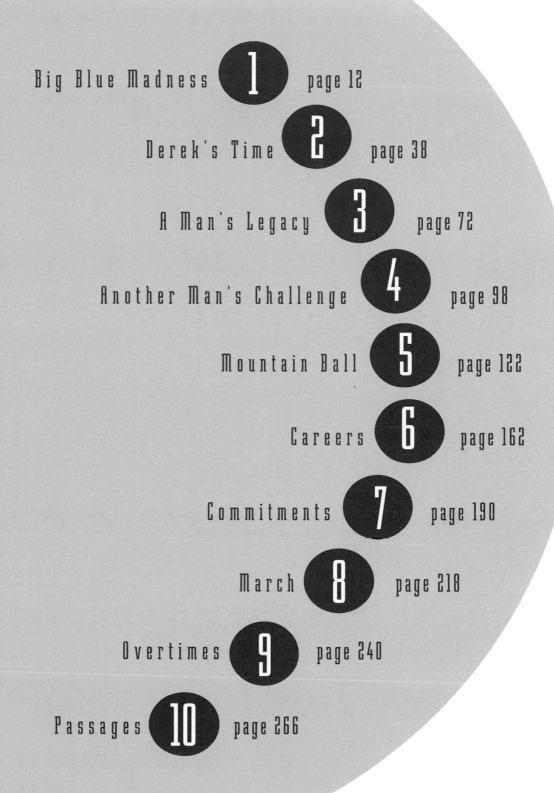

Big Blue Madness **1** page 12

Derek's Time **2** page 38

A Man's Legacy **3** page 72

Another Man's Challenge **4** page 98

Mountain Ball **5** page 122

Careers **6** page 162

Commitments **7** page 190

March **8** page 218

Overtimes **9** page 240

Passages **10** page 266

Blue Yonder

Cuba (1) Howie Crittenden, Doodles Floyd, and the 1952 Kentucky high school state champion **Brewers** (2) Coach McCoy Tarry's undefeated 1948 state champion **Earlington** (3) State champion 1967 **Madisonville** (4) Home of UK All-American and Basketball Hall of Famer Frank Ramsey **Owensboro** (5) Home of folk hero Rex Chapman. Home of UK All-American and Basketball Hall of Famer Cliff Hagan **Bowling Green** (6) Western Kentucky University Hilltoppers and legendary coach "Uncle Ed" Diddle **Hardinsburg** (7) Home of University of Louisville All-American Butch Beard **Brownsville** (8) Edmonson County High School, 1976 state champion **Louisville** (9) University of Louisville Cardinals. Eastern High School, 1997 state champion. Home of UK All-American Ralph Beard. Home of U of L All-American and Basketball Hall of Famer Wes Unseld. Home of UK star Derek Anderson **Edmonton** (10) Home of UK recruit J.P. Blevins **Campbellsville** (11) Home of Western Kentucky University All-American Clem Haskins **Midway** (12) State champion 1937 **Lexington** (13) University of Kentucky Wildcats, six-time NCAA champions and winningest team in college basketball, and Coach Adolph Rupp, recently eclipsed as winningest coach in collegiate history. Home of UK All-American Jack Givens. Home of UK walk-on Cameron Mills. Site of Memorial Coliseum, Rupp Arena, and 1997 Sweet Sixteen **Cynthiana** (14) Harrison County High School. Home of former UK coach Joe B. Hall **London** (15) Hazel Green High School, 1940 state champion **Manchester** (16) Home of folk hero Richie Farmer and Clay County High School, 1987 state champion **Harlan** (17) Home of UK All-American "Wah Wah" Jones and 1944 state champion **Hazard** (18) Home of UK All-American Johnny Cox and 1955 state champion. State champion 1932 **Carr Creek** (19) Famous state runner-up 1928 and state champion 1956 **Wayland** (20) Home of legendary "King" Kelly Coleman **Paintsville** (21) Home of prep hero J.R. VanHoose and 1996 state champion **Pikeville** (22) Home of legendary coach John Bill Trivette. Site of Region 15 tournament **Inez** (23) State champion 1941, 1954 **Ashland** (24) State and national champion 1928. State champion 1933, 1934, 1961

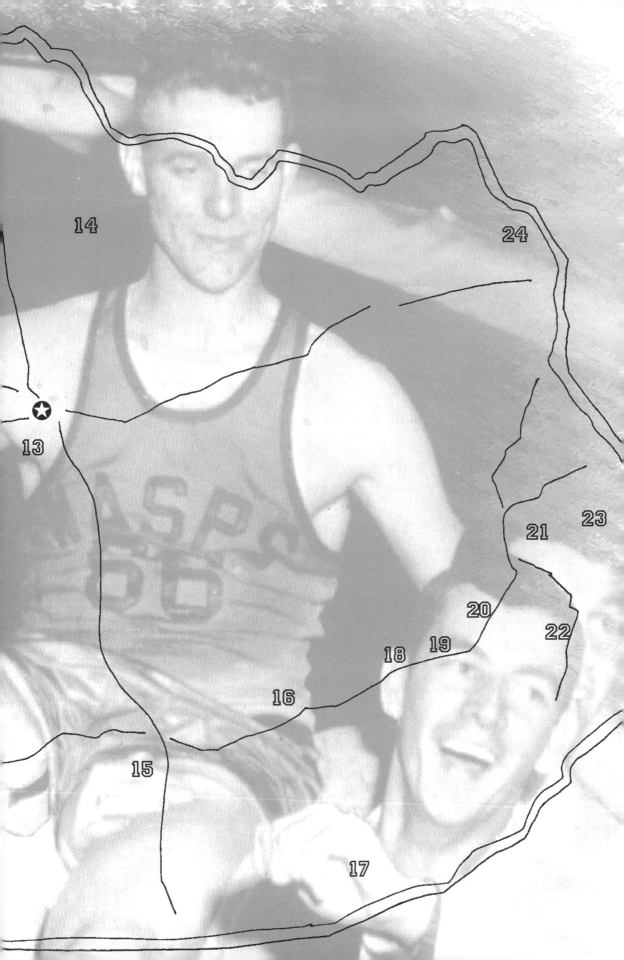

I just want to be buried in a Kentucky T-shirt.
I want them to play the UK fight song, *My Old Kentucky Home*, *The Dance* by Garth Brooks, and throw me in the holler.

—*Jason Ryan*

Introduction

In the dim morning light of April 2, 1996, less than seven hours after the University of Kentucky had defeated Syracuse for its sixth collegiate basketball championship, a man on his way to work in Franklin County, Kentucky, noticed a peculiar smattering of blue in the roadside cemetery that he passed every day. Slowing his car and pulling closer to get a better look, he made out the letters "UK" on balloons that bobbed above three graves. Somcone had tied them there in the night.

One can only wonder about the circumstances. Were the balloons placed there to allow the deceased to take part in the great moment that they had been deprived of in life? Were the night callers drawn to the graveyard because Kentucky basketball was for them a family thing foremost, its triumphs unsatisfying if not shared with the loved ones named on the headstones? Might this have been the fulfillment of deathbed requests? Or was it simply, in the local currency, the most meaningful tribute that Franklin County sons and daughters could pay their ancestors? Like most cultural phenomena, Kentucky basketball is visited by elusive whys and wherefores.

Whatever the particulars, the cemetery tableau was a dew-softened poster for those to whom Kentucky basketball has been handed down like a watch or a recipe or a certain way of stacking wood. For many of them, growing up in Kentucky involved two choices: watch the game or go outside and play. Such is the essential nature of Bluegrass basketball that it's often referred to as a religion, which speaks well for Kentucky's pastors. Blessed, indeed, is the church that is attended by as many Kentuckians as one of the coach's radio shows.

The fact is that basketball simply means more in Kentucky than it does anywhere else; that it has more to do with how the state thinks of itself. While other places take the game seriously, Kentucky takes it personally. To an almost frightening extent, basketball is the thing Kentucky chooses for its identity. The distilleries and the horse farms and the coal mines tell the tales of their own sub-states, but basketball is the collected works, the treasury within which the far-flung Kentucky profiles are collated and bound. Basketball is what the commonwealth shares. There are times—say, from mid-November to early April—when one could make the forgivable mistake of thinking that basketball is what the commonwealth *is*. Suffice to say, Kentucky is a place that grows and smokes tobacco, makes and drinks bourbon, raises and races horses, mines and breathes coal, and sleeps and eats its favorite sport. In Kentucky, they even have a name for the basketball offseason. They call it the Kentucky Derby. It lasts a little longer if the track is sloppy.

Kentucky is a place where pep rallies are carried live on television, where radio stations play game tapes in the summer, where a state legislator once moved that the flag be lowered to half mast after a twelve-year home-court winning streak was broken. It is a place that names babies for All-Americans (Kyle Macy) and streets (Richie Farmer Boulevard) for players who don't even *start*. It is a place where bad news about the Cats (i.e., the scandal that crumpled the program in the eighties, as first reported by the *Lexington Herald-Leader*) is cause for somebody to pull a gun on the paperboy. It is a place where a full-fledged, talk-show-dominating, front-page controversy breaks out when the university basketball team changes the shade of blue on its uniform. It is this: When Tony Delk, the leading scorer of the '96 championship team, announced that he would be attending UK, Kentucky fans flocked to his Tennessee high school—eighty miles from the state line—in such number that closed circuit television had to be set up in the cafeteria.

As for the trappings of obsession, Kentucky, of course, has notorious quantities of the basic stuff—weddings planned around the Cats' schedule, lifelong fans buried with pompons and autographed basketballs, blue and white caskets, inheritance battles over the season tickets, divorces complicated by two seats in the lower level, home libraries of game tapes, the Rick Pitino signature washer and dryer set . . .

Such is the renown of the Kentucky basketball fan, though, that those things have practically become clichés. Everybody has a "Kentucky room" at home. Everybody has a son named Kyle. More revealing are the subtle daily manifestations of basketball's reach. There was the 1997 afternoon, for instance, when two women of the garden-club variety were browsing at the fashionable Joseph-Beth bookstore in Lexington and the one in the furry hat spotted a new book by the legendary Kentucky announcer, Cawood Ledford. "Oh, there's Cawood's book," she said. Calling attention to the picture of a former player (Deron Feldhaus) in the cover collage, she asked her companion, "Now, who is that?" Standing nearby, I glanced at the picture and, noting the subject's dark hair and solid build, foolishly suggested that it might be Richie Farmer. "Oh," the lady replied, obviously knowing better but politely indulging my ignorance, "was that before Richie had his mustache?" I learned then and there never to presume to know more about Kentucky basketball than a Kentuckian, no matter what kind of hat she is wearing.

There was also the occasion in 1996 when an unfortunate Harlan County teenager swerved to avoid hitting a dog and encountered a utility pole instead, knocking out power for the towns of Loyall and Baxter. The cool-headed investigating officer, aware, naturally, that the UK game was about to come on television, withheld the youngster's name for fear of what some of the less accommodating citizens might do to him.

In Kentucky, the idea is to not let life interfere with basketball. That the game holds a higher office in Kentucky's value system than it does in any other state's is a fundamental fact that I accept on faith and certify after a year of close watching. This observation is not the result of empirical study, or even of thorough journalism; it is merely an irrepressible sense. If anyone in Indiana or Kansas or North Carolina prefers to hold onto the conviction that his state is the spiritual capital of basketball, I won't discourage him. I won't argue with him. This book is about provincialism, after all. So if a snapshot of Paintsville, Kentucky, comes out looking like Mulberry, North Carolina, Mulberry is more than welcome to stick it on the refrigerator. The search for the soul of Kentucky basketball is undertaken here as an adventure in Americana.

I attempted something like this once before, about ten years ago. For a book called *Bleachers*, I spent a summer in the Wrigley Field cheap seats to write an essence-of-baseball kind of thing about the culture of the Cub fan. After the book came out, I was invited to talk about it with Bryant Gumbel on the *Today* show. Not taking into account that Gumbel was a major Cub fan, I naively presumed that my literary efforts had gotten me there. The interview was going along nicely until Gumbel asked me about the partisanship that he assumed we shared. I mumbled something about actually growing up as a Cardinal fan. With that, Gumbel slammed down his papers in a display of exaggerated pique, and, perhaps wishing he were serious, declared the interview over.

So this time, I'll try to head off the misconceptions. I didn't take on this project as a Kentucky fan. I'd covered some games in Lexington and I'd picked up signals from Planet Kentucky on the Cincinnati sports talk shows, but I never developed a rooting interest in the Wildcats—if anything, the opposite. I was tired of them beating Tennessee by fifteen, Georgia by twenty, and Auburn by thirty. The only time they didn't do that, it seemed, was after they got caught cheating. I didn't empathize much.

It didn't help that my only personal brush with genuine Kentuckyness was just before Christmas in 1983, during one of Kentucky's Final Four seasons. Coach Joe B. Hall brought Sam Bowie, Melvin Turpin, and Kenny Walker to Cincinnati for a game against a very inadequate Bearcat team. Not surprisingly, Riverfront Coliseum was packed with Kentucky fans who for years had tried in vain to buy tickets at Rupp Arena. They were mightily piqued when Cincinnati's coach, Tony Yates, endeavored to make a game of it by devising a slow-down strategy that limited Kentucky's victory to 24-11, their outrage suggesting that Yates owed them the privilege of watching the Wildcats run up the score. After I wrote a column in *The Cincinnati Enquirer* to the effect that Yates's obligation was to Cincinnati's cause, not Kentucky's, piles of letters arrived with steam coming out of the flaps.

Consequently, the predispositions that I held toward Kentucky basketball were wary ones, at best. I knew, most of all, that the Big Blue community—which is to say, the state—was inclined toward concerted overreaction. Before the 1996 championship season, editors at *Street & Smith* found themselves under siege by correspondence from Kentucky fans highly offended that the magazine had picked the Wildcats *second* in its preseason poll. The most mail I ever saw at the *Enquirer* was in 1978, when the Wildcats won their fifth NCAA title and the paper's columnist, like many around the country, alluded to them as a collection of joyless brutes. Then there was the memorable *Herald-Leader* controversy, when the Lexington newspaper had the temerity to break Pulitzer Prize-winning stories about hundred-dollar handshakes and the like within the Kentucky basketball program. Although the series provoked no immediate sanctions—in retrospect, it was the harbinger of subsequent trouble that would result in Kentucky's NCAA probation three years later—it was so good that subscriptions were cancelled by the thousands. Death threats and dead flowers were delivered to the authors of the stories, a bullet ripped through the window of the newspaper office, vending boxes were shot up, and a paperboy (is this a job you would want your son to have if you lived in Lexington?) was chased off one customer's property with an ax handle. In an informal survey of forty-seven Lexingtonians, not one believed that the *Herald-Leader* series was justified. Regional sentiment was summed up by an erstwhile reader who wrote a letter to the editor and signed it "Blue Bleeder." Concluding his passionate epistle, Blue Bleeder shamed the editor for taking down Kentucky basketball and pointed out, poignantly, "It's all we got."

Therein lies the fascination that attends Kentucky basketball. It is obviously out of control in many respects. It is way too big, and too many people take it way too personally—as if their family name were on the line with every game and remark. But there is a disarming vulnerability even in their virulence. There is a depth of feeling that gets right to the human spirit.

It's that depth of feeling, that practically primal emotion, that drew me to this book. When the victory over Syracuse thumped shut the protracted ignominy of probation and sealed off eighteen tortured years—a Kentucky eternity—without a national championship, the commonwealth spread its arms, tilted back its head, and went off shouting and leaping in a sleepless festival of provincial joy. Kentucky basketball had long been a wonder of the world; at that moment, it became a story.

When I began researching this book shortly thereafter, I was fortunate to find on the Internet an engaging e-mail sports bar for Kentucky fans. Cat Chat went a long way toward relieving me of some of the baggage I'd gathered up for the journey, its amiable writers demonstrating that there are plenty of Bluegrass folks who vent their Catness in a sporting manner. Of course, there are exceptions—more, perhaps, in Kentucky than in other places where basketball is a more casual diversion. A Kentuckian here and there has been known to lose a little perspective, the sum of the aberrations constituting an image. Those who fancy themselves more sophisticated often find it fashionable to belittle the Kentucky fan—to cast him in the same kin-marryin', shine-drinkin', ball-bouncin', cable-watchin', welfare-drawin', barely-readin' stereotype that bedevils the mountain folks. There will be none of that here. The breaches of perspective to which I've been party will be passed along as an indigenous part of Kentucky's colorful basketball landscape, but to generalize on their basis would be to evaluate a racehorse as it walks away, or to judge a ballplayer by his agent.

The exercise here is not to pass judgment on Kentucky, but to try to figure the place out. Its customs are so singular and its sensitivities so acute as to make the commonwealth a cultural curiosity. Kentucky is an enigmatic corner of the country that, for its own personal, complicated, essentially uncharted reasons, puts a severe provincial spin on an internationally mainstream sport. There are no abiding explications as to why Kentucky is the way it is; there are only theories—some good, some overrated. Adolph Rupp, the legendary coach who put Kentucky basketball on the map (some would say put *Kentucky* on the map), represents a leading theory in this respect. The fact that the state has no major-league professional teams is another. Kentucky's image problem is a good one, tying into self-esteem and what basketball can do for it. The isolation of the mountain communities is an interesting thing to ponder in this context, specifically the smallness (basketball doesn't require as many players as other team sports), demographics (it's also cheaper than most), and jingoism (which fosters fierce competitiveness) that result when one part of the nation is cut off from the rest. The tradition of the UK program—it is the winningest in college basketball—obviously contributes to the culture, carrying with it a way-back, ancestral aspect. At the same time, the success and popularity of Kentucky high school basketball is a parallel dynamic that fits into the equation somehow and significantly.

High schools have much to do with the Kentucky basketball story and will consequently have much to do with the book. A couple of weeks before UK won its national championship in 1996, the Kentucky state high school championship—the famous Sweet Sixteen—was carried back to the Eastern Kentucky mountains by little Paintsville High, a monumental achievement in these fast times. The honor brought to the tucked-away town by way of basketball was not unlike that which the game bestowed upon Kentucky at large, and it was consequently evident that a portrait of one would end up looking much like the other. What's more, Paintsville's star center, J.R. VanHoose, was a celebrated underclassman whose accomplishments, reputation, and mountain background were sure to turn his recruitment—would Pitino, or wouldn't he?—into a Kentucky drama.

VanHoose's compatibility with the University of Kentucky, or lack of it, would become an especially intriguing subject in the context of The New Kentucky, the one that Pitino had successfully reinvented in the eight years since he had taken over a program whose magnificent legacy had been compromised by unyielding traditions of scandal and bigotry. While VanHoose was laboring to renew the heritage of the hill-country heroes who preceded him, Pitino's state-of-the-art basketball was personified by UK's Derek Anderson, a senior from Louisville whose talent and charm were breaking down barriers between the big city and the Big Blue. In an earlier day, Anderson would not have found a place on Kentucky's roster; in this day, could VanHoose?

The Kentucky winter of 1996-97 seemed uncommonly plot-thickened by the see-saw fates of its VanHooses and Andersons, by the caprices of Pitino, by injuries and overachievement and emerging personalities and hard choices and a breathless finish; but then, every season is uniquely dramatic in the commonwealth, where the story lines have a way of perennially rewriting themselves. As theater, Kentucky basketball is sufficiently rousing to engage even one with skeptical predispositions.

Knowing that, one of the Cat Chat scribes left a trenchant message in my mailbox before a particularly big night in late March, making note of his anxiety and commenting on what he rightly presumed was mine. "As for yourself—my friend, you are no longer a detached journalist," wrote Frank Dudley Berry from California. "Don't worry, I won't tell. But it is as Heisenberg and even Newton say—you can't observe something closely and intensely without being affected by the observations."

Taking the point a little further, I might add that Kentucky basket-ball is something you can't observe closely and intensely without *your family* being affected. This time, if somebody asks me about being a Kentucky fan, I can retain some professional detachment and say, at least, that I was with my son when he became one.

L.W.
November, 1997

1

Big Blue Madness

Jason Ryan punched out early on the afternoon of October 15, stopped at home long enough to say good-bye to his wife and baby, drove south fifty miles to Lexington, and parked his pickup truck smack in front of Wildcat Lodge, the piney dormitory of the University of Kentucky's basketball team. Every two hours for the next four days, he plugged the meter there while somebody in front of the Memorial Coliseum ticket window held his place in the line of people dressed top to bottom in blue. This, known in Kentucky as vacation, was in the interest of Big Blue Madness, which is what they call the public scrimmage that celebrates the beginning of basketball practice at the University of Kentucky. It also describes the condition with which the colorful land that Daniel Boone pioneered has become notoriously afflicted.

Ever since Ryan started welding Ford seat frames at Dynamec, not long out of high school, he had been taking his vacation at Big Blue Madness. This year, at twenty-one, he especially needed these few days in which he could lose himself in the thing he loved so desperately, surrounded by others who felt the same way. Unfortunately, his wife didn't feel that way, which was part of the problem they had been having.

Life had been swell for Ryan the previous April, when the Wildcats sweetened the Kentucky air with their sixth NCAA championship, but the ensuing months without basketball had been difficult. Things got worse after a thief broke into the Ryans' mobile home on Hog Ridge Road, outside the Grant County community of Williamstown. The place was trashed and the baby videos were taken along with almost every-

◀ *Big Blue Madness: October, 1996*

thing else, but what *really* set Jason off was that the disrespectful crook left his UK flag lying like a gum wrapper on the ground outside. The only consolation was that the robber hadn't appreciated the value of Ryan's most prized possession: the taco in the freezer. After the Florida game the previous February, Jason had been hanging around Rupp Arena for Rick Pitino's radio show and noticed that the mega-popular Kentucky coach, who did commercials for Taco Bell, wasn't interested in the 59-cent snack that somebody handed him. Ryan piped up and said he'd take it. When he got back to Hog Ridge Road, he sealed his cheesy treasure in a Ziploc bag and stashed it in the top of the frig.

Unlike Jason, Charity Ryan had not taken much solace in the fact that her husband's precious Pitino taco had been spared in the robbery. Nor had she felt much sympathy for him when he stood there crying at the discovery that his souvenir blue-denim bottle of Maker's Mark was missing. "Jason," she said, "they just took our television, our VCR, our stereos, Haley's videotapes—everything we owned and worked hard for. And you're crying over a thirty-dollar bottle of Maker's Mark!" The fact was, his Kentucky stuff had begun to symbolize their marital trouble.

The couple's problems had started when they were just married and living in one of the bedrooms of her parents' house. Charity came home from work one evening to find that all her "girly stuff," as she called it, had been taken down and replaced with Kentucky posters and pompons and prints and pillows and shot glasses and ticket stubs. She was a Kentucky fan, too, like everybody else Jason knew; he had assumed she would love the decorations. They argued about it for two or three days.

For the next few years, Charity could never quite shake the feeling that UK came ahead of her in Jason's priorities. But it wasn't just her own feelings that she was concerned about; she was troubled that he seemed to care more about the team than about his career, and she was disturbed by his moods after Kentucky defeats. He was uncharacteristically abrupt with her on those nights and had a difficult time sleeping. After a one-point Saturday loss to UCLA in 1994, he threw his boots against the wall, rode out to his grandfather's farm, and, all alone in the field, broke tobacco sticks until midnight—work that he normally tried to avoid. The previous March, when Kentucky was eliminated from the NCAA tournament by Marquette, he sat down and cried on the floor of a Foot Action store at the mall. He even cried when one of his UK Christmas ornaments broke. Ryan joked about ending up like a postal worker. Charity suggested, only partly kidding, that he get professional help. To this, Jason just shook his head. "She just doesn't understand," he confided. "This is more than a game; it's a lifestyle. It's serious. It's what Kentucky is all about."

By the time he arrived on the UK campus for Big Blue Madness, Ryan was hungry for some single-minded Kentucky companionship. There was no better place for it. He was fourth in line for the free tickets, which would become available when the gates opened on Friday evening, October 18. In front of him were newlyweds John and Kathy Matthews, who had married purposefully on September 6 (*9-6*) in honor of the '96 season and Kentucky's sixth national championship. A year earlier at Big Blue Madness, John and Kathy had made a pact: If the Cats won the NCAA, they would go ahead and get married after the season. John got a little queasy about the idea halfway through the schedule, when he took note of the way in which Kentucky was blowing everybody away, but Kathy said a deal was a deal. The groom wore Converse basketball shoes at the wedding. The cake was a duplicate of Rupp Arena. Pitino sent a bottle of champagne. As admiring Kentuckians gathered around him in the Big Blue Madness line, John Matthews showed off his wedding ring: five sapphires, to represent the previous championships, and a diamond in the middle for the great year in which he also got married.

Jason Ryan could only envy the mutual love of Kentucky basketball that was fundamental to the Matthewses' fresh marriage. Although John Matthews had only seen one real Kentucky game in his life—a loss to Mississippi State in 1962 that even the great Cotton Nash could not prevent—he was a regular at Big Blue Madness, and Kathy had every intention of continuing the tradition together. They could only hope that in another generation, they would be like the gray-haired couple in front of them in line, Jim and Betty Ryle.

Kentucky basketball was the way in which the Ryles chose to enjoy their retirement. Free of working obligations, they had been able to stake their place in line Tuesday morning, planning for the four-day siege as if it were a camping trip to Lake Cumberland. Jim figured he might even stumble on some customers while they waited for Friday night; he had built up a little retirement business making custom UK golf clubs. One of Betty's hobbies was finding UK ornaments for their six-foot Christmas tree that was decorated with nothing but.

As meticulous as they were to arrive at Memorial Coliseum on October 15, the Ryles were thirty-five days behind the first one in line. Wally
Clark had been there since September 10, the day he parked his camper
on the Avenue of Champions, a bounce pass from the Adolph Rupp historical marker that stood watch over the Memorial Coliseum plaza. A
Vietnam veteran and former plumber, among other things, who had been
drawing disability checks since a stroke six years earlier, the chesty, dark-
haired Clark was not going to be denied the pole position, plopping his
lawn chair in front of the ticket window several weeks earlier than would
have been necessary. In all likelihood, he could have accomplished the
same effect by arriving in early October—the year before, he was first in
line showing up seventeen days ahead of time—but to Clark, the mission
in which he was engaged was too sacred to be trifled with. For five of the
previous six years, the first in line had been Robert Vallandingham and
his family, of New Albany, Indiana. "I just wanted to beat those people
from Indiana," said Clark. "I couldn't understand why we would let somebody come from out of state and be the first in line." It was Kentucky
tradition, after all, to take such a thing—to take basketball—personally.

Kentucky tradition was a given in Clark's childhood, as much a
part of the landscape as dime stores and flat tops. He grew up two blocks
from the spot where he was now spending the heart of autumn, and as a
teenager he and his brothers would bike to the Coliseum to shoot around
with Pat Riley and Louie Dampier until Rupp chased them out. His brothers came back to sell popcorn and soft drinks while the Wildcats routed
the South. His mother worked at the university switchboard. On game
days, the Clarks charged a dollar to let people park in their front yard at
Clifton and Rose; two dollars for the back. The lot was closed at tipoff so
the crew could watch the game. Clark's take on Kentucky tradition was
summarized in two words: Adolph Rupp. "Why do you think JFK stopped
here on his Presidential campaign?" he asked. "I think he wanted to meet
Rupp."

As the 1996-97 season neared, Clark was increasingly troubled by
the prospect that it might be the one in which the dreaded Dean Smith of
North Carolina, with a deficit of just twenty-five victories, would eclipse
Rupp as the winningest coach in college basketball history. Fearful that
Rupp's legacy would be consequently diminished, he felt that it was a

time for the Kentucky basketball community to step forward in a manner that would defend the program's honor. His part was living on the Avenue of Champions for thirty-eight days. He was equipped for the task, with rows of Kentucky mugs and hats lined up on his shelves and enough necessities to last until a cousin brought more. He brushed his teeth in the Coliseum restroom. He talked a lot on the cellular phone that AT&T gave him for the occasion. He listened to the Kentucky marching band in the evenings, and occasionally he had to fend off random wiseguys wanting to know why he didn't have a job; a few of them jumped on the roof of his camper one night and slid down onto the hood. Boredom was a more intrusive visitor. But Clark believed in what he was doing, and he didn't at all mind the celebrity that went along with it. On top of everything else, he got to watch the Cats informally practice when (due to NCAA preseason restrictions) Pitino couldn't.

Every day for five weeks, Clark had wandered into the Coliseum as the Kentucky players gathered around two o'clock for their daily scrimmages. Often, he watched alone, from the top row of the lower level, as the point guards, Anthony Epps and Wayne Turner, hounded each other and went hard to the hoop; as the freshman center, Jamaal Magloire, played a less subtle game with Nazr Mohammed, his sophomore counterpart; as Jared Prickett posted-up Oliver Simmons, a battle of long-legged redheads; as Jeff Sheppard and Derek Anderson competed at a sophisticated level of jumpers, lobs, and no-look passes; and as sophomore superstar Ron Mercer worked his considerable stuff against former sophomore superstar Rex Chapman, now a veteran pro and Pitino's neighbor in Lexington's fashionable McMeekin Place subdivision.

Clark was there, also, on the day when the players fidgeted on the sidelines as Pitino, walking briskly from his upstairs office, appeared in the corner of the concourse level above and descended imperially down the aisle, his hair black and perfect as usual, his suit dark and impeccable. On the floor, photographers busied themselves adjusting lights and backgrounds, making everything excessively right for the cover of Pitino's upcoming motivational book. Wally saw the cover before the prints were even developed. For more than a month, nothing happened on the floor of Memorial Coliseum that Clark didn't see.

His thirty-seventh day was Media Day, and when Pitino discussed his latest team with the Kentucky press, it was incumbent upon him to discuss the ubiquitous Wally Clark, as well. "We've gotten to know Wally very well here," the coach said. "He showers and shaves here, comes in in the morning with no shirt on and has his coffee. I tell people back home [in New York] that he's camping here for thirty-eight days, and they ask, 'Why thirty-eight days? Couldn't he have done it with twenty days?' I say, 'Yes.' They say, 'Then why did he do it?' I say, 'I can't answer that . . .' "

Kentucky vacation: In line thirty-eight days for Big Blue Madness, Wally Clark slept in his camper and brushed his teeth in Memorial Coliseum.

○ ○ ○

While Jason Ryan spent his vacation in line for Big Blue Madness and Wally Clark lived there for the September pennant races, the league playoffs, and nearly half the football season, Bob Wiggins passed leisurely fall days puttering around his house in Falmouth, Kentucky. His seat for Big Blue Madness was already reserved—on the end of the players' bench. He didn't always get to sit there, but he always sat *somewhere*, which is why the basketball office had given him special privileges for the gala Friday night.

The season that would be initiated October 18 promised to be a big one for Wiggins. He was braced to break the record held by his late traveling companion, Steve Rardin, for most consecutive Kentucky games attended: 626. The 1996 national championship game in the Meadowlands had been Wiggins's 614th in a row, dating back to 1977. He hadn't missed a home game since it snowed nine inches in 1961. Seventeen years earlier, when he was sixteen, he'd had his first Kentucky ticket torn at the university's old Alumni Gym, driving a 1936 Pontiac fifty miles to watch the Cats beat Illinois by eleven. Since that February night in 1944, Wiggins had been to 1,102 games altogether. He knew this because he had been collecting programs since they were ten cents. He paid half a dollar for the program at the 1958 national championship game in Louisville, when the Wildcats got the best of Elgin Baylor's Seattle team.

Wiggins had worked forty-one years as an engineer for the Kentucky Department of Transportation, and most of the vacation days he earned over that time were spent on Kentucky basketball trips. Road-game mornings, he generally had breakfast with Kentucky's legendary equipment manager, Bill Keightley, and its more legendary announcer, Cawood Ledford (until Ledford retired in 1992), and after another Kentucky victory he would often drive all night—usually with Rardin—from Oxford or Tuscaloosa or wherever, *take off his tie*, and go straight to work. Rardin, a news distributor whose white hair and goatee resembled Colonel Sanders's, also wore jackets and neckties to Kentucky games. It was as if the two gentlemen were going to church.

Since Wiggins's retirement, his wife had been wintering quite a bit in Florida while her husband cavorted around the country—mostly by air now—watching basketball. "She does her thing and lets me do mine," he said in his immaculate brick home between Lexington and Cincinnati. "She knows that I'd be lost without Kentucky basketball. If I didn't do this, I don't know what I would do." In the offseason, he watched tapes of the games Mrs. Wiggins and others had recorded for him.

According to the schedule, Wiggins would break Rardin's record in early January. This would formalize the distinction that he already held unofficially: Kentucky's number-one fan. In his self-effacing way, however, Wiggins was the first to recognize that loyalty to Kentucky basketball, like any spiritual thing, cannot be quantified. Deducing from the heart, it was the common nature of the Kentucky fan to consider himself number one in the ranks; it was just hard to imagine anyone caring more about the Cats. And in truth, if none could match Wiggins's record, there were plenty who were at least his equal in depth of passion. Many—probably most—of the fiercest, caringest UK fans in the commonwealth eluded radar completely; they had never been to a game at Rupp Arena or Memorial Coliseum before it.

The Kentucky media has made a dutiful, gallant attempt to chronicle the peculiarities of the Big Blue constituency and even attach some names to it, but for every Bob Wiggins, whose consecutive-game streak was closely monitored, there were the thousands of Kentuckians who crowded the I-75 overpasses on a cold winter night in 1975 to wave at the team bus as it returned home from Dayton after the boys beat heavily favored Indiana in the Mideast Regional. For every Steve Rardin, whose Kentucky Fried Chicken look was a favorite of every cameraman, there is a quiet Kentuckian as profoundly attached to UK basketball as the elderly cancer patient who received a pair of tickets behind the Wildcat bench and just before he died wrote back to say that his life was now complete. For every Tombstone Johnny, who gained a little fame when he drove 775 miles from Iowa to watch games in Rupp Arena, there is an anonymous Kentucky lover like the widow in Hopkinsville who left the team $42,000 when she passed on. For every Ted Arlinghaus, who built a regulation-sized replica of Rupp Arena into his Northern Kentucky home, there is a lifelong fan like the grandmother in Falmouth who had an icebox full of notebooks in which she had kept score of every UK game for forty-five years. For every Simeon Hale, who was well-known at the age of ninety-one for his 24-hour excursions between Somerset and Rupp—he walked from his country home to the bus stop, got off in Lexington and walked to the arena—there is someone like the old woman in Hazard, who, after the Cats had played a preseason exhibition in her home town, edged her way toward the student manager and said, "I'm a-wonderin', I been listenin' to Kentucky basketball all my life . . . Could I touch that there ball?" For every Wally Clark, first in line and available for photo opportunities, there is a Wayne Washburn and one of his faceless phone friends.

Washburn had actually accumulated a little local celebrity himself, although few knew his last name. A soft-spoken 23-year-old rabbit farmer, he was known to those who listened to Kentucky's pre- and postgame call-in shows as Wayne From Mooresville. Dave Baker, one of the hosts of the radio shows, asked Wayne for the rabbit report every time he called. Wayne, in return, asked for the recruiting report. As often as not, he had as much information to share as the experts; rabbits were his livelihood, but recruiting was his life. It would not be an exaggeration to say that Wayne From Mooresville spent more time on recruiting than Pitino did. He took his cell phone with him when he went behind the house to feed his several thousand New Zealand Whites.

Wayne estimated that he spent six hours a day on the phone, which was about an hour more than he spent on the rabbits. He played a little basketball in the driveway—Anthony Epps's cousin came by occasionally for a game—and shot some nasty pool on the table inside his brother's auto garage next to the house, but there was no doubt as to what his days and life revolved around. "The large-screen TV, the radio, the cell phone—those three items are the most precious things I own," he said, smiling shyly as he sat around the wide-porched Washington County house in an old white T-shirt. His brother, father, and uncle all shared the house, but the phone and the remote control remained pretty much in Wayne's hands.

Unlike most recruiting junkies, Washburn didn't rely on newsletters for his information, just friends whose faces he had never seen. It started after he called a sports show in Louisville one night and his phone number went out over the air. Two hundred people called. Many of them kept calling. Before long, Wayne's modest country home five miles from the Lincoln Homestead State Park (the land on which Abe's father was raised and Nancy Hanks also lived before they married, now featuring an eighteen-hole golf course) had become the unofficial Kentucky headquarters of the underground recruiting network. There was a fellow from Hyden, Kentucky, who called twice a day. A guy from Paducah had a phone bill of $110 one month and Wayne was the only person he called. An Indiana friend checked in every other day, and another in Tennessee kept Wayne abreast of the gossip down there. A phone pal from Bowling Green, Kentucky, knocked on Wayne's door one day just to shake his hand. One from Tell City, Indiana, had a hard time picking up the Owensboro radio station one night, so he called Wayne and asked him to hold the phone up to Pitino's "Big Blue Line" show.

The constant ringing of Washburn's cell phone was evidence that there were others like him all around Kentucky and beyond. The others might have had less or larger livestock, and their glasses might have rested on their noses a little straighter than Wayne's, but they were one with him in basketball, and they were legion. And just as Wayne From Mooresville would have been if he didn't call the talk shows, they were anonymous. Even Wayne, tucked away in a Central Kentucky settlement not even on the map, *felt* anonymous; he was so distant in the basketball background that he was amazed when a letter showed up one day from Tennessee coach Kevin O'Neill. After Mercer had chosen Kentucky over Tennessee, Wayne said something about it on the radio that peeved O'Neill, who hand-wrote his response. "He told me to mind my own business," marveled Washburn. "I just kept looking at that thing. I couldn't believe I got a letter from Kevin O'Neill. Why would he write me?"

Not surprisingly, Wayne had never traded a word with anyone on the Kentucky basketball staff, to whom he was but one of the masses often heard from but seldom seen. Although Lexington was less than an hour away, he had never been to a Kentucky game. On the other hand, he had never missed one, either. He had taped every game for the past ten years and watched most of them again. In the few months since the 1996 championship game, he had already seen it fifteen times. On several occasions, he had watched most of the famous, heartbreaking Duke game in the 1992 regional final, when Christian Laettner made the remarkable buzzer shot to beat Kentucky in overtime, but he still couldn't bring himself to let the tape run to the end.

Watching Wildcat games was a sacred birthright to Washburn and tens of thousands like him who came by their Kentuckyness involuntarily. Wayne specifically credited his uncle for the way he was. "When I was a kid and my uncle had the game on, you had to go outside to play," he said. "I'm the same way. When the game is on, there's no conversation.

"I'll probably always be this way. It's just somethin' I grew up with and somethin' I feel pretty strong about. When you follow UK, there ain't nobody better than you. There ain't nothin' like Kentucky."

○ ○ ○

When it was completed in 1950, Memorial Coliseum was a basketball showplace so awesomely huge—it occupied a city block and seated 11,500 people—that skeptics doubted it would ever be filled. Instead, it was never *not* filled when the Wildcats played. A quarter of a century later, the Coliseum was so inadequate to handle the demands of the Kentucky program that the team moved off campus into what was then the nation's largest basketball facility. Rupp Arena was built for twenty-three thousand people in a city of less than two hundred thousand. For the first season, 1976-77, a hundred thousand people applied for tickets. Every year since then, newly available tickets—people move, people die—have been placed in a fall lottery, which awards approximately five to fifteen winners a year out of up to five thousand entries.

This leaves the vast majority of Kentucky fans at home for UK games, or at the local sports bar, where they vent their frustrations at the moderate level of noise that the huge Rupp Arena crowds typically generate. The Rupp audience—the lower section, in particular—is traditionally well-heeled, populated over the years by the likes of Lexington socialite Anita Madden, various members of the John Y. Brown family, and the politi-

The house that Rupp built: The Baron laid the cornerstone for Memorial Coliseum in 1949.

cians, bankers, coal operators, and horse breeders who comprise Kentucky's economic and social elite. With no major-league professional franchises to invest in or be seen around, Kentucky's sporting class gets its public gratification once a year at the Kentucky Derby and a dozen or so times at the state university's basketball games.

The UK program is obviously important to the moneyed alumni and business folks. They were the ones who, according to the controversial 1985 *Lexington Herald-Leader* series in which more than two dozen Wildcat lettermen were interviewed (most of them later recanted their statements), slipped the hundred-dollar bills into the hands of the players in the early 1980s, gave them $500 just to visit their homes, and bought their complimentary season tickets for $1,000. They were the coal barons who lent the coaching staff their private planes and the lawyers who hung around the basketball offices. They are the ones who stand to benefit financially from the commerce that Kentucky basketball generates and the statewide image it promotes. They are the movers and shakers of the Kentucky basketball community, but they aren't and never were the people who make Kentucky basketball Kentucky basketball.

"The real Kentucky fans," said media mogul and Wildcat announcer Ralph Hacker, Cawood Ledford's play-by-play successor, "don't come to Rupp Arena. They sell their tobacco for $1.92 a pound in Cynthiana, and if they come to a game, they pay a scalper way too much for a bad seat in section 228, row T, and sit there and cheer their heads off while the people down below sit on their hands. The real fans are in nursing homes in Hopkinsville and can't even see the TV anymore, so they listen to the radio like they always did when Cawood was announcing. It's a kid in Hazard who wore number four when Kyle Macy was playing and now maybe wears twenty-three for Derek Anderson.

"The farther you go from Lexington, that's where the die-hard fans are. The NCAA won't allow you to go more than fifty miles anymore to play a preseason scrimmage, but I remember when we had one in Elkhorn City [deep in the Eastern Kentucky mountains] and they were lined up at five o'clock for an eight o'clock game. On the way we stopped in Pikeville to eat, and I guess they found out where we were stopping because there were people lined up there just to see the players eat.

"In Eastern Kentucky, they know nothing about horse racing and little if anything about making bourbon. But all of the Kentucky coaches since Adolph Rupp have told us we know basketball. It's the one thing all Kentucky people know. There's very little in the state of Kentucky of a common interest. In Western Kentucky, with all the lakes and water, boating and fishing are very important, Central Kentucky has horses, tobacco, and the bourbon industry, and Eastern Kentucky is isolated from the rest of the state. And almost nobody in the state gets along with Louisville. The only thing everybody has in common is Kentucky basketball. You can go to Pikeville, Falmouth, or Fulton, and that's the common tie. Even in Louisville, every rating shows that Kentucky far surpasses U of L. The Kentucky basketball team is this state's pride and joy. You might find somebody on food stamps or W.T. Young [Lexington philanthropist and horse breeder] or Bruce Lunsford [CEO of Louisville health care giant Vencor], and all three of them can sit down and talk about whether or not it was a smart move for Rick Pitino to bring in Nazr Mohammed, whether Eddie Sutton was a good recruiter, whether Rupp was forced out of his job, and how many points Dan Issel scored against Mississippi State. Kentucky basketball is what all the people know about, much more so than whiskey, tobacco, coal, or horses. When you think in terms of common interests, that's all we got."

The inability of the common fan to get into a Kentucky home game at a reasonable price has led to the familiar phenomenon of outrageous crowds at sites beyond Lexington. Kentucky's Southeastern Conference road games are traditionally accented by folks in blue—Tennessee was so embarrassed about its fans being outnumbered by UK's that it made the Kentucky ticket available only as part of a multi-game package—and Kentuckians in general swarm around any chance to see the Cats. For *practices* they have held before occasional games at Freedom Hall in Louisville, the Cats have drawn crowds of up to 19,000. Tickets were in such demand that they were scalped after 6,500 of them sold out for an intrasquad scrimmage at Henry County High School in New Castle, population 893. In 1996, when the Cats were so loaded that Pitino organized a junior varsity team for the walk-ons and third-stringers, a throng of 2,500 showed up on a Sunday night to watch the JV play a junior college team at a neutral site in Owensboro. The UK freshman team used to regularly sell out Memorial Coliseum. Kentucky fans just can't get enough: In Ledford's last season as an announcer, he initiated the practice of conducting Pitino's postgame radio show at courtside, hooked up to the arena's public address system, prompting so many fans to stick around that the total of them outnumbered the *game crowds* for all but fifteen of the nation's teams. A few nights after that season ended so traumatically on Laettner's shot in the NCAA quarterfinals, 13,000 people showed up at Rupp Arena *for an awards ceremony.*

When a Wildcat game is in progress, small towns across Kentucky virtually shut down; convenience stores sell out of chips and the whole state hunkers down in front of the television that has only recently replaced the radio as the game-night centerpiece. One late night when the Cats were playing on the West Coast, an airline pilot passing over Lexington radioed down to find out what sort of disaster was in progress—the lights were on in virtually every home in the city. During the radio days, basketball fans in the dips and hollows of Eastern Kentucky grew up knowing the highest and best places around to get reception; when Cawood Ledford retired, one of the five hundred letters he received was from a couple whose first date, on a winter night back in the fifties, took place on a mountaintop that the girl mistakenly thought her boyfriend had picked out for romantic purposes. Rick Suffridge, a displaced Kentuckian living at the time in South Carolina, spent many winter hours in his car trying to pick up WHAS out of Louisville. When it was time for him and his wife to move on and they placed a For Sale sign in the front yard, a concerned neighbor came over to express her concern that the move signaled an impending divorce; she had seen Suffridge sitting alone in his car all those nights and assumed the couple was having marital problems.

Jason Ryan once delayed a dinner date with Charity until after the game was over, then broke it when the Cats lost and he didn't feel like eating or talking. After that, it was understood that their basketball nights would be spent somewhere that had nachos and a big-screen TV. But they were not in the least unique in arranging their relationship around UK games or regretting when they didn't. Countless Kentucky weddings have gone off in half-empty churches, the result of basketball-insensitive planning; the guests and family members simply shake their heads and say that so-and-so should have known better. Other vows have prudently been scheduled or rescheduled to avoid Big Blue conflicts. Tommy Puckett and Julia Gaskin took this option after Kentucky surprised Indiana in the regional finals in 1975, mailing out invitation corrections that said, "UK is No. 1, Puckett and Gaskin wedding No. 2. See you at the church and tipoff too." To many Kentuckians, there is no emergency like a close game. In 1995 a policeman near Lebanon, Ohio, a middle-class community that has accommodated large numbers of job-seeking Eastern Kentucky natives, noticed a man walking around a snowy cemetery in 15-degree weather. The nearest house was about a quarter of a mile away. When the officer inquired as to what was going on, the man told him that he was looking for a three-year-old girl who had wandered off and was apparently lost. The policeman proceeded on to the house, where he found seven men clustered around a television watching a Kentucky game. Asking about the little girl, he was told, "Oh, yeah. We'll look for her in a minute when the game's over."

Such stories, while poignantly common and eagerly repeated, truthfully count for little more than Bluegrass hyperbole. But the sum of them has produced a state persona that is loathsome to prideful Kentuckians, sports fans and not, who are offended by the image that such embarrassing narrow-mindedness gives to a population already stereotyped as unwashed and inbred. The specific notion to which many take vigorous exception is that basketball has been charged with the task of single-handedly raising the commonwealth's self-esteem. "It's hard for me to understand that there are Kentuckians out there who think that UK basketball is all they have to make them feel good about themselves," said H.B. Elkins, a former journalist originally from the mountain town of Beattyville. "I suppose I have my share of UK T-shirts and sweatshirts, and I do enjoy the games. Last year, when UK was playing in the SEC tournament, as soon as I learned when the first game would be I scheduled an eye exam for that morning so I could take a sick day from work. I guess I inherited an appreciation for UK basketball from my dad, who was a fan ever since I can remember. When the games weren't on TV, we had a little brown Channel Master AM radio that my dad nicknamed 'Coach Rupp.' We'd tune in to WHAS and listen to Cawood call the games. I enjoy discussing UK basketball with other fans at work or on the Internet . . . But my life doesn't come crashing down if the Wildcats lose. I have too many other things to worry about. I get my hackles up at the mention of the stereotypes thing."

Elkins and the not-so-silent Kentucky majority to which he belongs would maintain that the average, well-adjusted Cat fan is extreme not so much in the organization of his values but in his rooting interest and the appetite for information that goes along with it. In this respect, the Kentucky fan is much like any other, the difference being that his geographical tether is made of stronger stuff. Excepting the localized, comparative few who are loyal to the winning basketball traditions of such schools as Louisville and Western Kentucky, UK is without collegiate or professional competition for the state's sporting devotion. And whether or not they are appropriate, the cultural and educational stigmas historically assigned to Kentucky have made its citizens all the more aware of where they live and what they represent. These dynamics have in turn been quickened by six NCAA basketball championships. Kentuckians weary of finding themselves near the bottom of the national rankings for test scores and socioeconomic indicators can take heart when they see the list turned upside-down for basketball.

The UK fan is consequently eager for any news along these lines. The result is that the pre- and postgame talk shows last most of the night on Lexington and Louisville radio stations, and the state newspapers—in particular the *Herald-Leader*—cover UK basketball as both a program and a lifestyle. Along with the features about fans whose last wishes have to do with going to a Kentucky game and the investigations of who sits where at UK games, front-page stories in the *Herald-Leader* have included—in addition to the much-cussed Pulitzer Prize series—a Madison County judge's ruling on the custody of UK season tickets in a divorce dispute, the pouring of the subconcrete at Rupp Arena, a new uniform style for the Kentucky cheerleaders, and a rash of articles concerning the infamous color change in 1996, when Pitino outfitted the Cats in a denim shade that resembled, gasp, *North Carolina*. (The denim, however, was not so repulsive that it prevented Maker's Mark from selling 250,000 bourbon bottles labeled with it, exceeding the sales goal by 230,000. Noting that the bottles would never be opened, a company official commented that the distillery would have made a lot more money if it had filled them with tea.)

The demand for Big Blue information has been so intense for so long that in 1977 Oscar Combs, publisher of a small paper in the Eastern Kentucky town of Hazard, began to produce *The Cats' Pause*, the first and longest-lasting year-round publication devoted exclusively to the athletics of one university. Twenty years later, Combs was able to sell *The*

Cats' Pause and retire in style to Florida. His paper had become a slice of home to native Kentuckians whose family and occupational considerations had taken them out of the range of daily UK dialogue. Combs managed to cash in at about the time faraway fans were finding that they could stay in touch with Kentucky basketball through a modern variety of media, including cable television, recruiting publications, newsletters, and the numerous venues of the Internet. Some of the best information, though, still emanated from Kentucky.

"Press coverage of basketball in Kentucky is much higher in quality and much less superficial than it is elsewhere," said Dr. Jeffrey Burch, who, having lived in several states, had made a science of gathering information on the Cats from afar. "I've found the people at the *Herald-Leader* and *The Cats' Pause* much more knowledgeable about basketball than writers in much larger metro areas like Chicago or New York." A Kentucky grad and tournament chess player whose job at the Georgia Tech Research Institute consisted of developing computer aircraft and missile models, Burch, through his own enterprise and modern technology, had accommodated his craving for Big Blue information by joining the ranks of Kentucky basketball writers, electronically delivering a studious, comprehensive UK newsletter to subscribers on the Internet. (In fact, many of Burch's cravings were tied to basketball. During the championship season of 1978, he celebrated every Kentucky victory with a banana split, the result being that two decades later he was still reminded of Kyle Macy every time he buckled his belt.) Burch researched his newsletter with the meticulous skill of a scholar, knowing that it went out to a tough audience; many of his customers were acquaintances he had made through Cat Chat, one of several Big Blue discussion groups on the Internet.

To a large extent, the subscribers to Cat Chat were self-described information junkies like Rick Suffridge, a still-happily married recruiting aficionado whose move from South Carolina took him to North Carolina, where his partisanship remained unswayed by the powerful counterforces all around him; H.B. Elkins, whose strong feelings about Kentucky stereotypes reflected a conservative, regional activism; Jeff Crume, who, at a Nashville junior high school in the seventies, exchanged five-page Kentucky notes with the only other UK fan he knew there; Diane Massie, a niece of former UK football coach Jerry Claiborne and frequent traveler who, when unable to find a sports bar with the proper satellite feed for UK games, had been known to sit in her hotel room and watch the scores roll across the bottom of CNN Headline News; Deen Ipaye, a native West African (the Lagos State team on which he played in a Nigerian national sports festival was ahead 72-0 at halftime of the championship game when the other coach conceded) who came to Kentucky because he wanted to see what Lincoln's birthplace looked like and whose love for the basketball team was preceded by his love for the place; Frank Dudley Berry, a deputy district attorney in California who hadn't lived in Kentucky since he was four years old and thanked the Cats for keeping his heritage alive; Gary Powers, whose computer booted to the sound of former Kentucky governor Happy Chandler singing *My Old Kentucky Home*; and Daniel (Capt. Dan) Armstrong, a military weather officer stationed in New Jersey whose list of regular reading included *The Cats' Pause*, *Basketball Times*, *Futurestars*, *Bob Gibbons' All-Star Report*, *Ultimate Hoops*, all the preseason magazines he could find, and eighteen basketball sites on the Internet that he checked at least once a day. Never leaving home without an e-mail address, Armstrong had tapped into Cat Chat from computers in Bosnia, Africa, and various other hot spots around the globe. "I consider Cat Chat something of a lifeline," he said.

That was because, to Armstrong and the thousands he spoke for, life had a lot to do with Kentucky basketball. "In the cosmic order as I see it," the captain explained in an Internet message, "Kentucky basketball fits in way up there. God, family, Kentucky basketball. The difference between these is that Kentucky basketball requires a lot of extracurricular activity. Being a UK fan, an information junkie, and someone who can't get info soon enough, I really get a lot of use out of the Internet. Just as soon as they're available, I read the writeups and boxscores on ESPN, *USA Today*, or *Nando*. I also listen to games via the Internet on Audionet. Now, I just need to get a life."

Kentucky fanatics not as cyber-oriented spend unfathomable numbers of hours viewing and reviewing game tapes, many of them compiling their observations into critiques that they send along to the Wildcat coaching staff. During the championship run of 1996, Pitino said that he had received strategic suggestions from two thousand Kentuckians who, like him, passed their late nights breaking down film. An Eastern Kentucky man wrote the coach to say that he made a practice of analyzing each game tape three times. A Kentucky doctor sent him a Federal Express package containing notes on the team's unproductive tendencies in the half-court offense and its ill-advised passes on inbounds plays. Pitino express-mailed the gentleman back, advising that instead of watching the next game he open a bottle of red wine, put Sinatra on the stereo, and spend some quality time with his wife. The doctor tried that, but after a torturous half hour he had to turn the game on.

And then there are the quiet folks who keep their Kentucky basketball to themselves, treasuring it for simple, deeply held reasons that don't require the embellishments of game tape or electronic mail. When John Swartz retired from Wright-Patterson Air Force Base in Dayton, Ohio, he and his wife, Mary, moved back to Bethel, Kentucky, to live in the prefabricated home that Mary's parents ordered from a catalog in 1930 and to be with the people and things that were dear to them. Nothing else felt right. Kentucky, on the other hand, felt so good to John Swartz that he once, while living in Ohio, took the only ride home he could get—in the trunk of a 1944 Chevy. When they finally left Dayton behind and crossed the Ohio River for good, the Swartzes hung a UK flag from a tree in the front yard.

They had been content ever since. "Folks are poor around here," said Mary, who was born the year Adolph Rupp came to Kentucky. "Family and Kentucky are about all we got, other than horses. And I'm not a big horse person."

○ ○ ○

The dome tents started at Wally Clark's folding chair and by Thursday, Big Blue Madness Eve, formed a fast-growing community that stretched from both of the Memorial Coliseum ticket windows out to the Avenue of Champions and around the block. Warmed by an unseasonable October sun and bonded by the identical colors they wore, the squatters were in a festival spirit, tossing footballs, sharing pizza, huddling around portable televisions, and catching naps on the grass, right under Adolph Rupp's historically markered nose.

Clark and a few of the early birds just behind him, Jason Ryan included, had already been rewarded for their punctuality. The day before, they had been hanging around in their blue shirts when a couple of coeds from the pompon squad came by to say that they would like an audience for their rehearsal. So a dozen Madness types went inside and sat in the front row, where they cheered the girls and watched beyond the glass of the weight room upstairs as Rick Pitino put hard miles on the exercise bike. Pitino watched them watching him, and when he was good and sweaty he came over and invited the group to practice that night, provided they didn't tell the media. Attendance was a little over a hundred percent. After the practice, Pitino ordered the players to line up and sign autographs. Always ready for such a contingency, Jason Ryan had brought along a basketball he kept in his pickup. For him, it was a vacation to remember. The next morning, Ryan and his pals spotted senior forward Jared Prickett having breakfast at the student union and invited him over. Prickett impressed them with the amount of Chinese food he could eat before 8 a.m.

Prickett, a rebounder from West Virginia who had missed the previous season with a knee injury, figured prominently in the conversations that continually engaged the Big Blue enthusiasts as they waited for Friday. It was generally agreed that he and the big new center, wide-shouldered Canadian Jamaal Magloire, would have to supply the Cats with some sort of power game if they were to make a mark on the season ahead. The lineup, though not 1996's, was otherwise promising. The expectations for Ron Mercer were along All-American lines and Derek Anderson's star had twinkled a few times in the galaxy that was the national championship team. Anthony Epps was a proven point guard and Wayne Turner was a faster, creative backup. Jeff Sheppard and Allen Edwards were skillful players who seemed to give Pitino more perimeter personnel than he needed. This was all noted to death by those who had been counting the days until October 18, and the sum of it was a jolly, conditional optimism unburdened by the pent-up anticipation that the first title in eighteen years had finally released.

Jason Ryan was watching at home when Kentucky exorcised its demons in the Meadowlands six months earlier (before the semifinal game with Massachusetts he ate nothing but artificially blue-colored food all day) and when the deed was done he ran barefooted onto Hog Ridge Road, whooping and hollering. It was the first national championship in his range of memory, and it at last had put behind the dismal period of scandal and probation that had darkened his adolescent years. It is often and mistakenly said that Kentucky fans demand national championships,

Practicing: Jason Ryan's goal was to someday be the 'Y' after the UK cheerleaders form the first seven letters of "Kentucky."

tolerating nothing less; Ryan was only three the last time the Cats won one, and he tolerated just fine. He tolerated Kentucky basketball so sincerely, in fact, that it accounted for his life's ambition: He wanted, more than anything, to someday be the one who got to come out of the stands and spread his arms in the shape of a "Y" when the cheerleaders spelled out KENTUCKY. "Either that," he said, "or to be one of the guys who gets to wipe the sweat off the floor some night." Even his death's ambition had to do with Kentucky basketball: "I don't want a suit or anything. I just want to be buried in a Kentucky T-shirt. I want them to play the UK fight song, *My Old Kentucky Home*, *The Dance* by Garth Brooks, and throw me in the holler."

Such was Ryan's life-and-death concept of Kentucky basketball that he made sure his newborn daughter, Haley, was wearing a UK sweatshirt as she left the hospital. Charity Ryan went along with it, but it bothered her a little that Jason kept connecting the baby to basketball. He had a key chain that played the UK fight song, and during the course of her pregnancy he would play it while holding the chain against her belly. That was all right, but then, two weeks before her due date, he left for the 1994 version of Madness. "The doctor wouldn't let me go, so I spent the whole weekend nerve-racked," Charity said. "When he got back, I thought, 'Great.' He came to the doctor's office with me, and when the nurses were checking me out Jason was all excited, saying, 'I can't wait. Just eleven more days.' One of the nurses said, 'Isn't that great—he knows the exact date you're due.' And Jason said, 'No, that's the first UK game of the season.' It really hurt my feelings. Later he tried to make up for it by saying that he knew Haley was due two days before the first game. But it was too little too late."

Shortly after the baby arrived home, a friend of the Ryans brought over a handsome blanket that she had made for Haley. Jason admired the blanket until he noticed that the so-called friend had fiendishly stitched the tiny initials UL (for University of Louisville) into the corner. Not the least amused, he hadn't spoken to her since. He was generally annoyed by friends and people at work who made fun of his Kentuckyness, but even so, he made no effort to conceal it. When he had worked at IGA, he refused to wear the Hometown Proud apron because it was red. At Dynamec, his production fluctuated according to the state of the Cats. In the offseason, he welded about 800 to 1,000 pieces of seat frame every day. On a shift after Kentucky lost, he could manage only around 600. After a victory, he was good for about 1,400 pieces.

Because he had been told often enough, and because it was obvious, Ryan was well aware that his feeling for Kentucky basketball exceeded the norm. But in the two-block line that wrapped around Memorial Coliseum—whose ranks included Mary Frances Snyder Morrissey, a 1940 UK graduate whose presence at Big Blue Madness meant that she could cross the last item off her wish list—Ryan practically *was* the norm. Like him, the Ryles and the Matthewses and Wally Clark and Mary Frances Snyder Morrissey believed that basketball was the flag whose stars streamed gallantly o'er the ramparts when the commonwealth was bombed by ridicule, demographics, and stereotypes.

It was a sentiment whose resonance was out of the range of most ears not trained in Kentucky. Even Rick Pitino, despite what he said, had failed for seven years—until he had won a national championship and lived through Kentucky's response—to appreciate what the people in line felt so profoundly. But he finally had, and as the crowd continued to swell outside the Coliseum, inside, where three walls of curtains had been set up on the concourse for his Media Day press conference, the Ken-

It's only a practice: But the tickets are free.

tucky coach paused to pay tribute to the people he was only beginning to understand. "Winning the national championship, I think, is very, very special for what I think are the greatest lovers of basketball—that's the people of this state and the surrounding states that follow Kentucky," he said convincingly. A self-proclaimed gym rat, the stylish New Yorker had come to Kentucky only half prepared: He understood practically everything about basketball and practically nothing about provincialism. The Jason Ryans and Wally Clarks of his new world had unwittingly taught him the latter. "There's nobody that loves basketball like the state of Kentucky," he went on, converted. "No one comes close."

Media Day, however, was established to provide information about the team that would be introduced the next day, not the people to whom it would be introduced. And so, as Wally Clark gave another interview and Jason Ryan plugged the parking meter in front of Wildcat Lodge, Pitino did his best to size up Kentucky's prospects as defending national champion. "In this day and age," he said, "I think you need three NBA draft picks to win a national championship." His 1996 team had four— Antoine Walker (Celtics), Walter McCarty (Knicks) and Tony Delk (Hornets) in the first round and Mark Pope (Pacers) in the second—not counting the ones who would follow over the next two or three seasons. Whether the 1996-97 team had three would probably depend on who could hang with Ron Mercer and Derek Anderson.

Mercer's draft status was a question of when, rather than if, and had been ever since he left Nashville a year before as the best high school prospect in the nation. "I think Derek Anderson is also someone you'll see playing at the next level," Pitino said. "Derek, you know, has that great smile, a lot of charisma. He's also a very intelligent basketball player. Derek and Ron will come out only when they're having substantial attacks of breathing."

The more immediate question, though, was when Anderson would come out for Media Day. When Pitino concluded his preseason address—slipping out through the back curtain so that he couldn't be detained—the press repaired to the open portion of the Coliseum concourse, where the Kentucky players sat uncomfortably on hard chairs while reporters and photographers clustered around them. In the absence of Anderson, the thickest cluster was around Mercer, who looked his questioners in the eye and answered in short but thoughtful sentences.

After five minutes there was still no Anderson. Personnel from the basketball office were looking around curiously. Finally, a slim, rhythmic figure strolled pretentiously into the scene, wearing a six-inch Afro wig and a mischievous grin that the people of Kentucky would come to know very well in the months ahead.

2

Derek's Time

Derek Anderson was ten when he moved from Flint, Michigan, to Louisville, and eleven when the University of Louisville won its second national championship of the eighties. He assumed he would play there.

The city of Louisville—at least part of it, Anderson's part—was about the only place in Kentucky where a young basketball player might dream of wearing a uniform without the name of the state on it. The University of Kentucky was sovereign in the suburbs and blue-washed much of the city, but Anderson's perspective didn't line up with the prevailing one in the commonwealth; he was a Michigan toddler when UK won its only title of his childhood, and he was fifteen when the Wildcats were placed on NCAA probation. Compared to the stylistically and competitively eminent U of L, Kentucky was not a particularly compelling option for him or any of his friends around Algonquin Parkway in the city's West End. What's more, the best black players from Louisville had been avoiding Kentucky since Kentucky stopped avoiding them.

That would have been the sixties, when cranky old Adolph Rupp was persuaded to seek the services of a blockbuster center named Westley Unseld, whose decision to play instead for Louisville was seconded by Rupp's next black recruit, a silky guard named Butch Beard who played high school ball three counties west of the city. Neither was convinced of the sincerity of the Baron's offer, and their conspicuous rejections served to galvanize Rupp's reputation as the champion of segregation in Southern basketball. More than a quarter of a century later, the grandparents of Anderson's best friend, prized prospect Jason Osborne (the two of

◀ *Derek Anderson: Growing up in Louisville, he never thought he would wear the name of Adolph Rupp's university across his chest.*

them were so close and looked so much alike that they told everybody they were cousins, which somehow made it into the newspapers) informed Rick Pitino that no grandchild of theirs would set foot on the campus of Adolph Rupp's university. In the tradition that had begun with Unseld, Osborne went to Louisville.

Virtually every first-rate player Anderson knew had gone or was going to Louisville, which was the best reason he could think of not to. Anderson was a respecter of heritage, but his went deeper than Wes Unseld. It went back at least five generations to a slave named Jim Adams, who lost a brother and a sister on his fugitive flight from Tennessee, and to one of Anderson's great uncles in Central Kentucky, who, the story went, was hung for trading horses more skillfully than white men. That uncle's sister, who watched her brother die, raised the uncle, George Williams, who raised the basketball player in the family spirit. "My whole thing was my great-grandmother and George," Derek said. "I didn't want to ever disappoint them." The uncle—whom he called Dad—and the great-grandmother impressed upon Derek not to be a follower. He didn't follow the guys in the West End who drank beer and used and sold drugs, and he didn't follow the ones who went to the University of Louisville.

Anderson had nothing against the U of L. He was friends with many of the players there, having competed against them on playground and indoor courts all over the city. What bothered him was that the teams he and Jason were on—they never separated—nearly always won. He didn't think that should happen. "I was in high school and I was playing harder than these college guys sometimes," he said. "A lot of guys just played to shoot, but Jason and I played to win. It just seemed to me that the U of L guys were underachieving. I know, if I'm in college I'm not letting anyone younger or older outdo me. When we started beating them, that sort of took the magic away about Louisville." For Anderson's uncle, Louisville's magic went poof when Denny Crum failed to materialize in the prospect's living room. The head coaches of Western Kentucky and Ohio State and other schools made the effort to get there, and George Williams found it inexcusable that Crum couldn't find his way across town to pay a courtesy call.

So when it came time to take his game from Doss High School to the next level, Anderson looked around for a place where the respect went both ways. His options would have probably been more plentiful if he had attended the summer camps or played for a higher-profile high school team. As it was, the slender forward was considered the best senior in Louisville, but his reputation stopped there. Kentucky's interest in him seemed only cursory. Tubby Smith, an assistant coach at UK, left his card one time late in Anderson's junior year at Doss, but Derek didn't call back, and Pitino's staff moved on to other players. Meanwhile, Anderson was hearing plenty from his friends in the neighborhood, who had heard plenty from their parents and grandparents, who remembered the way UK had been back when. "It was a tradition of the Louisville players never to go to Kentucky because of all that," Anderson said. But he didn't agree. He even told Jason Osborne as much. "I just think we shouldn't hold grudges of that nature. If that's the way we're gonna be, we shouldn't be in America, because there's racism all over the place."

Anderson's lenience toward Kentucky might have suggested to his friends and elders that he was unconcerned about history or lacking in racial sensitivity, but that was hardly the case. On the contrary, he had made a personal study of Martin Luther King and was especially partial to the works and biographies of Malcolm X. George Williams had devoted his nephew's teenage summers to commemorating the civil rights movement, taking him once a week to the library, where Derek read the black history books that he didn't see at school, and having him eschew the big-time basketball camps for trips to Birmingham, Atlanta, and Washington. What Anderson learned most about history was to leave it behind. "To George," he said, "everything is a circle of life. He sees the past in the past and the future in the future." What that meant for Derek was that modern-day Kentucky would not be held accountable for the fifties and sixties. It would be held accountable, though, for its contemporary indifference. When, as a senior, he had begun to look away from Louisville and his uncle suggested that he return the call to Tubby Smith, Anderson's pride said no. "I thought they were interested in me," he said, "but they thought they could get a steal . . . just come in and have whoever they wanted."

One weekend, Anderson visited Ohio State and Monday morning showed up at Doss dressed head to foot in scarlet and gray. The Buckeyes' NBA-bound junior, Jimmy Jackson, had shown him around, played some ball with him, and given him a nickname, "Smooth." Smooth was impressed by Jackson, by Ohio's State's two hundred miles from home—

what good was home if Denny Crum wouldn't even cross town?—and by its pharmacology program.

Arriving at OSU without much hullabaloo, Anderson put up numbers of every stripe, made a dent in the Big Ten, and raised his reputation significantly as a freshman and sophomore, establishing himself as one of the top underclassmen in the country—he was MVP at the Olympic Festival—until he tore up his left knee late in the second season, two days before his daughter, DeAsia, was born. Then he watched the program lose its equilibrium through a disorienting series of criminal cases, player defections, and a year of NCAA probation for recruiting violations. If he was going to sit out a season rehabbing his knee, better to do it someplace where scandal was at least a few years removed. Again, he figured the place would be Louisville, but Crum, perhaps feeling jilted from the first time around, courted him only casually. Anderson was unconventional enough to get serious about Kentucky and, by that time, player enough for Kentucky to get serious about him; he had scored twenty-three points against UK in the 1993 Maui Classic.

The year he sat out was the one which prepared the Big Blue for the national championship that would ensue. In 1996, as the Cats cut a mean swath through their schedule, Pitino would say that his team had learned much from the poorly played loss to North Carolina that ended Kentucky's 1995 ambitions in the regional final. Anderson, who watched the Carolina game with his girlfriend in Louisville, also learned something that day—something very disturbing—about the team he would be part of the next year. "I saw hate between the guys on the team," he recalled. "I saw players mad at each other before the game was over. You could see it in their eyes. The game was like eight on two or seven on three, never five on five. I had practiced with those guys, I knew their attitude and their moves, and you could see it out there.

"When I saw that, I took it on as my mission for the next year: I wanted everybody on the team to feel comfortable with each other. If they were gonna point a finger, I wanted them to point it at me. That's the way I want to be when I'm on a team." Anderson believed that his teammates, the fans—everybody—should love the game as much as he did. The love was obvious when he played. His was passionate basketball, a joyful, thoroughly engaged kind of style that—and this was unique—celebrated fundamentals and whimsy at the same time, at once intelligent (Anderson scoped the floor with the same analytical vision that he used to solve Rubik's cube), technically sound, and delightfully creative. He couldn't wait to put on the blue.

It worked out that Anderson became eligible to play for UK at the same time as Ron Mercer, the gifted freshman with whom he would be linked for the next two years. The pairing was inevitable; they were both sleek, vertical, and extra-sensory. They roomed together and seemed to play with the same brain. Anderson's lobs invariably ended up in Mercer's hands, and vice versa; they were interchangeable. During one of the pre-season scrimmages in 1995's October, Anderson rushed down on the fast break, spotted Mercer on the wing, noticed the defender edging over to defend the alley-oop, and, improvising quickly—the two of them were interchangeable, after all; why not?—lofted a pass off the glass *to himself*, catching it two strides later and hammering it down with obvious satisfaction. (Later, the coaches presented him with a videotape of what they labeled "The Dunk.") Mercer took his turn on the next break, his slam being one-handed and sufficiently spectacular. Anderson explained their connectedness as if he were breaking down game film: Unlike other players, he said, neither of them stopped running on the fast break.

The only trouble was that they were *too* interchangeable and consequently, in Kentucky's excessively stacked lineup for 1995-96, played the same position, negating their uncanny synergy but giving Pitino a composite small forward with all-conference numbers and all-encompassing capabilities. With four NBA draft picks shouldering the load, the four-legged newcomer essentially work-trained for the greater responsibilities ahead. "We had Antoine, Delk, McCarty, Pope . . . all those guys had been there," Anderson reflected. "I realized I couldn't shoot ten or fifteen times a game. I told Ron, 'Our time will come.' That's why neither of us complained all year. I told him, 'You're a freshman, I'm a junior; we've both got next year. Let's stick this out.'"

Mercer ultimately put his imprint on the championship game with a season-high twenty points and Anderson, characteristically, was the one who summarized Kentucky's accomplishment in a sound bite. "You have to enjoy this now," he said when the nets had been cut down, "because when you're fifty, you won't be dunking on people . . . I don't drink, so I think I'll just get a wine bottle and stare at it."

With the championship seniors off to their NBA camps the following fall, Pitino made it clear that the floor now belonged to the thin twins. "I think Ron Mercer is getting ready to bust out and have an incredible year," he said on the October afternoon when dome tents populated the Coliseum plaza. "He's a remarkable talent. He knows his time will come. I think Derek Anderson is also a terrific talent. Overall, if there's a person more suited to our [full-court, frenetic, legs-and-hands] style of play than Derek Anderson, I don't know who it would be." The upshot was that there would be no splitting of time between the two of them in 1996-97. In fact, there would be nothing at all between them except for the transparent cable that seemed to link the modems in their heads.

The next day, Anderson and Mercer were on the same team for Big Blue Madness, which was more stunning than fair. It wasn't really a game, anyway, as much as a show (for the fans and also for the recruits whom Pitino had invited, conspicious among them being a regionally celebrated junior center named J.R. VanHoose from Paintsville High School, the defending Kentucky state champion), with those two as the show-stoppers. They played their elevated micro-game, finding each other regardless of proximity, altitude, or circumstance. Together, with the blessing and strategic encouragement of their modernistic head coach, Mercer and Anderson brought Kentucky basketball to the cutting edge, their contemporary craftsmanship all the more provocative in light of the company that evening.

The theme for Big Blue Madness was "Back To Tradition," and for it the Wildcats had brought back representatives of their NCAA championship teams to ceremoniously place trophies on pedestals. Cawood Ledford, the very voice of tradition, narrated, as Ralph (no relation to Butch) Beard was introduced first, walking out self-consciously to handle the hardware from 1948. Beard represented not only Kentucky's first NCAA champion, but an age when even the cities turned out white players. A three-time All-American and cover boy of the first issue of *Sports Illustrated* in 1949 (five years before *Time* bought the name and began publishing continuously), he was the best to come out of Louisville—at least the best that everybody knew about—until Unseld and the great black athletes who followed; some would argue that his stature remains uneclipsed. Bill Keightley, the longtime Kentucky equipment manager known as Mr. Wildcat, had remarked a few days earlier that, over the six decades from which his observations were drawn, the only UK player

Long before Deion: After setting the national scoring record as a basketball player
at Harlan High School, Wah Wah Jones became a three-sport hero at the University of Kentucky.

who might have been as quick as Derek Anderson was Ralph Beard. Sadly, Beard also symbolized Kentucky's notorious dark side, having been implicated in the program's first scandal, a mid-century point-shaving episode that cost the Cats a collegiate season and cost Beard a professional career. Kentuckians, collectively blessed with an uncommon understanding of gambling and various types of illicit profiteering, had mostly forgiven the great guard, whose culpability was of some dispute anyway.

Beard's teammate, Wallace "Wah Wah" Jones, carried the 1949 trophy. Like Beard, Jones was extraordinary in several sports, reflecting a time when specialization was only for those with fewer options. Large and rugged, Jones may have gained more fame in football had he grown up farther north or south, but as a Kentucky mountain boy he was a basketball legend, leading Harlan High School to the state championship while setting the national high school scoring record. In the same manner that Derek Anderson was the perfect athlete for Pitino, Wah Wah Jones was the quintessential Rupp player. Anderson and Jones were approximately the same height, and they wore the same colors, but after that the comparison veers into the evolutionary patterns that reconfigure a young sport in half a century.

Doing the honors for 1951 was Frank Ramsey, the famous sixth man of the Boston Celtics who was coupled in Kentucky history with Cliff Hagan. Ramsey and Hagan were high school rivals on the western side of the state (Madisonville and Owensboro, respectively) and All-American forwards at UK whose association is perpetuated in the Basketball Hall of Fame. Ramsey's presence at Big Blue Madness was a reminder that Mercer and Anderson were merely the latest in a roll call of prestigious Kentucky pairings that also included Beard and Jones, Vernon Hatton and Johnny Cox of the Fiddlin' Five (1958), Louie Dampier and Pat Riley of Rupp's Runts (1966), Kyle Macy and Jack Givens from the 1978 national champions, and, even in the unfortunate eighties, twin towers Sam Bowie and Melvin Turpin.

Adrian Smith, a small-town guard who became MVP of an NBA all-star game, walked the floor representing 1958 and country guards who could shoot. James Lee, who arrived at UK with Jack Givens as the university's first black players from Lexington, stood in the spotlight for 1978, personifying Joe B. Hall's muscular teams and the breaking of the hometown color line.

There would be two more public scrimmages before the first game, and two games going on simultaneously in each of them—Mercer/Anderson's and everybody else's. In one indelible scrimmage moment, Anderson maneuvered for an offensive rebound on the baseline and softly tossed the ball over several large people and the entire basket apparatus, whereupon Mercer ascended from the floor, put an outstretched hand on the top of the pass, and deposited it quite hard into the hoop. Anderson was probably the only person in the auditorium who even knew that Mercer was *there*. Afterwards, he elaborated. "It's like he's a brother," he said. "I know when Ron's coming around the corner now. It's like e-mail. You just send it and you know it's going to get there."

When that intrasquad game had ended, Pitino excused the crowd and directed the players to the baseline. Anderson, and Anderson only, was not among them. Through technical precision that only Pitino could appreciate, number twenty-three had managed to skillfully circumvent the coach's personalized penalty system by which a player earned sprints according to how many mistakes he made, most of which were defensive. The sprints had to be completed in a certain time or they didn't count. After all the other Wildcats had sweated off their debts, sophomore Oliver Simmons remained on the floor, running to midcourt and back, then to the other baseline and back, trying desperately to make it in twelve or fourteen or however many seconds Pitino put on the clock. Time and again, he crossed late. As he dragged himself to the line and fought through yet another sprint, his teammates watched painfully and shouted their encouragement, imploring him to beat the clock. He couldn't. After countless failures, reserve guard Cameron Mills joined Simmons and stayed on his heels the entire route, unexpectedly shoving him at the finish, sending the bigger player sprawling across the baseline, just in time.

"That team out there tonight," Pitino said afterwards, not happy, "was one that would get knocked out in the NCAA tournament, definitely. The good news is that we are there offensively. Derek Anderson, in particular, really gets Ron Mercer going. It's rare today when you coach a possession basketball player like Derek Anderson, somebody who tries to do something positive on every possession."

Despite his general disappointment, Pitino was so enamored of Anderson's performance—of Anderson in general, really—that he admonished the referee for nullifying one of Anderson's jaw-dropping, fly-over dunks with an offensive foul call. "If a guy does something that spectacular," the coach said, "the ref should give him the benefit of the doubt."

○○○

Wes Unseld was preceded at Seneca High School by his 6-foot-7 brother, George, who graduated in 1961. George wasn't quite the object of desire that his big little brother would become three years later, after two state championships, but he looked good to Kansas, Notre Dame, and Purdue, among others. There was one Kentucky school that was interested in him, too. It was located right there in Louisville. The name was Bellarmine.

He ended up choosing Adolph Rupp's university. That is, the university Rupp *played* for—Kansas—back in his home state, under the great Phog Allen. There was no chance of going to the school where the Baron *coached*; Unseld didn't even entertain the concept. "I really thought that would never happen for an African-American player with Adolph Rupp being there," he said.

It was not altogether certain that it would happen at the University of Louisville, either, with Peck Hickman being there. Hickman had coached at Louisville since 1944 without recruiting a black player, despite the fact that Johnny Unitas played with several on the Cardinal football team in the early fifties. There were alumni at Seneca High who campaigned for Hickman to break the color line with George Unseld, but Unseld was never recruited. "People are always mad at Kentucky for being segregated so long," he reflected after a long career as athletic director of the Jefferson County (Louisville) public school system, "but you've got to look at Louisville like people look at Rupp. To me, they're two peas in a pod—at least at that time."

The pod snapped apart, scattering the peas, when Louisville integrated its program a year after Unseld left for Kansas. Perhaps in an attempt to clear the way for the next Unseld, in 1962 Hickman signed Wade Houston—the future Tennessee coach and father of the New York Knicks' Allan Houston—out of Alcoa, Tennessee. With that precedent in place, Wes Unseld, Butch Beard, and their successors chose to elevate Louisville's program instead of Kentucky's. "I became a U of L fan because my brother played there, and after that they had all those African-American kids," said George Unseld. "But when I was coming out of high school, U of L's reputation was just like Kentucky's. To this day, I know people who would not walk across the street to a UK game. I attended my first one two years ago. I had to do some soul-searching. I decided I liked Pitino and the way he dealt with kids. But it took me a while; I don't think you can ever forget about the way Kentucky was."

Every school in the South was that way in the fifties and early sixties, but Kentucky's problem was that it stayed that way too long—in the state, longer than Louisville and Western Kentucky; in the Southeastern Conference, longer than Vanderbilt and Auburn; longer, even, than its own football team, which integrated the SEC in 1966 with Nat Northington. The difference between Louisville signing Wade Houston in 1962 and Kentucky signing Tom Payne in 1969 was the difference between Louisville's ultimate reputation, even a generation later, as a sanctuary for the contemporary black basketball star, and Kentucky's as a place where Jason Osborne's grandparents wouldn't let him set foot.

"I think if people are going to talk about Kentucky, they should talk about Louisville," said Julius Berry, the preeminent Dunbar High School (which had an all-black enrollment and staff) star to whom Lexington's black players looked up in

Playing above the rim: Julius Berry did it in the fifties for Dunbar High.

the late fifties. "Peck Hickman didn't come to my door, either. In fact, the only Kentucky school that recruited me was Morehead; their president came to my house. When it comes to Kentucky, I look at things a little differently than the way you always hear about them. Adolph Rupp had a boss, [athletic director] Bernie Shively, and Bernie Shively had a boss [university president Frank Dickey]. Whatever category you place Rupp in, you have to place all three of them in the same category. I think you have to look at it from that perspective." In fact, it was Shively who, during a game at Memorial Coliseum in the mid-fifties, escorted Berry's highly respected Dunbar coach, S.T. Roach, out of the lower-level seats he and the Dunbar principal had acquired. Rupp, on the other hand, was noticeably accommodating to Roach, offering him occasional use of the Coliseum for practice sessions.

"I talked to Coach Rupp one time," said the 6-6 Berry, who on weekends played at the city's Woodland Park against such UK standouts as Cotton Nash, Vernon Hatton, Johnny Cox, and Billy Ray Lickert, as well as Duke All-American Jeff Mullins, a Lexington resident. "One of my teammates and I were on our way back from St. Louis in 1959 after visiting St. Louis University. Coach Rupp was on the same plane with Oscar Robertson, Jerry West, Johnny Green, and Johnny Cox, coming back from an all-star game in Kansas City [where Rupp had obviously coached black players]. When the plane touched down in Louisville, we had to change planes. So I was sitting there waiting for the next plane with my teammate, Henry Jones, Johnny Cox, and Adolph Rupp. Coach Rupp told me that he would love to have me but he couldn't play colored boys in the SEC. He said that if he were me, he'd go to Idaho State. I don't know why Idaho State, but that's what he said." Rupp also told Dayton coach Tom Blackburn that he would be crazy not to recruit Berry, which Blackburn successfully did on the Baron's advice, winning out over 150 schools that sought the Dunbar hero's celebrated services. (Oscar Robertson was responsible for showing around Berry and Covington's Tom Thacker at the University of Cincinnati. He took them to a public batting cage, where the two recruits sat quietly and watched The Big O pound fastballs from the pitching machine.)

Thacker had a similar encounter with Rupp the very same year. Although there was no specific pressure to recruit Thacker—as part of Greater Cincinnati, Covington was not as Kentucky-based as the rest of the state—Rupp made a point of approaching the Grant High School star after a 1959 all-star game at Memorial Coliseum. "I remember Rupp came out on the floor congratulating me on how high I could jump to be 6-2," recalled Thacker, who went on to play for two national champions at Cincinnati and make a few All-American teams. "He was saying, 'I wish we could take you at Kentucky, but we go down South and I don't think they'd like that.' Sure, I would have loved to go to Kentucky because I was a basketball player. It fascinated me. But the attitude was, we knew it wasn't highly possible. Everybody had that attitude about UK being racist. UK was South. It was a Southern school."

It was, in many ways, the definitive Southern school. More than its latitude, it was Kentucky's association with and domination of the South that fixed its geographical orientation for basketball purposes. For most of Rupp's forty-two years at UK, Kentucky was the alpha and omega of Southern basketball. The Man in the Brown Suit won twenty-seven Southeastern Conference championships and every national title the league ever claimed until newcomer Arkansas brought one home in 1994. To its football-minded brethren of the SEC, against whom Rupp was not inclined to hold down the score, Kentucky was a basketball beast without remorse. And while the South resented Kentucky for its uncompromising basketball, the rest of the country was offended by its uncompromising Southernness.

Historically a border state, Kentucky's basketball chronicles would have followed a different script entirely had the school gravitated toward its Northern neighbors instead of its Southern, joining Ohio State and Indiana in the Big Ten Conference rather than Tennessee and Vanderbilt in the Southeastern. Had that happened, the program, keeping pace with its conference, would have been more swiftly urbanized and consequently integrated; it would have been challenged harder on the court by large Midwestern schools that placed a higher premium on basketball than those in the South; and all in all it wouldn't have been considered so frightfully big, bad, and bigoted.

Rupp's association with the South figured so prominently in his image that, although he spoke in a flat Midwestern manner picked up from Austrian parents on a Kansas plain, he was often imitated with a Southern accent. Even his actions were interpreted with a Southern accent. His failure, for instance, to bring in Wes Unseld or Butch Beard or any black player until 1969 has left him with a posthumous reputation as the Bull Connor of college basketball. As political correctness has expanded its horizons in the nineties, Rupp's conservatism in the area of race has painted a bull's-eye on his name for the potshotting contemporary journalist. *Sports Illustrated* called him "a white supremacist" and "a charming p.r. rogue [whose] politics leaned more toward the KKK." Columnist George Will referred to Rupp as "a great coach but a bad man."

The race issue dogged Kentucky's program throughout most of the fifties and sixties, when black superstars such as Wilt Chamberlain, Elgin Baylor, Bill Russell, and Oscar Robertson carried their college teams to national glory and went on to greater acclaim in pro basketball. The most humiliating defeat Rupp ever suffered came in the final game of 1950, when—although the outcome was later revealed to be under the taint of gamblers and their Kentucky business partners—the City College of New York annihilated UK 89-50 with a lineup that included four black starters.

The first black to play in Lexington was Solly Walker of St. John's in 1951, an occasion which prompted Rupp to call the *Herald-Leader* and request that the paper, on his behalf, appeal to the Kentucky crowd to treat Walker hospitably. The top-ranked Wildcats routed the second-ranked Redmen then, but St. John's and Walker got more than even when they ended Kentucky's season in the NCAA tournament. In the 1958 NCAA championship game, Rupp and his staff figured out a way to beat Elgin Baylor's Seattle team and postpone the pressure to recruit a black player. The SEC was still nearly a decade away from integration.

The 1958 national championship was Kentucky's fourth in eleven seasons, on top of which the Wildcats were undefeated in 1953-54, when they chose not to participate in the NCAA tournament because Hagan, Ramsey, and Lou Tsioropoulos were ruled ineligible for having already graduated (they completed a year's worth of work when UK's 1952-53 season was blacked out by the point-shaving scandal). Over that period, no other team in the country was close to matching Kentucky's success, a fact that made Rupp leery of radical change. In the early sixties, however—and this is an onus by which Rupp has been uniquely judged—UK did not have the luxury of letting some other institution blaze the trail; as the standard-bearing program and northernmost school in the SEC, Kentucky was the one from whom the others took their lead. Jim Crow laws in the Deep South states prohibited blacks and whites from playing together; Alabama, Mississippi State, and Auburn surrendered berths in the NCAA tournament due to state legislation, and other schools would have done the same if they'd had the opportunity. Kentucky had no qualms in that regard, going to the tournament once in Alabama's stead (1956) and twice in Mississippi State's (1959 and 1961), but when it came to integrating his own team, it was convenient for Rupp to defer to the customs of the places in which the Wildcats had to travel and compete.

"You also have to consider that Coach Rupp did very well with white ballplayers," said Julius Berry, whose years as an administrative aide in the mayor's office served to deepen his understanding of Lexington's dynamics. "If he had brought black players onto the team at Kentucky, the floodgates would have been opened. And if that had happened, Kentucky's dominance probably wouldn't have been there. Look at some of the black high schools in the South like Parker High School in Birmingham—a huge school. With all of the black athletes available in places like Birmingham and Atlanta and all over the South, really, it would have certainly leveled the playing field."

It was a complicated time and issue, and one that evidently left Rupp conflicted. There are indications that he was actually an early advocate of integration—certainly no Bull Connor—but unfortunately a timid one, not secure enough in his position to do the deed and damn the consequences. It is a fact that he tried to recruit black players long before he succeeded (it was difficult to resist; there was so much talent in Louisville that a kid named Cassius Clay swept the floor at halftime of Central High School games), but there is a legitimate question as to how hard.

Truth and fiction tend to commingle after thirty years, but one rumor had Rupp willing to pull out of the SEC in the late fifties if it meant that Chamberlain would come to Kentucky. In the spring of 1961—after Julius Berry and Tom Thacker had gotten away—Rupp started dropping hints, publicly and privately, about signing at least two black players from Kentucky and daring other SEC schools to forfeit their games in protest. Later, however, when he realized the vigor of the South's resistance, he recanted on those remarks. Had Rupp dug in his heels at this point, history would be much kinder to him and Kentucky. But the considerations of that day were not like those of this day, and the fact is that Rupp had an easy out. Given the prevailing politics of the Deep South states and the raucous nature of the crowds in their tiny gymnasiums (Auburn played in a World War II Quonset hut and seated its football team behind the Kentucky bench; at Mississippi State, where the fans rang cowbells and pulled the hair on Cotton Nash's leg when he took the ball out of bounds, Rupp found a dead skunk under his seat), he could say with reluctance, visible regret, and palpable justification that, despite his efforts to bring everybody else around, in the final analysis it was simply not feasible to use a black player in the SEC. Besides, while the

Baron was working the media to get a better sense of the landscape, UK president Dickey, also president of the SEC, broached the subject of conference integration with the other university presidents, who let him know that the time was still at least five years away.

This is not to suggest that the SEC was entirely to blame. The Baron had underestimated the segregationist sentiment even in Lexington, where in 1961 black members of the Boston Celtics and St. Louis Hawks, in town for an exhibition game, caught the next plane out of town after they were refused service in their hotel dining room. Temple cancelled a game at UK for the same reason. These accumulated incidents evidently persuaded Rupp that bringing a black player to the campus would cause more problems than it would answer. Resolved for the time being not to involve himself with black prospects, Rupp phoned the *New York Journal-American*, reached a young sports clerk named Jimmy Breslin, and asked if the paper would be so helpful as to indicate "colored" high school players with asterisks so he would know whom not to recruit.

In Kentucky, meanwhile, it was easy to tell which great players not to recruit: They were all on display at the state tournament. In 1963 alone—six years after the black high schools became eligible—the Sweet Sixteen included Wes Unseld and his Seneca teammate, Mister Basketball Mike Redd (a sensational 6-3 guard who introduced fellow Kentuckians to the dunk), as well as future NBA players Clem Haskins, Bobby Washington, and Greg Smith (whose teammate and brother, Dwight Smith, appeared to be headed for stardom in the pros until he was killed in an automobile accident shortly after the conclusion of his senior season at Western Kentucky University).

"Dwight Smith might have been the best player to come out of Kentucky in the sixties—better, maybe, than Clem or even Wes," said Butch Beard, who later played and coached in the NBA. "Mike Redd was also way before his time; he was doing shit in the sixties that you didn't see until the eighties. Overall, with Dwight and Greg and Clem and Mike Redd and Wes and Tom Thacker and Charlie Taylor and George Wilson and Bobby Washington and all of them, that was as good a group of talent as you would find in one time and one place. I think that's why there's a lot of bad blood from the older blacks in the state of Kentucky. I think that for all those great players to come out of the state and for the University of Kentucky not to get any of those players . . . I think the older blacks resented that; I really do. And there still might be some of that resentment."

A few weeks after the 1963 state tournament pulled out of Louisville's Freedom Hall, the NCAA Final Four came to town. It was the commonwealth's uneasy privilege to host a national championship game that went into overtime before Tom Thacker and Cincinnati, angling for their third consecutive national title, were taken down by a Loyola team that started four black players. To get to Freedom Hall, Loyola had overcome Kentucky's SEC conqueror, Mississippi State, which, for the right to play in its first interracial game, had defied state legislation by tiptoeing out of Starkville in the dark.

All in all, it was a bad year for segregationists. Kentucky had been able and very content to put on a Southern face until Dickey was replaced as UK president in 1963 by Californian John Oswald, whereupon Rupp found himself pressured from within for the first time and frustrated that Oswald's liberal instincts were not in touch with the Kentucky reality with which he had learned to live. The result of this frustration—which was compounded by the fact that the Wildcats dropped all the way to fifth place in the SEC in 1963, the fifth consecutive year in which they failed to win the conference title after taking ten of the previous twelve—was the incident that to this day does the most damage to the famous coach's reputation.

In his 1979 book, *Adolph Rupp As I Knew Him*, longtime Rupp assistant (and later Rupp's boss as athletic director) Harry Lancaster set forth a damning account of the conflict between Rupp and Oswald over the color of Kentucky's roster. Throughout the course of several meetings in which the coach and the president exchanged views on the subject, Oswald pointed out that the basketball team was the last component of the university to remain segregated and that the program's obstinacy was possibly costing UK millions of federal dollars. "Oswald was putting on pressure to integrate," Lancaster wrote. "Adolph would come back from those meetings and say to me, 'Harry, that son of a bitch is ordering me to get some niggers in here. What am I going to do? He's the boss.' I didn't see where we had much choice but Adolph had never been around blacks and I think he worried about the unknown. He told me one time that he had told Oswald he would sign a black player as soon as he could find one that was sure to start. He didn't want the blacks sitting on the bench.

He told me that Oswald told him the blacks could sit right there on the bench with the white players." Arguing that he had tried in vain to attract black players to Kentucky, Rupp suggested to Oswald that if he could do a better job of recruiting them, he should "hop to it."

During the same stretch of the early sixties, Rupp suffered through a recruiting slump that saw him lose coveted big men such as Jerry Lucas, Gary Bradds, and Bill Hosket, who turned in succession to Ohio State. Out of options and excuses and losing his grip on the SEC, he belatedly undertook the pursuit of the imposing and widely publicized Unseld, Kentucky's Mister Basketball of 1964 and the top center prospect in the nation. Desegregationist parties in Louisville, Unseld's hometown, lobbied hard for the Seneca High School star to make history at UK—harder, perhaps, than Rupp did. Rupp visited the Unseld home at a time in which he knew that the big center was occupied with a speaking engagement. Word got out the next day that Unseld had not been courteous enough to even attend the meeting. Convinced that Rupp's interest in him was only token, Unseld ultimately enrolled at Louisville, where he became an All-American on his way to the Hall of Fame.

The sting of Unseld's rejection was aggravated when the Cats, rated No. 1 in the country late in the season, lost back-to-back games in the 1964 NCAA regional (the second one for third place) to Ohio University and Loyola, both of which started multiple black players. The calls to integrate began to ring constantly in Rupp's ears. In 1965 and 1966, Kentucky became the first SEC school to enroll black athletes in track and football, and Vanderbilt broke the color line in basketball by signing Perry Wallace of Nashville, an eventual all-conference player, and Godfrey Dillard of Detroit. (In their first freshman game, at Mississippi State on February 27, 1967, the crowd threatened to lynch Wallace and Dillard, spat on them, and for some curious reason let a chicken loose in the gym.) Even after losing Unseld, Rupp would have beaten Vandy to the punch if he had been able to sign Beard out of Breckinridge County in 1965, when he was Kentucky's Mister Basketball and one of the most heavily recruited high schoolers in the nation. UK star Pat Riley showed Beard around campus and Rupp's son, Herky, who was coaching high school basketball in Louisville at the time, met with the smooth guard in an earnest attempt to get him to Kentucky. The Baron himself sipped iced tea in the Beard home and told the family about being cursed at

Tennessee and having bottles thrown at him in Alabama. Although Beard was a Kentucky fan—"I grew up listening to Cawood Ledford call the games on the radio," he said—he was not reassured by these accounts.

"I had announced that I was going to stay in the state of Kentucky," recalled Beard. "The state university was certainly one of the places I was considering. I promised my parents I would stay in Kentucky so I wouldn't be too far away; otherwise, I would have played

Sweet prospect: In 1964, after leading Seneca High to its second consecutive state championship, Wes Unseld was recruited by nearly every major basketball school in the country, including Kentucky.

in the Big Ten or somewhere farther away. I had about two hundred scholarship offers. I remember I was watching Lew Alcindor on TV announcing that he was going to UCLA, and as I was watching the phone rang. It was Coach Wooden. He asked me to come out to UCLA for a visit. I didn't make the trip, because I knew that if I did, I'd go there. It was probably the biggest mistake I ever made."

Beard has no comparable regrets about the missed opportunity at Kentucky. In his estimation, it wasn't much of an opportunity. He made visits to the UK campus and was very interested in going there, but hadn't met Rupp until the famous coach came to his home in little Hardinsburg.

Later, at a track meet in Lexington, he told the Baron he was coming to UK, but ultimately thought better of it and accepted an offer to Louisville, where he joined Unseld on some of the All-American teams. "I really don't think Rupp wanted a black player," Beard said. "There were maybe some alumni who wanted Kentucky to be first in the SEC, but I don't think he did. I'm just judging by what he said, the statements he made. I don't want to go through all that bullshit again, but I remember it. I did not feel comfortable about going to the University of Kentucky after he came to my house and made the statements he made."

Rupp was wobbling under a burden that he didn't enthusiastically shoulder, and by November, 1965, his exasperation had built to the point that he fired off an angry letter to a UK alum from Louisville who had written him to criticize about his recent recruiting record:

Dear Mr. Jones:

I was glad to get your letter because I want some of our great alumni to get a picture of some of our problems here at the university. You signed as a disappointed UK fan. I personally am ashamed of you as is every other loyal Kentuckian, because we still have the winningest record of any team that has ever picked up a basketball. It is because of bellyachers like you that we haven't been able to do better in recent years. I think I know what we need here at the university possibly better than any other coach, and one of those things is less criticism and an active participation by some of our alumni to help us get some of the material that you spoke about in your letter. How many boys who are athletes have you brought to the University of Kentucky campus at your expense? How many of their families have you entertained in Louisville and told them about the advantages of coming to the University of Kentucky? Some of the advantages you have apparently forgotten about. Please don't come from Louisville to Lexington to see us play. Go out to see U of L play because they have a boy by the name of Westley Unseld on that team who we made 13 trips to Louisville to interest in coming to Kentucky. Before you continue with more bellyaching, let's get something done on your part to make a contribution to the university that gave you a fine education. We only beat Tennessee 3 of the last 4 games in spite of the fact that we didn't have a big center. You apparently overlooked this also.

In tough times, Rupp took heart when his undersized 1965-66 team, which he fondly nicknamed "Rupp's Runts," overachieved all the way to the NCAA championship game. To get to the Final Four, Kentucky had to get past Michigan and its great black star, Cazzie Russell. After the Cats eliminated Duke in the semifinals, they found themselves going for it all against unheralded Texas Western, which would be the first team ever to start five black players in an NCAA title game.

The history made in College Park, Maryland, on March 19, 1966, would not have been so profound had the opponent not been Kentucky; had it not been Adolph Rupp. There were plenty of all-white teams in the country (North Carolina, for instance, which was in the process of signing Charlie Scott) and tournament. Color lines, in fact, had not been broken on the other teams in the Final Four, Duke and Utah. Except for the Rupp factor, the sociological particulars of the championship game would have been much the same if Duke had been able to beat Kentucky the day before. That has turned out to be a colossal irony: Having eluded the microscope under which the 1966 championship was placed, Duke has gone on to enjoy a reputation as perhaps the most enlightened of the Southern basketball schools. Kentucky, meanwhile, has not altogether enjoyed the entirely different reputation it has been saddled with ever since that fateful occasion.

The difference lay heavily in the fact that Kentucky had a face to attach to the moment. It was round, fleshy, unsmiling, and a little hook-nosed, and people around the country found it easy to see racism in that visage. They could see it also, if they chose to, in his baronial manner. They didn't take into account that Rupp, unlike so many of his SEC counterparts, scheduled games against integrated teams. They didn't know or care that Rupp had coached a black player in an Illinois high school. They didn't know or care that he distributed circus tickets every summer to kids in a black section of Lexington; that he had a black farm manager, an unconventional hiring for that time and that place; that he conducted clinics for black coaches. They knew only that Kentucky was very proud, very Southern, and very white. Kentucky was the dour man in the brown suit.

Largely because of him, there has never been another basketball game in which race was so overt and celebrated a theme. To basketball fans black and white, gathered around television sets in bigger groups than usual, it was the equivalent of Joe Louis fighting Jack Dempsey. "To this day," said Butch Beard, "I still root for Kentucky except when they play Louisville. But I sat in my dorm room that night pulling hard for Texas Western." The coaches themselves did little to minimize the race angle. Whether or not Rupp privately made racist comments before the game—there are conflicting reports concerning the derogatory terms he may have used in referring to the opponent's personnel—it is certain that Texas Western coach Don Haskins told his team that he did. The Miners were consequently on a mission. On the first play of the game, a Texas Western player dunked on Riley and said, "Take that, you honky [something or other]." At halftime, Rupp allowed *Sports Illustrated's* Frank Deford into the Kentucky locker room for background purposes only. Deford later revealed that he was startled to hear Rupp tell his players, "You've got to beat those coons," and command center Thad Jaracz to "go after that big coon."

The underdog's 72-65 victory is still considered one of the searing moments in American sports history, and every time its significance is recollected in print or on videotape, Rupp's reputation takes another hit. The drama of that night in Maryland is heightened in proportion to the degree of malevolence assigned to Kentucky's notorious coach. The fact is that Rupp's symbolic Southernness is what makes the story great.

So personal were the ramifications of that famous game that those close to Rupp noticed a change in his coaching afterwards. Harry Lancaster wrote that Rupp panicked more easily after 1966 and became so defeatist in close games that he was unable to function as he once had. Near the end of his time, he once woke up in the middle of the night wondering what he could have done differently against Texas Western. In a day of civil rights and consciousness-raising, the cantankerous old coach with the unfortunate first name was an unwitting symbol for everything that the new age was trying to put behind. As their team was beating Rupp's in the 1969 Mideast Regional, Marquette fans shouted him down with cries of, "Hey, Hitler!"

That summer, able to suffer it silently no longer, Rupp was compelled to write a letter to the *Louisville Courier-Journal* explaining that, despite his self-interest in the best basketball players available, the SEC and the foibles of recruiting had collaborated to keep black players off his roster; and yes, he had wanted Wes Unseld very badly.

While Rupp continued his weary public search for a black player who would come to UK—Kentucky was the watched pot that wouldn't boil—Louisville rode Unseld and Beard to a number-two national ranking and Western Kentucky also joined the ranks of the country's top teams with a nucleus of black Kentuckians. In the early sixties, legendary Western Kentucky coach "Uncle Ed" Diddle, whose colorful career at the Bowling Green school covered more than forty years, put together a native roster that included black stars Clem Haskins of Campbellsville (an All-American) and the Smith brothers, Dwight and Greg, of Princeton, Kentucky. By the time Diddle had retired and Wayne Chapman, Rex's father, had transferred to WKU in 1967, the Hilltoppers had a team that would have challenged for the Final Four had not Haskins broken his wrist late in the season. In 1971, Western actually got to the Final Four behind Jim McDaniels and four other black starters (Rex Bailey, Jerry Dunn, Clarence Glover, and Jim Rose) from rural Kentucky, losing to Villanova in double overtime before beating Kansas for third place (its tournament victories were later annulled due to NCAA violations). Rupp, who had tried in vain to recruit Rose out of Hazard (the mayor of Hazard delivered Rose to Rupp's office) and the 6-11 McDaniels out of Scottsville, Kentucky, could only curse his bad fortune when McDaniels scored thirty-five points and the Hilltoppers humbled the state university 107-83 in the 1971 Mideast Regional.

The humiliated team that lost to Western Kentucky was an SEC champion and top-ten club with five starters who averaged in double figures, including the black center who had at long last broken UK's color line. Tired of losing recruiting battles for post players and desperate to find a successor to Dan Issel, the school's all-time leading scorer, Rupp had located the young man whom he thought would put a resounding end to the program's segregationist policies and the bad publicity that went along with them: a raw but athletically impressive 7-footer from Louisville named Tom Payne. Payne was not a high school superstar in the tradition of Issel, Unseld, Lucas, or McDaniels—in fact, he had played comparatively little basketball—but his size and strength alone made him a professional prospect as an underclassman. On the basis of talent, Rupp had done well to find Payne. The cause of racial pioneering, however, was not one that the big guy embraced in the spirit of Jackie Robinson. Embittered by the racial slurs he endured—at Tennessee, teammates Larry

The color line: Tom Payne was the one who finally broke it for the Kentucky basketball program. It was an unfortunate choice.

Steele and Mike Casey told the officials they would walk off the court if the verbal abuse didn't stop—and fascinated by the money available, Payne cut short the Baron's late and poorly executed experiment, declaring himself a hardship case after his sophomore (and only) season. He signed with the Atlanta Hawks for $800,000, but played for only a year before he was arrested for a series of rapes and sentenced to fifteen years in prison. In 1986, Payne was convicted of another rape charge in Los Angeles, where he had been working as an actor.

When Payne left UK, he left it, ironically, as the only SEC school without a black player. For the 1971-72 season, Rupp's last, a pair of black UK football players, Darryl Bishop and Elmore Stephens, played for a while as walk-ons before they were kicked off the team for missing a flight. (Stephens has since stated that he discerned no racism in Rupp and was treated the same as his white teammates.) Rupp's successor, Joe B. Hall, was a more vigorous recruiter, and his enthusiasm to maintain Kentucky's competitive standard was not impaired by racial conservatism. He swiftly signed three black players from the Western Kentucky region—Larry Johnson,

Reggie Warford, and Merion Haskins, Clem's brother—and when he recruited James Lee and Jack Givens together, Hall went a long way toward unifying Lexington's black and white communities under Kentucky colors. The relationship was reaffirmed when Melvin Turpin and Dirk Minniefield stayed home to play for UK. On the national scale, meanwhile, Hall kept the program current by bringing in such African-American stalwarts as Pennsylvania's Sam Bowie and Georgia's Kenny Walker.

Strangely, however, the vast resource of the state's biggest city—its *only* big city—went virtually untapped after the unpropitious choice of Tom Payne. It wasn't as if Louisville lacked talent. The list of outstanding collegiate players turned out by the city—many of whom hung around to play for the U of L, some of whom didn't—included the likes of Wesley Cox, Darrell Griffith, Rudy Macklin, Herb Crook, Felton Spencer, Allan Houston, Jason Osborne, and DeJuan Wheat. In 1983, Hall signed Winston Bennett, the Mister Basketball from Male High School, but he was the only black player from Louisville to put on the blue and white uniform in the entire quarter century between the departure of Tom Payne and the arrival of the skinny kid who came from Flint and moved onto Bennett's street in the West End.

○○○

As a coach who liked to put his players' individual talents to their best advantage, Rick Pitino had a role for Derek Anderson that was elaborate in detail but simple in principle: Be everywhere, do everything. Pitino's hair-afire press was the perfect vehicle for Anderson's rangy, playful derring-do, a fact which became apparent a few minutes into Kentucky's first game of the 1996-97 season, when number twenty-three flashed into a pass that one of Clemson's guards intended for another and then lobbed the ball to Allen Edwards for a dunk that resembled what went down the year before. A minute later, Mercer came off a pick to hit a fadeaway jumper that was not humanly defensible.

The Clemson game was the second of a doubleheader at the RCA Dome in Indianapolis, which, after winter had come and gone, would be the destination toward which Kentuckians pointed their hopes, the site of the 1997 Final Four. (Although the doubleheader initiated the season for all four teams, the evening had a midseason feel to it by halftime of the first game between Connecticut and Indiana. That was when Bobby Knight introduced himself to the timekeeper. "If you can't keep the goddamn clock," the Hoosier coach screamed on his way to the locker room, "get somebody else to do it!") The Final Four coincidence supplied a ready theme for the Kentucky folks on hand, and they began contemplating an early spring return to the Dome about the time Anderson spotted Edwards in flight to the hoop for the first basket of the season. They should have taken into account, however, that the latter was playing power forward at 6-5, 205.

Opting to start neither of his young 6-10 centers against 20th-ranked Clemson, Pitino had opened the season with Jared Prickett in the pivot alongside Edwards and Mercer, two light-eating forwards. The big freshman, Magloire, debuted after about eight minutes, picked up some fouls, and went back to the bench, where the big sophomore, Mohammed, could be found for the full forty-five minutes, including overtime. Prickett, who had not appeared in a game since he injured his knee twelve months before, went the grueling distance, but at 6-9 and 235, he was not enough Wildcat to hold off the hefty men whom Clemson rushed at him in numbers. The Tigers inevitably figured out that they could overwhelm Kentucky near the basket, which they did to abolish a ten-point deficit in the second half and dominate the overtime for a 79-71 victory that many of their followers considered to be the biggest in the history of the program; beating Kentucky was often that.

The outcome was technically an upset, the Wildcats having been variously rated between second and eighth in the preseason publications, but Pitino insisted that it really wasn't. "It's going to take some time because we're playing four guards," he said afterwards. "It's a two-edged sword for us right now. We have to press because we're so small, but we don't have enough depth to really do it the way we need to. This is probably the least amount of basketball ability we've had since my first year at Kentucky. We'll get some help . . . But in the meantime, we've got to make sure we don't get so many of these losses early in the season that we don't make the NCAA tournament."

Over the next few days, as Pitino reviewed tapes of the Clemson game with his assistants, his concern deepened. Kentucky's relentless style had been spectacularly executed by the infinitely talented national championship team, but without sufficient depth—for a lack of available legs and fouls—it would prove impractical. The depth problem, in part, was Anderson's fault. His game was so vital to Kentucky's scheme, and his presence on the floor so necessary, that Pitino had elected to redshirt senior Jeff Sheppard, whose best position, like Anderson's, was shooting guard. Sheppard's professional aspirations were not unrealistic—a leaper and shooter, he had played significant minutes every year since arriving at UK from Georgia—but they would be severely compromised if he were to spend his senior season on the bench. When Pitino announced Sheppard's redshirt before the opening of the season, he said that the decision would not be revisited unless a major injury on the squad pressed the veteran back into service.

Of course, the coach would think again if Sheppard grew four or five inches before Christmas. As it was, Pitino could see himself being cornered into a position of having to play big men whom he didn't consider nearly ready. Magloire could block shots in the dark, but the rest of his game was still Canadian prep. Mohammed, whose touch was considerably better, was just getting accustomed to playing with a waistline. When he recruited Mohammed out of Chicago, Pitino hadn't anticipated the gentle fellow contributing much until he was at least a junior and more likely a senior. To need him now was to be genuinely worried.

It worried Pitino further that the Kentucky fans *weren't* worried; that they wouldn't even consider the possibility that the Wildcats would fall short of the NCAA tournament. He called it Kentucky arrogance, and what really frightened him was that his players might come under its influence. The feeling around the commonwealth was that Kentucky would always be Kentucky, no matter how many players left for the pros or how many were redshirted or how much the power forward weighed. Pitino had tried to warn the public and especially his athletes that the challenge of Kentucky's schedule would not be answered by merely putting on the colors. The next opponent, for instance, was Syracuse, the very team that the Cats had encountered in the NCAA finals less than eight months before.

The matchup with Syracuse had been orchestrated as the main event of the first round of the Great Alaska Shootout. It was set for Thanksgiving night, which meant that turkey dinner was a pregame meal for about six hundred Kentuckians who found themselves in ten inches of Anchorage snow. Many of them had made the trip (at least one couple—an optometrist and his wife from Pikeville, Kentucky—*driving* the more than four thousand miles) because it was easier than getting into a game at Rupp Arena.

Any tournament that involves Kentucky takes on a distinctively Kentucky look and sound. In faraway events involving numerous teams (in this case, eight), it's not uncommon for UK fans to outnumber all the others combined. The effect is amplified by the fact that each Kentuckian feels compelled to wear between one and about seventy-five Big Blue items on his or her person. "Oh, I love that pin," said the lady in blue to the other lady in blue as they descended in the elevator of the Anchorage Hilton. "I have the earrings to go with it," replied the second, turning her gaze to a man wearing a Kentucky coat and carrying another that one of the Alaskan fur dealers had offered—in vain, of course—to take in trade for one of his, even-up. (At this point, the elevator paused to let on a small, elderly man who, in a thick accent apparently Russian, asked if there was room for him. "If you're a UK fan," answered a UK fan, causing the Russian gentleman to wonder why all the friendly people from the United Kingdom wore blue.)

Among the ubiquitous Kentucky fans indulging in an Alaskan Thanksgiving were Jack Bailey, a UK grad from the early fifties who hadn't been able to get into a home game since then . . . and Jim Mitchell of Cairo, Illinois (but he worked in Kentucky), to whom the 300-mile drive to Lexington was forbidding on a regular basis but who had made the trip to Maui three years earlier and would do it again the next year . . . and a lady from London, Kentucky, who wore a sweatshirt with UK spelled in sequins and clutched a Kentucky-blue moose she had bought in the hotel gift shop. (Another woman, seeing it, had hurried into the shop, only to be informed by the clerk that for the first time ever they had sold out of blue moose. The second lady was not entirely discouraged, however. Working the lobby, she had acquired the autographs of Allen Edwards, Anthony Epps, and assistant coach Winston Bennett.)

Jason Ryan was not among the Kentuckians in Anchorage—it was mostly an older crowd—nor, strangely, was Bob Wiggins. By Wednesday afternoon, when Pitino, Mercer, and Anderson stopped to have their picture snapped in front of the stuffed grizzly bear at the hotel's front door, Wiggins almost certainly should have been sighted taking a meal or two with Bill Keightley in the coffee shop or passing through the lobby with

Ralph Hacker and Kyle Macy or hanging out with members of the Committee of 101, an organized band of UK boosters and volunteers who were all over the place. Thanksgiving wouldn't stop him; surely not now: The three Alaska games would put him within single digits of breaking Rardin's record. Nor would the snow: Wiggins had made it through far worse conditions over his 615-game streak.

As a fan who had earned his special privileges, Wiggins undoubtedly had tickets waiting for Wednesday's coaches' banquet in the Sheraton ballroom. The others would shop and scope the lobby and visit the glaciers, but Wiggins would surely be at the Sheraton to hear the eight coaches make obligatory jokes around the Kentucky theme. "They had something in *USA Today* about my salary," said Syracuse's Jim Boeheim, who, twenty years before, had interrupted Pitino's wedding night for a job interview and then hired him as an assistant. "Rick saw me outside and laughed."

"We were in the UK Invitational Tournament a few years ago," added Charlie Bruns of the host team, Alaska-Anchorage. "I'd heard you couldn't get a seat at a Kentucky game. Yet I looked in the stands during the game and there was an empty seat a couple rows behind our bench. At one point I turned to the fellow sitting next to the empty seat and asked him why that was. He said, 'Well, my wife passed away and I gave her ticket to my best friend.' That didn't make a lot of sense to me, so I asked him, 'Why isn't he here?' The guy said, 'He's at the funeral.' "

But Wiggins heard none of that. He was not at the Sheraton. He was not at the Hilton. He was not at the glacier. He was in the hospital back in Kentucky, having suffered a heart attack on the day before he was to leave for Alaska. His condition was okay, but the streak was over. He would not break Steve Rardin's record. Ironically, Rardin's streak had also ended with a game against Syracuse.

While the lobby fretted over Wiggins, Pitino spent much of the afternoon worrying about his sophomore point guard. Martin Buser, the Iditarod champion, had invited the UK team out to some federal land near his place to go snowmobiling and Pitino had accepted nervously, realizing it might not be the most prudent activity to undertake on the day before a big game but figuring it was Alaska, after all, and kids like Wayne Turner might not ever be there again. A tightly bundled playmaker whose game was distinctly citified, Turner was a Boston product who hadn't seen a lot of open tundra in his time. "The guys were taking turns on the snowmobile," Pitino said later, when he had calmed down considerably. "Then Wayne Turner took his turn, but he didn't come back right away. It was one of the scariest things I've ever seen. Three o'clock, no Wayne. Four o'clock, no Wayne. Now it's dark. We've sent three guides, we're calling the police. Finally Wayne [who was extremely lost] sees this house and he goes up and knocks on the door. They answer the door, and Wayne says, 'There's this famous dude I'm trying to find, a guy who won a big race . . .' Fortunately, the people knew who he was talking about."

When Turner turned up safe, Pitino resumed worrying about Syracuse and the unsettling prospect of being 0-2 for the season. His expectations, already checked by Clemson, were further tempered by the fact that he had decided on a lineup he feared might not be his best at the moment. But sooner or later, the Wildcats would have to put a real center on the floor, so he took the plunge and started Nazr Mohammed. It was only an experiment. A few minutes later, he took out Mohammed and put in Magloire. He wanted to put Mohammed back in, but he couldn't take Magloire out. The freshman scored, he rebounded, he blocked shots. He even played the press. With the long Canadian lurking in the rear and Anderson materializing in several parts of the floor simultaneously, the Kentucky press was its former self again, taking Syracuse completely out of its rhythm and the game.

The Cats' half-court offense, meanwhile, had never been better, finding Anderson for twenty-five points while Pitino screamed, "Set legal screens! Set legal screens!" The Orangemen were practically spectators as Kentucky bing-bang-boomed to a 22-point halftime lead and a breezy 34-point victory. Curiously, Syracuse had played Kentucky much tighter in the Meadowlands. The Orangemen had lost All-American forward John Wallace and point guard Lazarus Sims from the runner-up team, but Kentucky's loss was greater in number, minutes, statistics, and NBA draft choices. It didn't add up. Boeheim's explanation was that, "Our freshmen were not ready for that kind of full-court pressure. I don't think any freshman point guard is ready for that. Kentucky played at the level of a Final Four team . . . I think they'll have a chance to be as good as last year."

Bob Wiggins would be back at courtside long before Kentucky lost again. The Wildcats were not challenged in their next two games of the

Great Alaska Shootout, putting a lesson on the hosts and having their way with a veteran College of Charleston team that had turned some heads by knocking off highly regarded Stanford. Charleston was on a mission but Kentucky was on a roll, winning by twenty-seven. For leading the team in scoring in the championship game, Mercer—who was still Kentucky's biggest name—wrested the tournament's Most Valuable Player award from Anderson, who deserved it. More significantly, Mohammed and Magloire combined for twenty points and ten rebounds in the Charleston game. "In two weeks," said Pitino, "they've gone from dropping passes to doing jump hooks and up-and-under moves. There's a night and day difference between this team and the one two weeks ago. Now I feel terrific about our basketball team. It's been astonishing."

But Kentucky had not yet seen astonishing. That would come later. Astonishing would be what the Wildcats did in Freedom Hall to Indiana.

First, there were thirty points from Mercer and a solid victory over Purdue in Chicago, where the team stopped on its way back from Alaska. In the fuss over his best collegiate performance, Mercer deflected the credit to his alter ego. "The leading light on this team is Derek," he said. "He has the experience. He knows what he's doing out there. I try to learn from him. I'm a step behind." Mercer's modesty was refreshing, but Pitino put it more bluntly. "Derek Anderson," he said at the end of a night in which Anderson's numbers had been relatively ordinary, "is our best basketball player."

The Indiana game was next, with more than twenty thousand people—Bob Wiggins prominent among them—making a red and blue spectacle of Freedom Hall. It was the sort of color scheme that Derek Anderson, growing up, had imagined seeing in the famous arena when he played there (in his dreams, however, the red was Louisville's, and he was wearing it), and the sight of it was as compelling as the matchup, which pitted inter-conference, comparably obsessive regional rivals and Top Ten teams as well: the reborn national champions against the undefeated champions of the preseason NIT. Kentucky's difficult seven-point victory over Indiana the previous season had broken a 19-19 tie in the series, which was known for its grueling struggles. The fortieth game would also be a contest of coaching styles headed in opposite directions. While Pitino endeavored continually to reinvent the modern game with pressing strategies and open-court innovation, Bobby Knight seemed determined to prove that he could still win the same way he won (three national championships) in the seventies and eighties, when he succeeded in a fashion borrowed from the fifties and sixties.

Despite his stubbornness, Knight was still a masterful game coach, and he made a concession to Kentucky's speed in his opening lineup, starting three guards in a concerted attempt to break the press. The problem was that two of the guards, Michael Lewis and A.J. Guyton, were freshmen. The third, junior Neil Reed, was so ineffective against the pressure that Knight soon lifted him and resorted to bringing seven-foot freshman Jason Collier into the backcourt as a tall passer. Basketball purists had a tough time watching. Kentucky's lead exceeded twenty with more than six minutes left in the first half. At halftime, the Hoosiers had thirty-one points and Anderson, who sat out three minutes, matched the number he had chosen for his back (which, not coincidentally, was also Michael Jordan's) with twenty-three.

By the second half, the game was so out of hand that the Indiana fans lost all ability to heckle. When one of them teased Jared Prickett for missing a breakaway dunk, the Kentucky senior just looked into the red shirts, pointed up, and said, "Scoreboard." Anderson, releasing five years of pent-up hometown emotions, answered the Hoosiers in his own way. After a particularly precocious slam in the second half, he lapsed into a shoulder-shimmy dance that, in Kentucky's over-scrutinized micro-history, would long be associated with his (thirty points) and his team's (99-65) memorable performance.

At the end, Knight was slumped back passively in his chair and the Cats, respectful of the rivalry, were straining to hold their score under a hundred. Reporters walked softly into the interview room afterwards, but the Hoosier coach was more resigned than angry at the sum of the evening's events. "I don't think there's anything we could have done to change the outcome of this game," he said. "We were beaten in the first five minutes by a much better team. By the second five minutes, the game was over. This team and this coach play this kind of basketball about as well as any team could play it."

He might have added that the hometown shooting guard, with his killer combination of court sense and drop-dead creativity, played Pitino's style of basketball as well as any player could play it. Pitino as much as said that. His appraisal of the Indiana game was essentially this: "I think

Derek Anderson is the premier two-guard in the country. What we see every day from him in practice is incredible." Pitino, who had ordered walk-on Steve Masiello to dribble out the final twenty seconds, didn't approve of Anderson's dancing but couldn't bring himself to criticize his irrepressible senior star. Anderson, meanwhile, apologized his way—with the coy smile that had become his signature. "I talked to 'Toine [Boston Celtic rookie and former Wildcat Antoine Walker, a slam-dunk dancer of some repute] the other day," he explained sufficiently.

An hour after the game had ended, seventy-five Kentucky fans of all ages waited politely behind Freedom Hall for a last glimpse of their heroes as they boarded the team bus. There were no policemen to hold back the crowd, and none necessary; the Kentuckians courteously kept their distance, permitting the players to climb on without delaying them for autographs or otherwise interrupting the music in their headphones. Settling into their seats, the Wildcats stared back through tinted windows and waved. When the bus pulled out, the fans made no sudden moves to disperse. The moment was too good to leave behind just yet.

It was just as good for the hundreds of thousands who weren't there. In their homes, at their parties, on the radio, over the Internet, they talked about never expecting such a game in their wildest dreams. They discussed Anderson's dance—the nays had it—and Dick Vitale's remark that Anderson and Mercer were the best one-two punch in the country. They also compared the two inseparable stars to each other—the votes were split—and thanked the basketball gods that Kentucky had them both.

3

A Man's Legacy

In 1946, the owners of the sixteen major-league baseball teams voted 15-1 to keep Jackie Robinson off their playing fields, the one exception being the team that had signed him, the Brooklyn Dodgers. The vote was not binding, but the Dodgers' mastermind, Branch Rickey, knew that his great experiment would die a quiet death unless he received the backing of the former Kentucky governor who was then the commissioner of baseball, Albert "Happy" Chandler. In an inspiring moment of civil libertarianism and professional defiance, the colorful Kentuckian told Rickey to go ahead and bring the fellow on if he was good enough. "I'll have to meet my maker some day," he said years later. "If he asks me why I hadn't let this fellow play and I say because he was black, that might not be a sufficient reason." If Robinson was the pioneer of baseball integration and Rickey its impresario, Chandler was at least its executor.

Forty-two years later, at a committee meeting of the University of Kentucky trustees, the subject of Zimbabwe somehow came up, to which the 89-year-old former governor and baseball commissioner issued a regrettable response. "You know Zimbabwe's all nigger now," Chandler said. "There aren't any whites." The unfortunate comment naturally provoked an outcry on several fronts and the old Kentucky icon only made it worse when he said that black folks back in his hometown of Henderson showed a preference for the epithet he had used. Chandler was out of touch with the times, certainly, and ill-advised in his language and attitude, but it was coldly ironic that the very executor of baseball integration should be singled out and even marched against four decades later as

◀ *Icon and son: Herky Rupp has stepped up to refute contemporary attacks on his father.*

73

an enemy of civil rights. If he was an enemy of civil rights, what were the fifteen tycoons who owned major-league baseball teams? And while it is highly doubtful that the black citizens of Henderson, Kentucky, liked being called what Chandler called them, it is not at all doubtful that he somehow *thought* they did. It was not the old man's heart that put him out of touch, but his place and time. The word that was anathema to so many was simply common in the where and when from which he came.

And so it was with one of Chandler's best friends, of whom the former governor said, "Every time Rupp got, as I like to say, his tit in a wringer, I got it out." Unlike Chandler, Adolph Rupp had not been raised in small-town Kentucky, but he, too, was a rural turn-of-the-century product whose learned behavior in racial affairs was awkwardly old-schooled. Southerners and some European-Americans, in fact, might have been taught ethnic tolerance from the same primer. Even in today's age of political correctness, racial epithets are not uncommon among the senior citizens of nearby Cincinnati's German community, for instance—witness Marge Schott. If Rupp's choice of words betrayed deep-seated thoughts that made him a bigot by definition, then a bigot he must have been; but he was not the Aryan villain that myth so eagerly purports. His racial attitudes approximated those of his environment. So institutionally bigoted was the time and place in which he worked—which, in fact, he *represented*—that a local sportswriter stood up at the team banquet after the 1966 season, which ended in the title-game defeat to Texas Western, and declared that Kentuckians could all be proud of having the best *white* team in the nation.

Having succeeded in uniting the state over basketball, Rupp was not interested in dividing it over integration. Even his champions acknowledge that the Baron was by no means a social reformer. Rupp himself acknowledged that when he integrated the high school team he coached in Freeport, Illinois, he first had to be satisfied that the player in question would conduct himself in a manner that would meet with the approval of the local spectators. Yet despite his record of racial conservatism—he was timorous perhaps to a fault in the matter of recruiting black athletes for Kentucky—there is ample evidence to suggest that Rupp was not a hateful bigot. He was probably not even a voluntary one.

This is not to advance the fantasy that his use of the term "nigger," as pointed out in Harry Lancaster's book, was an isolated or misrepresented instance; to the contrary, it was possibly habitual and perhaps revealing. Columnist Dave Kindred has shared a conversation he had with Rupp as a Kentucky sportswriter in 1974, when the Baron, two years retired, was recollecting his first visit to Lexington in 1930 and the impression made upon him by a neighborhood he passed through on his cab ride to campus. "Bear in mind," Rupp said, as reported by Kindred in *The Sporting News*, "that where Memorial Coliseum now stands, there were fifty-five little nigger one- and two-room shacks then. They took me to eat at the university cafeteria, and out the third-floor window I could see all those little nigger shacks. I wasn't used to anything like that . . . I said, 'Good Gawd almighty, what kind of place is this Kentucky?'" Kindred reported this not to join the journalistic firing squad, but to place the old coach's remarks in the appropriate context, calm the trigger fingers, and promote the point of view that Rupp's racial attitudes were apparently neither malignant nor defining. He pointed out that in the hundreds of times he spoke with the Kentucky folk hero, it was the only occasion in which he heard Rupp use a racist term. Although this is not a perspective that has gained unanimous favor in Kentucky's black community, it reflects the strong sentiment of most of those who worked with the man and knew him well.

"In today's society," said UK athletic director C.M. Newton, who played for the Baron at mid-century, "Coach Rupp would be considered racist. That is, if he operated today in the way that he operated then. But I guess that's where I pick a fight with a lot of young critics. They don't do their homework to look back and see what it was like in that context. Having played for Coach Rupp and been around him and coached against him, I can say that he was not a racist. He made some tough decisions about who to recruit and who not to recruit, but he was not a racist. There were tough decisions back then about whether to take a black student to some of the places he'd have to go to play. I know because I integrated the program at Alabama and I took Wendell Hudson to Auburn and Ole Miss and heard some of that stuff. So I don't have a lot of patience for guys writing today who don't really understand the conditions. It keeps getting written about nowadays in a totally different way than it actually was back then."

If anything, Adolph Rupp was an equal-opportunity bigot. His character flaw lately perceived as bigotry actually had its roots in something else entirely. For Rupp, discrimination was more a personality trait than a racial attitude; his language disparaged people and players of all walks. The coach routinely referred to his second- and third-string players as "turds," for instance, using the term in a manner not intended to be amusing. "That's wonderful," Rupp would shout to a reserve player who didn't meet his practice standards. "That's why you'll always be a turd." The ugly name reflected a distinct class system by which he operated. Second-line players were second-class citizens in the Kentucky scheme of things and were never allowed to forget it. When a couple of them returned Frank Ramsey's physical play with a few rough moves of their own during a practice session, Rupp roared at them, "Christ, let's don't hurt the All-American. You turds have all year to get well, but if I lose an All-American, damn!" The undefeated 1954 team was painted with the same brush when it voted 9-3 to participate in the NCAA tournament after stars Ramsey, Cliff Hagan, and Lou Tsioropoulos were declared ineligible by virtue of having already graduated (Ramsey, Hagan, and Tsioropoulos being the three dissenting votes). Rupp promptly overruled the election, declaring, "We won't allow a group of turds to mar the record established in large measure by our three seniors." So institutionalized was the name "turds" that for one public scrimmage the second-teamers came out with large T's taped to the backs of their shirts. (The newspapers the next day reported that Rupp was already looking ahead to Tennessee.) In general, Rupp's attitude toward players who couldn't perform at high levels was that they were basically in the way. During halftime breaks, when he devised his strategy for the rest of the game, he often told the turds that they might as well just stay out on the floor and shoot some baskets. (Georgia Tech's reserves did the same thing, and one night the two squads started up their own impromptu halftime game until the cheering of the crowd disturbed Rupp's locker room lecture and he ordered an immediate stop to their impudence.)

Often, Rupp either didn't know or care to mention the names of his bench players, referring to them instead by hometowns. When freshman Doug Flynn, the future major-league baseball player from Lexington's Bryan Station High School, hit three straight jump shots in a scrimmage against the varsity, Rupp stopped the action and shouted, "Hey, are you that kid from Lafayette?" When Flynn said no, the Baron turned to his sidekick, Harry Lancaster, and asked, "Who the hell is he, Harry?"

Never one to confuse his team with his family, Rupp saved his soft side for home and community, environments in which he waxed paternal. On the court, however, neither he nor Lancaster were early advocates of touchy-feely. At Kentucky, the pecking order was not only apparent but colorfully articulated, as well, by the two taskmasters in their khaki uniforms who presided over joyless, practically silent (but famously efficient) practices. The only words they wanted to hear were their own, Lancaster's delivered in the assistant's blunt, military manner, Rupp's with cleverly turned, unforgiving humor. The players who could take the double-barreled abuse were stronger for it; the others wilted or left. On occasion, the coaches' insults were calculated to run the player away. One story had Lancaster calling a young man from Tennessee into his office and telling him, "Son, I've tried to embarrass you, to humiliate you. You have no pride. You don't know an insult when you hear one. We can't use you here, so I want you to get your stuff and go somewhere else." The player wasn't easily bullied, however. "Coach," he replied politely, "tonight I'll have a little talk with God and I'll let you know tomorrow whether or not I'm leaving." The next day at practice, the fellow advised Lancaster that he'd had a long talk with God and was staying in school. "Son," said Lancaster, "I've talked with the Lord since you have, and you're leaving."

Rupp's sarcasm is legendary among those who played for him, most of whom remember well when they were its object. He told Milt Ticco, after the latter missed an easy shot that would have tied Ohio State at the end of regulation, that the Buckeyes ought to be awarding him a varsity letter. He told Dickie Parsons and/or Tommy Kron (depending on who's doing the remembering), "Did you know that I'm writing a book entitled *What Not To Do In Basketball*? The first two hundred pages are going to be about you." He told C.M. Newton and/or Gayle Rose, "You look like a Shetland Pony in a stud horse parade." He told John Crigler, "John Lloyd, a hundred and fifty years from now there will be no university, no fieldhouse. There will have been an atomic war, and it will all be destroyed. Underneath the rubble there will be a monument, on which is the inscription, 'Here lies John Crigler, the most stupid basketball player ever at Kentucky, killed by Adolph Rupp.'" He told mountain-boy Ernest Sparkman during the 1944 NIT, "Sparkman, you see that center circle? I want you to go out there and shit. Then you can go back to Carr Creek and tell them at least you did something in Madison Square Garden."

In the master's artful possession, sarcasm was both an offensive and defensive weapon. Its versatility was exercised even upon the occasional irreverent fan who had the temerity to question the Baron's performance. Upon receiving one particularly derogatory dispatch, Rupp wrote the offender back with an eloquently characteristic retort: "I thought you'd like to know that some SOB wrote me criticizing my coaching," he replied, "and he signed your name to it."

The apparent disrespect with which Rupp treated his turds and detractors might have seemed anecdotal and even gratuitous at times, but there was a revealing pattern at work—the blue lines on his personality map all emanated from a place called Personal Pride. When he interviewed for the UK job as a Midwestern nobody, Rupp declared emphatically that he was the best damn coach in the country and believed it so fundamentally that the dozens of better qualified applicants seemed to shrink in comparison. Such was the force of his pride that he could simply not tolerate anything that would undermine his eminence. In his estimation, the fumbling pivotman represented a horrifying threat to overthrow that which the Baron held sacred, and the critical correspondent suggested that the same had already been overthrown, if indeed there was anything to it in the first place. His contempt for poor performances and ineffectual players arose out of the overriding fear that they made him look bad. Rupp was quoted often to this effect. Before the Cats came from behind to beat Vanderbilt in the last game at Alumni Gym, their eighty-fourth consecutive home victory, he told them, "Boys, a man spends a lifetime compiling a record, and in one given night a group of bums like you are about to tear it down. If it looks like we're going to go down in defeat tonight, I want you to know that I am personally going to do something to this facility before the game is over and before you get out of this gym." The suspicious 1950 NIT loss to integrated City College of New York was so awful for Rupp—he took every defeat personally, just as Kentucky fans all over the state did and still do—that he told his squad, "I want to thank you boys. You get me selected Coach of the Year and then bring me up here and embarrass the hell out of me." After the Cats were beaten badly at Alabama in 1955 and the team had to rent several automobiles after the bus broke down, one of the cars of Kentucky players rammed the rear end of one driven by an elderly woman, who fell out of her vehicle onto the side of the road. Rupp rushed over to find that she wasn't badly hurt. "Lady," he said, "if you think this is bad, you ought to see what those bastards did to me back in that Coliseum." (The corollary, most likely apocryphal, is that Rupp once bumped into a woman at the airport on the way home from a mediocre performance. "Sorry ma'am," he said. "No offense." "And damn little defense, either," she replied.)

Those who were not disfigured by Rupp's wit have suggested that the coach could have been a stand-up comedian; but he was not a comedian: he didn't play for laughs (except occasionally with the press, which was treated to the more sanguine side of his humor). This may or may not have resulted from the fact that he often didn't *feel* like laughing. Rupp's incessant health problems included diabetes, an ulcerated stomach, back troubles that led to a spinal operation, various infections, and the cancer that he ultimately died from. On top of all that he was not, by nature, a jolly guy. On the basketball floor, he wouldn't countenance a smile from himself or his men. He once told a whistling player that there was no room for happiness on the basketball court; stop being happy, damn it, and play some ball.

"This pretty much explains his coaching technique," said Joe B. Hall, the assistant who ultimately succeeded Rupp as head coach. "It was the year of Rupp's Runts, and we were coasting along undefeated, number one in the country, and all of a sudden complacency hits the team. We had a horrible practice one day—one of those horrendous ones when all the windows are getting broken out, we're kicking the ball all over the floor, nobody is working very hard, nobody is getting back on the fast break. And Coach just walked out onto the floor in that Army uniform of his, put his arms up and said, 'Cease! Cease this disgraceful exhibition! These hallowed halls have never witnessed such a deplorab . . .' and he stopped, got down on one knee, and he took his finger and wiped something off the floor. 'By Gawd,' he said, 'a drop of sweat! One of the janitors must have dropped that when he was sweeping.' That's how he got your attention—with that kind of sarcasm and humor. But he never laughed and you never laughed. You bit the side of your jaw, but you didn't laugh."

Unlike his Wildcat teammates in the late fifties and early sixties, Adolph Rupp Jr.—"Herky" Rupp—was able to experience the coach's many sides without Lancaster at his side or the khaki shirt on his back. He saw him in the easy chair reading *U.S. News & World Report* or in his Shriner's hat headed out to raise more money than anybody else for the crippled children's hospital. He saw him out registering his calves—for sixteen consecutive terms Rupp was president of the state Hereford association—on the farm that Herky still runs. He sat with his dad in the upper deck at Ebbets Field (they were on a mission to visit every major-league ballpark together), rode with him to Shrine conventions in the cities and hotshots' homes in the hills (stopping to eat at places like the Sanders Motel in Corbin, where the Colonel himself came out of the kitchen in his apron to wait on them), and countless times was at his side walking across the parking lot to Alumni Gym three hours before a game when the coach stopped to visit with the blind pencil vendor who recognized the sound of his footsteps as he approached. He also knew him at practice, from the perspective of one of the turds.

"It was hard to keep a straight face when Daddy was telling you off," said Rupp's only child, who, from his home near UK's football stadium, has joined his own son and daughter in an extended campaign to restore the once-great name that late-breaking racist charges have broadly besmirched. "He might say you're a big damn clown or whatever, but it wasn't a personal thing against you or your family. Most people don't really know my father. He was a lot different than most coaches that I know today in that he was multi-dimensional. Basically, basketball was at the Coliseum or Alumni Gym, and when he got home he did other things."

One of the things he did *not* do when he got home, according to Herky, was demean or otherwise demonstrate discernible prejudice against black people. The family line is that if he had done that—if he had handed down racism as an operating principle—the remaining Rupps wouldn't be so profoundly offended by the image that has been perpetrated upon their patriarch, and so deeply committed to correcting it.

It's a good point. So are these: If Kentucky had joined a Northern conference and gone along with the status quo, as it did in the SEC, there wouldn't be an image problem; if Rupp hadn't dominated the South and consequently been expected to lead the way in all respects, there wouldn't be an image problem; if Kentucky hadn't beaten Duke for the right to play Texas Western in 1966, and if the nineties media had been content to let bygones be bygones, there wouldn't be at least so celebrated an image problem. And this: If Rupp had signed a black player five years earlier than he did—if only he had been bold enough to break the color barrier in the South—neither he nor Kentucky would have the image problem that still attends and complicates their names. If he had done that, the Baron's record would have been more articulate than his language, and he would gone down in history like his old pal Happy Chandler . . . with one major difference in his favor. The governor only gave Kentucky his life; the coach gave it 876 victories.

The Baron and the colonel: Kentucky fried legends

○ ○ ○

The record shows that the man in the brown suit won four NCAA championships (1948, 1949, 1951, 1958), one NIT title (1946, when the NIT was at least comparable in prestige to the NCAA tournament), one Olympic gold medal (1948), coached twenty-three All-Americans in his forty-two seasons at Kentucky, was inducted into the Basketball Hall of Fame in 1969, and involuntarily retired in 1972 as the winningest coach in college basketball history, a distinction that North Carolina's Dean Smith (another Kansan) was seriously challenging headed into the 1996-97 season.

In a way, though, Rupp *couldn't* win. His mastery over the South was so categorical that it not only made him thoroughly despised around the SEC (the strength of this sentiment might have been mitigated somewhat if Rupp, upon seeing his lead reduced from thirty to twenty-eight or thereabouts, had not been so frequently inclined to stomp and shout, "Who the hell is guarding that man?"), it also diminished the weight of his professional accomplishments. The reasoning goes that the preponderance of his victories were registered against lame, cracker-gym Southern teams that had virtually no chance against his precise, superabundantly talented Kentucky machine (after the war, the Wildcats had so many star players that two previous All-Americans found themselves riding the bench). This would be a sensible argument but for one question: Why wasn't Kentucky one of those lame Southern teams? Obviously, because Adolph Rupp coached there. Under circumstances that kept other SEC schools at a disadvantage (footballs being awkward to dribble), Rupp forged UK into a regional and national powerhouse. Skeptics might counter that Kentucky was different than the rest of the South because its football was of lesser mettle, but they would be forgetting where Bear Bryant coached from 1946 to 1953, when Rupp won three of his four national championships and would have probably absconded with another one or two were it not for the point-shaving scandal that temporarily did him in.

The scandal occurred in the wake of Kentucky's greatest glory. Its 1948 team, the Fabulous Five, brought honor not only to the state of Kentucky but to the entire country, combining with the national AAU champion, the Phillips Oilers, to bring an Olympic gold medal back from London. (Rupp, who made the trip overseas as a very visible assistant, never forgave the boys for costing him the head coaching position by losing a close game to the Oilers on a spectacular night when a basketball floor was temporarily installed at UK's football stadium.) Such was the popularity of the Fabulous Five that Herky Rupp remembers, as a grade-schooler, riding the train with the famous team as it traveled to the NCAA tournament in New York City and the players standing in the back of the caboose, waving to the crowds that gathered and the bands that played at small-town stations between Lexington and Ashland; and then the triumphant return home, where the lamp posts at the train station were decorated with life-sized photographs of each starting player. Herky named his kittens after those players: Beard, Groza, Jones, Barker, and Rollins. That was the team that married Kentucky and the Wildcats for eternity.

The 1949 Wildcats, after a puzzling loss to Loyola in the postseason NIT at Madison Square Garden, righted themselves for the NCAA tournament (it was rare for a team to be invited to both) and won it again behind Beard, Jones, and Groza. In 1951, with another of Rupp's crisp-passing, fast-breaking teams, Kentucky became the first school to bring home three national championships. The great seven-footer, Bill Spivey, was a junior that season, and the sophomore class included the Kentucky natives and future Hall of Famers Cliff Hagan and Frank Ramsey. The program was so flushed with success that Rupp and Bear Bryant, the university's hot (if somewhat jealous; he knew what kind of sports state Kentucky would always be) young football coach, whose 10-1 team upset top-ranked Oklahoma in the 1951 Sugar Bowl, joined in a ceremony renaming the street that ran between the stadium and new Memorial Coliseum: Euclid Avenue became the Avenue of Champions.

Point-shaving scandals were making big news in college basketball that year, hitting Bradley University and four New York area schools—City College, Seton Hall, Long Island and Manhattan—but when asked in August about Kentucky's vulnerability to the gambling virus, Rupp shrugged it off in his customarily haughty manner. "The gamblers couldn't touch my boys with a ten-foot pole," he declared. Two months later, the Baron was in Chicago coaching a group of college all-stars in an exhibition game against the Rochester Royals when two members of the crowd were taken into custody as they left Chicago Stadium. They were Ralph Beard and Alex Groza, who had become player-owners of the NBA's Indianapolis Olympians. The former All-Americans were charged, along with UK teammate Dale Barnstable—then coaching at Louisville's Manual High School—with fixing the suspicious Loyola game in the 1949 NIT.

The erstwhile Kentucky heroes admitted that they had made an arrangement with gamblers before the game, but insisted that their deal was only to manipulate the point spread, not to deliberately lose. Observers at Madison Square Garden, however, had wondered at the time how it was that Groza was so inexplicably ineffective that night, thoroughly outplayed by an obviously inferior opponent. Although his ineptitude was the most conspicuous, Groza had plenty of company in his conspiratorial performances. Jim Line and Walt Hirsch, reserve players from 1949 who became starters the next year, were also implicated as the grand jury investigation spread to other games between 1948 and 1951.

The wreckage that ultimately piled up from the case had little to do with criminal penalties. Barnstable, Beard, and Groza were given suspended sentences, but the latter two were banned from continuing professional basketball careers that had begun in big ways; both had made the all-NBA team in only their second season with Indianapolis (in one personal duel, Beard outscored Boston great Bob Cousy 24-2). As for the great institution of Kentucky basketball, meanwhile, there was little that the Manhattan district judge, Saul Streit, could do to the program legally, but the thunder of his judicial opinion reverberated from the Appalachian hollows to the halls of the NCAA.

In a 63-page, 80-minute speech—Kentuckians considered it a diatribe—at the conclusion of the trial, Streit ripped the UK program up one side and down the other. If his criminal punishments of Kentucky players were relatively light, his moral indictment of Rupp was a bullwhip to the bare back. The judge devoted eighteen pages of his report to the famous Kentucky coach, stating publicly that Rupp "aided and abetted in the immoral subsidization of the players. With his knowledge, the charges in his care were openly exploited . . . [and the coach] failed in his duty to observe the amateur rules to build character and protect the morals and health of his charges." Even more damningly to Kentucky—and by extension to Rupp—Streit called the UK program "the acme of commercialism and overemphasis . . . I found undeniable evidence of covert subsidization of players, ruthless exploitation of athletes, cribbing on examinations, illegal recruiting, a reckless disregard for the players' physical welfare, matriculation of unqualified students, [and] demoralization of the athletes by the coaches, the alumni, and the townspeople."

The investigation revealed that Kentucky players had received money on more than a dozen occasions from numerous and sundry sources ranging from the coaching staff to boosters to gamblers—and that was not counting the many times Lancaster stood at the back door of Alumni Gym doling out fifty cents so the fellows could eat at the bowling alley across the street. Rupp and even school president Herman Donovan acknowledged that the coaches had periodically handed the players fifty dollars of spending money after road games, including a couple in New Orleans, where the Wildcats frequently played in the Sugar Bowl tournament. Barnstable later commented that it was common for players to receive fifteen or twenty dollars from the school after a good game, which made it seem not too bad to take another twenty or fifty or even a couple hundred to ensure a victory that exceeded the point spread. (Asked by the grand jury whether Kentucky was as generous in defeat, Barnstable replied, "No sir. You were lucky to get something to eat then.") In general, there were no red flags to discourage the UK players from chasing their financial options. Gambling itself was practically institutional in Lexington, where parimutuel wagering was a trademark industry and one of the nation's largest bookmaking operations was run from a room above the Mayfair Bar on Main Street. The state of Kentucky had no laws governing the exchange of money over sporting events.

The bigger money, of course, was available when the point spread was tinkered with in the other direction. For the Loyola game that got out of hand and turned into an incriminating disaster, Barnstable, Beard, and Groza reportedly received two thousand dollars delivered to Groza's car under a viaduct. It also seemed that the bigger money was available when Kentucky and other teams played in Madison Square Garden (UK's horrific, hard-to-fathom NIT loss to City College in 1950 was a prime exhibit), an item that naturally didn't escape the people of Kentucky, who noted—and Donovan made specific mention of this in his public reply—that in all of Streit's sixty-three pages, there was not a single indictment or even a passing remark about New York's role in the point-shaving epidemic.

Kentuckians were convinced that the whole ordeal was mostly another case of New York being out to get them. In this sentiment, they took their lead from Rupp, who refused to ever play in the Big Apple again despite the fact that he had always loved its nightclubs and the attention of its press, which he capably charmed (one player said you could lead the coach all over town with a flash attachment). The persecution theory underwent a geographical expansion when other accusers began to come forward from around the land. The SEC, citing payments made to players between 1946 and 1951, voted to prohibit Kentucky from participating in the 1952-53 season, and the NCAA asked its members not to schedule the Wildcats that year. The NCAA made it clear that its penalty could be spared if Donovan were to fire Rupp, but the president declined, maintaining that the Baron was an honorable man who had done nothing that wasn't common practice.

Half a century later, Rupp's relationship to the scandal remains something of a curiosity. There is no question that it came as a shock to him, leaving him sobbing in his hotel bed on the October night when Beard and Groza were apprehended at Chicago Stadium. He was so disillusioned by what those two, in particular, had done to his program and to his memories that he unretired their jerseys and evidently saw to it that their Wall of Fame pictures disappeared one night, along with the photographs of the Fabulous Five and the all-conference mementos of Jim Line and Walt Hirsch. It was twenty years—the end of his career—before he was able to forgive or even speak to the players who were implicated in the point-shaving. "I guarantee you," wrote Lancaster in his book, "both of us were convinced that none of our players had been involved . . . [Then we] thought of the Loyola game when Groza had been outplayed by a stiff and wouldn't even move to the ball, like he was hiding behind the defender . . . "

Even without his specific knowledge of what went down, however, Rupp's accountability can easily be taken to task by a more cynical analysis. And it doesn't require much cynicism to conclude that his innocence is compromised if not by what he did, at least by what he *didn't* do; i.e, he didn't adequately represent the principles of intercollegiate athletics by discouraging the relationship between basketball and bucks. In addition to the Sugar Bowl money and Barnstable's mention of regular post-game rewards, several players confirmed—Hirsch said it to the grand jury—that the coach had given them fifty dollars after their resounding victory over Kansas in December of 1950, a game in which Rupp had desperately wanted to beat his mentor, KU coach Phog Allen. He was also known to have been friendly with Ed Curd, the big-time bookie who ran the huge Mayfair Bar operation. Rupp went to Curd's house at least once to solicit a donation for the Shriner's children's hospital and was seen with the gambler at least twice in New York nightclubs after Kentucky games there. If New York was the epicenter of the sports gaming world, as Rupp insisted, what sort of message was sent when he was seen openly socializing—in New York, no less—with the most notorious bookmaker in the South? The signals that the Baron transmitted in this respect were at best confusing. The gambler who first contacted Kentucky players, a New Yorker and one-time UK football player named Nick "The Greek" Englisis,

Towering figures: In order to beat his famous mentor, Kansas's Phog Allen, Rupp came up with a taller center. Bill Spivey (right) cooperated by outplaying Clyde Lovellette (left).

was photographed by a Louisville newspaper sitting at the end of the Kentucky bench during a conference tournament game in Louisville, which he almost certainly could not have done without Rupp's permission. While there is no hard evidence to link Rupp to basketball gambling, it is difficult to argue with Judge Streit's assertion that the Baron "aided and abetted in the immoral subsidization of the players."

Rupp's best and only defense lies in the fact that he apparently was not privy to what transpired between his players and the shadowy figures who bribed them. As news of the investigation broke in the fall of '51 and continued to leak into the season, the coach became wary of certain players on his roster. Bill Spivey, the All-American center from Georgia who had been named national Player of the Year as a junior, was the object of scrutiny by the grand jury while he rested a knee injury sustained as he was making a clinic film for Rupp during the summer. Nonetheless, the 1951-52 team, which included Hagan, Ramsey, and junior star Shelby Linville, rose to the top of the polls without Spivey and had every intention of repeating as national champion when the big fellow returned. Those ambitions were adjusted on Christmas Eve, shortly before he was ready to re-enter the awesome Kentucky lineup and shortly after the assistant district attorney from New York had come to Lexington to broaden his investigation, when Spivey requested that he be removed from the eligibility list until his name was cleared. He later asked to be reinstated, but when March arrived and the country's best center still hadn't been exonerated, the university athletics board suspended him.

Without Spivey, the team's top returning frontcourt player figured to be Linville, an agile 6-6 forward from Middletown, Ohio. Linville had started every game as a junior and was named on the all-conference second team, but strangely he saw only occasional action as a senior. "I was out for a little while with an injury, then came back and had a good game," recalled Linville, builder and pastor of Middletown's Roselawn Baptist Church, whose congregation consists largely of Kentucky-born folks. "The next game was against St. Louis. Coach Rupp put me in, I tipped in a basket, and he took me out. That was the last time he talked to me for five or six games. Then he put me back as the sixth man and never said anything about it. That spring, after the trial and everything, I was watching a Kentucky baseball game and [athletic director] Bernie Shively saw me. He said, 'Shelby, will you speak to Adolph? This thing has really hit him hard.' So I sat down with him. I told him there were times when I could have just hit him and left. But the whole reason why he wouldn't play me didn't dawn on me until later. My name had been brought up in rumors in New York because I had roomed with Hirsch, Line, and Barnstable. Three of us were from Ohio and one from Indiana. The connection was obvious. During those five or six games when I didn't play, that was when I was being cleared in sworn statements by those three players. They said they were afraid of me, that I was too true blue. When I sat down in Coach Rupp's office that day, he said, 'Shelby, I owe you a public apology. I probably kept you from being an All-American.'

Shelby Linville (right): "...the only one that Adolph ever apologized to."

I told Ralph Beard about that conversation and Ralph said, 'You're unique. You're the only one that Adolph ever apologized to.' But I could tell that the whole thing hurt Coach bad, real bad.

"The thing is, I roomed with all those fellows and I didn't know anything about what was going on. They put on a good front. I remember Hirsch even borrowed money from me. As far as I knew, scandal wasn't even in our language. But one time against St. Louis [at the Sugar Bowl tournament in December, 1950], I remember when Walt went in for the winning goal and almost broke the backboard. I was going in for a shot, but Walt had a better angle and he was my roommate, so I flipped it off to him and he slammed it off the board. Rupp cussed him out that night like nobody's business."

For Linville, whose devotion to the Wildcats is so enduring that he brings in guest speakers and stages a UK Conference at his church every July for the countless Ohioans who haven't forsaken their Kentucky roots, the scandal had multiple repercussions. The program of which he remains so proud was permanently stained; his opportunity for personal achievement and even a professional career was wiped out; he watched good people—notably Spivey—taken down unnecessarily; and he can't rid himself of the notion that he might have played on the best team in Kentucky history. "Figure it out," Linville said as he stretched out his long legs in the church office, where UK mementos shared the walls with his ministerial trappings. "If it hadn't been for the scandal, Kentucky would have had a run almost like UCLA. I really think we would have been another UCLA. [As it was, in the seven years surrounding the scandal, UK recorded three national championships and completed another season undefeated.] If the '52 team had had Spivey and no scandal, it would have been the greatest Kentucky team of all. I really believe that."

Spivey's tragedy was similar to Beard's and Groza's—Hall of Fame careers that didn't happen—except that he never accepted any money and passed a lie detector test to prove it. But he was *offered* a bribe, and his failure to report it—an act that would have entailed turning in his friends—and his indictment on perjury charges, for which he was acquitted, kept him out of the NBA. "I was walking on the Avenue of Champions one day," Linville said, "in front of the girls' dorm, and Bill stopped me in tears. He said, 'Shelby, so help me, I hope you don't think I was involved in all of that.' These men who banned him from playing, I'd like to see them in a situation where they had to decide whether or not to rat on their friends. I don't believe I could have reported them.

"It really hurt me to see Bill go out that way. He'd have been the number-one pro center in his time. He lost his whole career just because he wouldn't rat on his buddies." Spivey, who as a gawky high schooler had played in three pairs of sweat socks (often called for traveling as he slid to a halt) until he discovered that he could fit into a pair of size-12 gym shoes by cutting the toes out, pursued his case in court for a while, played for the Washington Generals (the Harlem Globetrotters' foils), kicked around some two-bit pro leagues, ran a bar and held a few public jobs in Lexington, dropped out of sight, and eventually lost himself in alcohol. Linville recalls a team reunion in which he and Lou Tsioropoulos walked on either side of the seven-footer to keep him upright. In 1995, Spivey died down-and-out in Costa Rica, where he had an apartment.

The Kentucky program, of course, proved much more resilient; such is its history. Even the year in which it was banned from competition was somehow triumphant; the Cats held four intrasquad scrimmages, three of which were sell-outs, the fourth drawing more than six thousand people to Memorial Coliseum on a cold, icy night. The first game of the following season brought an overflow crowd to see Cliff Hagan score fifty-one points against Temple, breaking his own school record, Spivey's Coliseum record, and the SEC record of LSU's Bob Pettit. The Wildcats were so intent on marking their return with glory that they purposely missed free throws to allow Hagan to score more points on the rebounds.

Casualty: Spivey's loyalty to his friends probably kept him out of the Hall of Fame.

Playing with a vengeance that reflected the spirit of both its coach and its constituency, Kentucky never lost in the 1953-54 season. After being shut down for a year, it was supposed to lose. It was supposed to suffer. But there was still Hagan, there was still Ramsey, there was still Tsioropoulos, and there was still Rupp. Unfortunately, there was still an NCAA, as well, and it had the final word when it ruled the three veterans ineligible since they were no longer undergraduates, setting a curious precedent that actually discouraged student-athletes from completing their course work in four years. Of course, it wasn't actually quittin' time till Rupp said it was quittin' time, which he did in spite of the players' vote, informing his turds that he was not about to let them undo a perfect season by blowing it all in the NCAA tournament.

The Baron had sworn that he wouldn't retire until the man who said Kentucky couldn't play in the NCAA—that would have been NCAA executive director Walter Byers—handed him another national championship trophy. He no doubt thought that with Ramsey and Hagan, et al., the first opportunity would be the only one he needed to make good on his vow, but the NCAA's unforeseen decision meant that he had to wait four more years (along the way suffering Kentucky's first home defeat in twelve seasons to a Georgia Tech team that Rupp hadn't even bothered to scout) until Byers forked over the hardware. Johnny Cox, Vernon Hatton, Adrian Smith, et al.—the Fiddlin' Five (they weren't concert violinists, Rupp said, just pretty good fiddlers)—brought it home in 1958 at the expense of Elgin Baylor.

It was the last national championship Rupp would win. The sixties were hard on him in every way. In the early part of the decade he had a cover boy, Cotton Nash, to whom he didn't really cotton at all, and in the latter part he had the Wildcats' all-time leading scorer, Dan Issel, and political problems the likes of which he had never imagined when he left behind the high school wrestlers he had been coaching in Iowa. On top of all that, his best team of the decade, the lovable Rupp's Runts of 1966, would ultimately, unwittingly, by virtue of its overachievement and fate's mischievous matchmaking in the NCAA finals, heap infamy upon the Kentucky way.

Four full decades were obviously enough, but Rupp wanted no part of retirement; it was inconsistent with his mission and unacceptable to his ego. He certainly wasn't going to step down after the humiliating loss to Western Kentucky in the 1971 Mideast Regional; he was way too proud to leave the program that way. The next year wasn't much better—Florida State closed him out handily in the Mideast—but this time, state law and university policy left him no choice. He fought it, of course, turning his forced retirement into a statewide melodrama that provoked numerous Kentuckians of repute, such as attorney John Y. Brown Sr. and Colonel Sanders, to take up the battle at his side. Although it was inconceivable that any basketball or athletic official on the Kentucky campus would have influence to rival his, Rupp suspected that Joe B. Hall, the assistant who was in line for the job, was somehow forcing him out. A curmudgeon to the end and beyond, Rupp stubbornly held on to his television show the next year, often using it to openly criticize Hall's work. Once again political correctness had found, in Adolph Rupp, a reason to live.

The old man was ornery for five more years. He lived to see—well, perhaps to *hear*, perhaps not—himself honored on December 10, 1977, on the street named for James Naismith, the man who invented basket-

Champions: Rupp and one of his prized Herefords

ball, in the fieldhouse named for Phog Allen, the great coach whom Naismith taught and Rupp learned from. It was Adolph Rupp Night in Lawrence, Kansas. In Lexington, Kentucky, meanwhile, the honoree was unconscious in his hospital bed, attended by family. The game between the team he played for and the one he practically invented was on the radio, Cawood Ledford announcing. Rupp died with fourteen seconds to play. Kentucky won by seven. He was seventy-six.

It's been twenty years since then, a quarter of a century since the grouchy old icon was retired against his will, but in the land that he made in his own image, the name remains bigger than life. To this day, it is the Baron's complicated network of legacies that separates Kentucky basketball from every other kind. The tradition of winning: Rupp is, of course, responsible for that. The exaggerated pride and insufferable arrogance (in the view of many) that accompany Kentucky's tradition: hmmm, where could that have come from? The racism by which the program is controversially identified: all about Rupp. The history of scandal that has characterized Kentucky basketball: it, too, had its genesis under the controversial watch of Adolph Rupp.

In much the same way that Rupp's race-related shortcomings were largely passive in nature—a matter of whom he didn't enthusiastically recruit—the questions about his integrity emanate from the fact that he appeared disinterested in the straight and narrow, choosing instead to have public drinks with Ed Curd and entertain Nick the Greek on the end of his bench. Nevertheless, he knew right from wrong. Herky Rupp recalls a recruit from Pittsburgh who sat down in the coach's office and said that the offer Rupp had to match was $14,000, whereupon the Baron promptly showed him the door. When it came to enticing players to Kentucky, Rupp didn't need to cheat. He already had plenty of head-turning recruiting tools, notably Kentucky's tradition and the legions of willing boosters at his disposal. While not commissioning the boosters to make illicit offers, Rupp wasn't the least bit shy about bringing the force of their numbers to bear. Late in his career, he encouraged the formation of the Committee of 101 and dispatched the eager Kentuckians to the recruiting trail. Nearly a hundred of them chartered a plane to fly to Philadelphia and sit in their blue blazers as they watched a burly center named Jeff Ruland play a high school game; the coach wanted fifty or sixty committee members to attend the games of every Kentucky recruit.

In virtually all ways, it seems, the issue of the Baron's honor is a complicated one fraught with the uncertainties of perspective and degree. If he was unbending in his refusal to cheat for recruits, he was a little more pliant in the matter of fundamental truth-telling, particularly as it might pertain to the outcome or final analysis of a basketball game. When he heard before the Cats' 1958 NCAA semifinal matchup with Temple, for instance, that Owls star Guy Rodgers would be taking the floor with a mild back injury, he inquired of all his starters as to which of them might be nursing a similar debilitation; when none reported any afflictions, Rupp advised the press that Johnny Cox had an injured arm and instructed the star forward to go along, thereby evening the excuses and ensuring that there would be no asterisk by Kentucky's victory. (When it came to gaining a competitive edge, there was much that Rupp was not above, superstition being high on the list. He carried a lucky buckeye in his pocket and placed such a high value on finding bobby pins on the way to a game that rascally players would drop them in his path. Then, of course, there was the famous brown suit—actually, three or four of them that looked about the same—that he wouldn't play a game without. Anything that might help: If the Cats were playing a Catholic school, he'd be sure to have a priest on his bench, too, just in case.)

The liberties Rupp took with the truth were generally innocuous and often as not humorous. Lancaster liked to tell of the occasion in Chicago when he came into the locker room at halftime to find the Baron backed against the wall by a hefty stranger who was screaming in his face. Lancaster knocked the intruder down and ushered him out, but moments later the unwanted visitor came barging back in, prompting the rugged ex-Marine to hit him again with such force that he broke a finger. Later that night, as Rupp regaled visitors in his hotel room—as was his custom after road victories, lounging in his red pajamas and nursing big glasses of bourbon—the coach informed everybody of how he had decked the large assailant with the same sort of right cross with which he had won the heavyweight boxing championship as a Jayhawk.

This harmless fabrication, of course, and others of a similar nature, do not make Rupp an evil man, nor do they impact significantly upon his legacy as a basketball coach. He was not, as George Will wrote, a great coach and a bad man. Nor was he a great coach and a great man. He was a great coach and an uncommon man, a complicated man, a brilliant man, a flawed man, a vain man, a baffling man.

The harsh contemporary characterization of Rupp—the portrait of the Southern coach as a heartless bigot—was too late arriving to have much effect upon the Baron's considerable ego, but it has hurt the family deeply and the state of Kentucky nearly as much. Like the great coach, Kentucky is a fundamentally insecure state, to which extent it places great store in the name of the man who carried it to the top of *something*; the man who took on New York; the man who showed 'em. Every time another arrow lodges in the old coach's reputation, a little more blood drips from the wound on Kentucky's psyche. In effect, to vilify Rupp is to lay siege on all that he meant to and for Kentucky, most of which is fiercely guarded pride. "What he accomplished was something that through the years the people of Kentucky could be proud of," said the proudest of them, Adolph Rupp Jr. "They could stick their chest out and say that we're better than you; basketball is the one thing we do better than you. That has to be the result of what my father did. He was the one who put Kentucky on the map, who took them to New York and Chicago to play the teams that people around the nation had heard of. And here's a team out of a Southern state going into the big cities and beating those teams, and they have Kentucky on their uniforms. It's something the people can stick their chest out about and say, 'That's us.'"

So Adolph Rupp did that for Kentucky, and he had reason to believe that he had really done something. On the other hand, he had no reason to believe that, by the end of the century, his legacy would be about something else altogether. A basketball coach twenty years dead should not have to undergo perpetual character analysis; he is a *basketball coach*, after all. But this is not just any basketball coach of just any basketball team. This is Adolph Rupp, and this is Kentucky.

The latter would say of the former that he was a great coach, leave it at that. And the latter would have a case. Unfortunately, that doesn't work for Kentucky. To some—to many—the state university will always be the school that Rupp built. This is a perception that carries with it a ponderous amount of baggage and, consequently, has not been entirely helpful to the ensuing coaches in their attempts to protect or restore (whichever the case may be at the time) the Wildcat tradition. In fact, for Rick Pitino, a substantial part of whose job was to knock on the doors of the best high school basketball players in Louisville and Nashville and Memphis and Lexington, etc., it was a problem that had to be dealt with.

4

Another Man's Challenge

By the time he won a national championship, Rick Pitino's postseason flirtations had become an annual spring diversion in the Bluegrass, the Pitino Derby rivaling Kentucky's more traditional one for air time and newsprint. Since leaving the New York Knicks for UK in 1989, he had turned down contracts of roughly two million dollars a year from the New Jersey Nets, two million from the Indiana Pacers, two million from the Atlanta Hawks, four million from the Los Angeles Clippers, and five million from the Los Angeles Lakers. The Nets' second offer was just a measly million a year more than the Lakers', but it was for five years—thirty million—and it came after Pitino had won his first championship of any kind.

After seven seasons, the time seemed to be at hand for his considerable ambition to take over. Everyone was well aware of the New Yorker's fast-tracking from the beginning; he walked it, talked it, wore it on his Armani sleeve. Before he won a national title at Kentucky, it was apparent that he probably would someday if he stuck it out, and there was reason to believe, consequently, that he might hang around for the ring; but all bets were off after the triumph in the Meadowlands. By his own account, Pitino was ready to accept New Jersey's outrageous proposal until he went to play golf in Ireland with some Kentucky boosters, chief among them being his wife, who whispered late one night that he should follow his heart. He did, back to the place where thirty million couldn't buy what was his, which was anything he wanted.

The profoundly grateful citizens of Kentucky were already be-

◀ *City boy, country boy: One of Rick Pitino's many challenges at Kentucky was communicating with the likes of Richie Farmer.*

holden to Pitino for taking over the UK program at its lowest point—lower, even, than 1953, when the whole Wildcat season was called off. That time, the Cats practiced all year and whupped up on everybody the next. The scandal that hit in 1989 was much more devastating. Not to individuals—there were no Beards or Grozas or Spiveys involved—but to Kentucky basketball, and to Kentucky.

The 1989 scandal is often confused with the *Lexington Herald-Leader* investigation that preceded it by four years, but the two events were related only in their implications, not in their particulars. In 1985, the *Herald-Leader* interviewed thirty-three former UK players who represented a span of thirteen years and got them to testify about such shenanigans as selling their complimentary tickets for up to a thousand dollars each, being paid exorbitantly for speaking engagements, finding money in Christmas cards, and shaking hands with boosters—a Corbin physician, for instance—and coming away with a hundred dollars or so in the grip.

The thirteen years happened to coincide with the stewardship of coach Joe B. Hall, who had retired at the end of the 1985 season, right around the time the *Herald-Leader* began its investigation and seven months before the series was published. Although the players' observations concerning Hall's responsibility were checkered—some said he spoke out vigorously against accepting money, others said he looked the other way—he was also implicated in some of the ticket irregularities; one player sold his, at a substantial profit, to Hall's attorney. It wasn't the first time Hall's program had been exposed. In 1976, his available scholarships had been reduced by two for two years due to recruiting violations uncovered in a probe that hit the Kentucky football program even harder. Hall, a Kentucky native and former Wildcat who worked, willed, and hounded his players to the 1978 national championship, was an uncommon coach in the respect that his partisanship toward UK was as irrepressible as that of the zealous boosters he was disinclined to suppress. In both investigations, Hall's problems emanated from the over-friendly accommodations he made for many of Kentucky's more generous supporters; Wildcat practices and locker rooms were commonly visited by horse breeders, coal operators, and other blue-blooded professionals. Their misplaced enthusiasm was at the heart of the wrongdoing that the *Herald-Leader* brought to public attention in the fall of 1985.

The series painted a picture of ongoing sugar-daddy relationships that boosters maintained with Kentucky players, often pairing up with an apparently pre-designated athlete as soon as the latter arrived on campus. The exchange of money wasn't enormous—one of the more prominent Wildcats (and one of the few who remained unnamed in the articles) estimated his career gross at about ten thousand dollars—but it was disturbingly commonplace, which accounted in part for the relative openness with which the players discussed what went on. (The illicit payment of Kentucky players was so institutionalized that former center Melvin Turpin confided to the *Herald-Leader* as to how he was highly offended at having not received what he considered to be his share of the booty.) Most of the players later denied their statements, and the newspaper refused to release the reporters' tapes, but the articles were so well-documented that the *Herald-Leader* won a Pulitzer Prize.

The investigation naturally led to another one by the NCAA, but after a couple of apparently fruitless years, no sanctions were imposed. Embarrassed to not find the misdeeds that the Lexington newspaper had turned up—it was suggested that many of the players were persuaded to disavow the incidents that the *Herald-Leader* reported—the NCAA could only snarl and wrist-slap the university for its reluctance to cooperate in the investigation.

The case was ostensibly closed at that point, but two months after the perfunctory reprimand an express envelope fatefully came unglued at the Emery Air Freight terminal in Los Angeles. The *Los Angeles Daily News* reported that the package, sent by UK assistant coach Dwane Casey to the father of prized recruit Chris Mills, contained a thousand dollars in crisp cash. The NCAA Committee on Infractions, already in the mood to fry Kentucky for the next parking ticket, was only too happy to renew the investigation, which became juicier as it ripened. There were accounts of improprieties in the recruitment of Shawn Kemp, Sean Higgins, and Lawrence Funderburke and, more damningly, falsification of Eric Manuel's ACT exam. This time, the NCAA had the goods.

Its sentence included a two-year ban from postseason competition, a one-year prohibition on live televised games, restrictions on scholarships, the nullification of two tournament victories in which Manuel appeared as a freshman, and a five-year personal probation for Casey, whose actual culpability (he claimed the package contained no money and was not sealed when he placed it on the secretary's desk in the basketball office) remains a Kentucky controversy to this day. In its lengthy ruling, the NCAA pointed out that Kentucky's attitude adjustment—i.e., its new willingness to cooperate with the investigation—spared it the death penalty. "Because of the nature of the violations found in this case," the report said, "the committee seriously considered whether the regular-season schedule for the men's basketball program should be curtailed in whole or in part for one or two seasons of competition. In the judgment of the committee, the nature of the violations found would justify such a penalty. However, this case was also evaluated in the light of the university's actions to bring itself into compliance."

Even so, the whole ordeal left the UK program in critical condition. This was a result not of the sanctions the NCAA imposed, but of the time it took to impose them. With most of Kentucky shut down to watch, its breath gathered in its chest, the judgment was formally and finally announced more than a year after the Emery Express envelope curiously came apart in Los Angeles. During that year, the Kentucky coach (Eddie Sutton) and athletic director (Cliff Hagan) resigned under pressure, most of the top players in the program (Mills, Manuel, Kemp, Sean Sutton, and LeRon Ellis) left school, new recruits gave UK a wide berth, and the Cats disgraced the Kentucky name with a scandalous won-loss record of 13-19, the worst since the spring Babe Ruth set out to hit sixty homers. For the depression-gripped commonwealth, it wouldn't have been any worse if coal had ceased to burn and thoroughbreds had lost their will to run.

The enduring symbol of the whole sorry episode was a *Sports Illustrated* cover story, printed in May of 1989, that carried the humiliating title of "Kentucky's Shame." The article called national attention to not only the latest impropriety but also to Kentucky's considerable tradition in that area: " . . . the Kentucky basketball program didn't invent cheating; the Wildcats merely perfected it." The bottom line was expressed in a quote from Georgia Tech coach Bobby Cremins: "[Kentucky's conduct is] a great example of winning at all costs," Cremins said. "The expectations of the Kentucky basketball fans have created a monster. Basketball is just too big at Kentucky; too big and too important. I would hope this will get it back in perspective."

Perspective, however, was not a commodity that the people of Kentucky were much inclined to acquire. Their reaction to the original *Herald-Leader* series had included the wholesale cancellation of subscriptions (including one fellow who didn't even have one but insisted he reserved the right to cancel anyway), a bomb threat at the newspaper's office, and other random promises of violence. Although the paper placed no money in the Emery envelope and was never in the vicinity of Eric Manuel's entrance exam, some Kentuckians still blamed it for UK's belated probation. Others considered the principal traitor in the program's downfall to be university president David Roselle, whose grievous act of treason was cooperating inordinately, in their eyes, with NCAA investigators. Part of the commonwealth's problem with Roselle might have been that he was a Duke graduate, but more significant was the fact that his response was the antithesis of Kentucky character. The indigenous Bluegrass instinct has always been to fight back. That is the very purpose that Big Blue basketball has historically served, after all—a way through which the state can retaliate against anybody and everybody who would try to bring Kentucky down.

Being more perspective-minded than the collective taxpayers and charged with purging the basketball program of its troublesome excesses, Roselle set his cap for Alabama coach C.M. Newton, a former UK player, as the university's new athletic director. Newton, who had integrated Alabama basketball and also raised it up, was considered to be above reproach as an intercollegiate citizen. His first task would be to hire a basketball coach with comparable integrity.

Seven years later, with the university's sixth national championship in the fold and its reputation redeemed on all counts, it was apparent that Newton's selection of Pitino was nothing short of inspired. At the time, though, and in light of the overriding ethical considerations, it was an interesting one. While Newton must have read some character between the lines of Pitino's resumé, to most observers the young coach's probity had been obscured by the glare of his upward mobility. Or perhaps it was just underdeveloped at that stage of his headlong career. During Pitino's highly publicized courtship—just a few days after the NCAA announced Kentucky's sentence, in fact—information came out connecting Pitino to eight of the sixty-eight rule violations with which the NCAA cited the University of Hawaii when he was an assistant there under Bruce O'Neil. Pitino had angled for O'Neil's job when the mess hit the fan, but part of

O'Neil's subsequent deal with the university was that he wouldn't get it. The NCAA seconded this, recommending Pitino's "permanent and complete severance of any and all relations . . . with the university's intercollegiate athletic program." He wound up as an assistant to Jim Boeheim at Syracuse—the interview took place in the lobby of the hotel where Pitino spent his wedding night, with his bride, Joanne, waiting impatiently upstairs—and moved on to the head coaching job at Boston University at the age of twenty-six. His rise from there was arresting, as he took a profoundly inauspicious Providence team to the Final Four and turned the New York Knicks around in two startling seasons.

By then, the Hawaii business had been left in the dust kicked up along Pitino's career track. When it emerged again while Newton was interviewing Pitino, the coach offered to pull his name out of consideration but the A.D., satisfied with his own background checks, told him it was unnecessary. Besides, at the new Kentucky, there would be no possibility of impropriety—Newton wouldn't have it, Pitino wouldn't need it, and the situation wouldn't permit it. In the years since Hawaii, Pitino had succeeded in establishing a reputation that placed him above such a thing, anyway; at least in his own mind. "There's no one in this business with more integrity than Rick Pitino. You won't have to worry about cheating with Rick Pitino," he declared during the gala press conference at which he was introduced to his rapt new constituency. Then he added the other thing they wanted to hear. "I promise to you people in this room today, you'll see Kentucky on the cover of *Sports Illustrated* once again. And it will be cutting down certain nets."

So the distant past was treated distantly and Kentucky snuggled up to the dapper Noo Yawker who was preeminently capable of restoring glory to its precious basketball team. A steady procession of Wildcat fans, a hundred cars long at one point, drove slowly through the tony McMeekin Place subdivision as the coach's new house went up, some of them stopping to collect souvenir lumps of dirt. On the surface, it was an unlikely infatuation. Pitino was an unapologetic Yankee and his Armani suits and Gucci shoes were as peculiar to Kentucky as his Big Apple accent ("Rupp Arener"), but all of that was superseded by two things: he was a *basketball* Yankee, which made him all right—in fact, Kentuckians saw in him a total devotion to the game that they could uniquely appreciate—and he was a Yankee with a sense of humor about it. As he acclimated himself to the job, he joked about spending twelve minutes on the phone with Richie Farmer, a beloved guard from the hills of Eastern Kentucky, and only understanding two minutes of the conversation. (Farmer said *he* could only make sense of about thirty seconds.)

The cultural clash between Pitino and Kentucky could never be entirely surmounted, but it was forgiven as soon as the home team starting winning its share, which, to everyone's surprise, was right away. With most of the big-time recruits having frantically squeezed through the same door that Sutton left open on his way to Oklahoma State, Pitino's first team was given little chance of even matching the unseemly record of the previous year. Most of the players who stayed were reserves and Kentuckians—notably Farmer, John Pelphrey of Paintsville, Deron Feldhaus of Mason County, and Reggie Hanson of Pulaski County, along with Sean Woods, an Indianapolis high schooler with strong family ties in Kentucky. But the Cats, relying on frenetic defense and liberal use of the three-point shot, lost by only two points to Indiana and were actually 3-1 when they went to Kansas and were beaten so brutally, 150-95, that KU coach Roy Williams suggested to Pitino that he call off his full-court press. Later in the season, Kentucky matched 6-7 Hanson against 7-footer Shaquille O'Neal, 6-7 Feldhaus against 7-footer Stanley Roberts, and every guard on the roster against the great Chris Jackson. Somehow, the Cats beat LSU, 100-95, and Pitino's Bombinos went on to a 14-14 record that kept the home folks delightfully entertained.

It was apparent then that if he stayed around long enough to see the job through, Pitino's stature in Kentucky would swell to epic proportions. Never in the history of college basketball had a coach taken on a mission of such magnitude as his. Joe Hall succeeded Adolph Rupp at a time when the Baron's grip had loosened, and Gene Bartow had no scandal to complicate the task of replacing John Wooden at UCLA. Pitino's burden was not only competitive at the highest level, it was culturally messianic; he was being asked to uphold the tradition, raise the spirit, and restore the self-esteem of an entire state. His multi-dimensional challenge came down, really, to three things: winning, winning right, and winning soon.

By the second year of his tenure, he was obviously well on his way. Although still ineligible for the NCAA tournament, Kentucky had become a top-ten team behind the bluegrass boys and the fast company of

Pitino's first impact recruit, New Yorker Jamal Mashburn. Mashburn's arrival in Lexington would turn out to be a signal event for both Kentucky and Pitino. For the former, it occasioned a re-entry into the top tier of college basketball. For Pitino, it was a symbolic declaration that Kentucky's past was exactly that. He had gone to the nation's biggest city—the one that UK had specifically avoided since Rupp's fellows got into so much trouble there—and brought back the kind of player he believed he had to have if Kentucky's place in the modern basketball universe were to approximate its place in the old one. He admired Farmer and Feldhaus and Pelphrey and he was appreciative of their devotion, but he needed Mashburn. He needed city players.

In that respect and virtually every other, Pitino's challenge was to begin a whole new Kentucky tradition. He was hired to raise the program from the ashes of scandal, but he instinctively knew that his bigger job would be to surmount the racist reputation that still hovered over Kentucky from the Rupp years, tethered in place, perhaps, by the schools that recruited against UK (particularly Louisville). Pitino's game plan was built on quickness and pressure. He couldn't do what he had to do with the white boys that Rupp used to recruit out of the mountains; he just couldn't. But that's what he essentially had in the beginning. And they were the ones, along with Mashburn, who had to tide him over until he had transformed the Kentucky reputation and redefined the Kentucky player.

That's what made "The Unforgettables," as Pitino dubbed them, so unforgettable. They had all the stuff of folk heroes. In them—in these underdogs, these leftovers from the dark age, these Kentuckians and their friends—had been entrusted the revival of Kentucky's most sacred institution. They took that trust and fashioned a legend out of it. By 1991-92, the Unforgettables had played together long enough and well enough to be respectfully regarded, but nobody expected them to win the SEC, to win twenty-nine games, to be in the NCAA quarterfinals against defending and soon to be two-time national champion Duke, to be in overtime against Duke, to be a point ahead with 2.1 seconds remaining, Duke's ball out of bounds under the Kentucky basket after Woods's remarkable clutch shot in the lane. The catch and turnaround jumper that Christian Laettner made to incredibly win the game (he didn't miss a shot all night) was recently ranked by ESPN as the top sports moment of the decade.

The Unforgettables: Mashburn, Farmer, Woods, Feldhaus, and Pelphrey restored the Kentucky spirit.

Even in defeat, The Unforgettables had lived up to their name. For shaking Kentucky out of its nightmare and nearly living out the impossible dream, Pitino, in a wonderful and teary bluegrass moment, retired the jerseys of his overachieving seniors—Woods, Feldhaus, Pelphrey, and Farmer—none of whom would otherwise rate even a fleeting mention in a discussion of the university's great players.

If the 1996 championship restored the glory of Kentucky basketball, The Unforgettables restored its spirit. Pride in the program was disproportionately swollen in the mountains, which had given the team both Farmer, the schoolboy icon whose famous name was placed on a boulevard in Manchester, and the lanky, reddish-haired Pelphrey, a former Mister Basketball and an unlikely all-conference selection. The natives innately understood that such a Kentucky-flavored team would probably never again grace Pitino's court, and they treasured The Unforgettables all the more for it. They understood that the program was moving uptown, but in the meantime it did their hearts a world of good to see their Sweet

Sixteen high school heroes out there playing their Big Blue tails off for the button-down Easterner with his salon-styled hair. No other kind of team would have been able to so endear Pitino to his provincially proud constituency. It went against their grain for Kentucky folks to warm up to a pretty-boy from New York, but he did what he did with their people; that meant a lot. The Unforgettables made Pitino so popular that the *Herald-Leader* and the *Louisville Courier-Journal* went to court over the right to publish excerpts from his book, *Full-Court Pressure* (ultimately, both papers excerpted it simultaneously).

He was on the roll of his life—rolling every year, that is, until the final game. His fourth team lost narrowly to Michigan's Fab Five in the Final Four. His fifth won a game at LSU that it trailed by thirty-one points with fifteen minutes to play, the greatest road comeback in Division I history. His sixth took home a fourth straight SEC tournament and was ranked second in the country when it self-destructed against North Carolina in the regional final. Informed and motivated by the Carolina loss, Pitino's seventh team was something to behold, a cutting-edge concoction of talent, selflessness, and contemporary style.

It was doubtful that he would ever be able to put together a better team at Kentucky; doubtful, perhaps, that anybody would be able to put together a better college team anywhere. Certainly, the Wildcats would not be able to maintain such a rarefied level of performance. The NBA draft selections of Antoine Walker, Walter McCarty, Tony Delk, and Mark Pope reduced Kentucky's talent pool to a more reasonable level after the championship season, a consideration which would have seemed to work in the favor of New Jersey's offer. When Pitino ultimately turned down that one, like all those before it, the pattern indicated that he was developing roots for the first time in his professional life.

In spite of the unrelenting skepticism about the coach's staying power—he always stopped just short of categorically denying his interest in another pro job—it looked as though Pitino might have found the role and the place in which he could make his mark in basketball history; certainly there was no other spot on the planet where his accomplishments would be treasured as dearly. Perhaps, also, he had found the place in which to raise his family. A foundation and homeless shelter had been set up in Owensboro in the name of the Pitinos' son, Daniel, who died of a heart defect in Providence at the age of six months. Their youngest son and only daughter were born in Lexington. Joanne, thankful for the relative stability and softened by Kentucky's breathless adoration, became noticeably more congenial toward her Southern surroundings after she took an apartment in New York City that she visited on a regular basis.

Pitino, not as able as his wife to spend time back home, instead brought touches of home to Kentucky. He arranged for a priest to sit on the Wildcat bench. He hired his black-shirted Providence trainer, Fast Eddie Jamiel. He opened his own Italian restaurant. And he played host to a colorful entourage of East Coast, Damon Runyon friends whom he was seldom without: John the Horse, Larry the Scout, Joey C, Johnny Joe Idaho, Jersey Red, and his brother-in-law, Billy Minardi. The Pitino pals were not shadowy, back-room figures; they were visible, cordial characters who frequently quizzed Kentucky media types on what they thought exactly about the coach: Was he the best around? The best ever at Kentucky? The best ever, period?

The most familiar of the Runyon clique was Jersey Red, a.k.a. Ken Ford, a high school culinary arts teacher in Fall River, Massachusetts, who became friends with Pitino when he cooked meals for the coach's old UMass fraternity house. When Jersey Red was home in Massachusetts with his teaching responsibilities, Pitino, an information junkie, called him two or three times a day for updates on the Celtics, Antoine Walker, UMass, the Big East, and anything else Ford might have heard that Pitino hadn't. As soon as school was out for the week, Jersey Red would be on a plane to Lexington, generally at Pitino's expense. There, he would provide the coach with the kind of companionship that Pitino's celebrity wouldn't allow him to cultivate locally. At Pitino press conferences, Jersey Red could often be spotted standing off to the side, curiously older and obviously citified, his red hair turning white, wearing blue nylon sweat pants that gave him the appearance of an assistant coach or trainer.

"I've been good for Rick," said Jersey Red, repairing to the edge of the Memorial Coliseum concourse, where he could smoke, after one of those press conferences. "I bring him back to earth. On numerous occasions, I've had to tell him who he is. He's never fully understood his clout in Kentucky. It's crazy. He needs four state troopers just to get to his car. He has no life down here. In New York, we'll be on the street and maybe a cabby will recognize him and say something like, 'You asshole, reber when you blew the point spread against the Pistons?' But it's not like that here. We tried to go to Kroger's once, and we absolutely couldn't get out of there. Around here, he's Elvis. I can see it in the people's eyes. He's Elvis.

"Back North, people think this is as sick as it gets. We've got friends who call the people here goobers, hillbillies, yahoos, all kinds of things. But I'll tell you what. They've got something here that people in New York and New Jersey don't have. They have passion. Whatever Duke is, this is five-fold. Whatever Indiana is, this is ten-fold. Rick refers to Kentucky as the Roman Empire of college basketball."

If Jersey Red and the likes of him were good for Pitino, he was even better for most of them. Before the coach was a coach, he had turned around Ken Ford's life. "I was twenty-nine years old, drinking a quart of Jack Daniels a day, and I was visiting a friend at UMass on my way to a job in Florida for the winter," said Jersey Red. "We were talking with a bunch of frat guys from Lambda Chi Alpha, and Rick tells me they just lost their fraternity cook, why don't I come cook for them? So I go back there and the kitchen looks like it was from the movie *Twister*. I made them some beef Stroganoff and afterwards Rick comes in and says, 'We just had a meeting. We'll make you the highest-paid fraternity cook in America, a hundred dollars a week.' If you'll listen to Rick's interviews, you'll notice he loves to use the word 'America.' Anyway, I told him I could make more than that in Florida, so they had another meeting and Rick offered me a hundred and thirty-five a week and said, 'The president of the fraternity has agreed to give you his room, and you can have all the Jack Daniels you can drink.'

"We became inseparable. You've got to realize, this was UMass; he was the only one in the house from New York and I was the only one from New Jersey. I think the only reason Rick was there was to play basketball with Doctor J; he was from Long Island, too. And then Doctor J left early to play in the ABA. So it was just him and me. The rest of the guys are all pocking their cahs in Hahved Yod. Anyway, I cheated him one time at cards. We were playing gin for grinders—what you'd call subs here—and I dropped a card on the floor. It was the maddest I've ever seen him. He jumped me and pushed me back against the plate-glass window with his hand clenched. He said, 'I can't believe you would do this to me, Jersey. After all I've done for you. I can't believe you'd cheat me. I want you out of here right now.' Of course, he forgave me, but that was the biggest wakeup call I ever had."

Jersey Red had become something of a celebrity himself through his friendship with Pitino. He wrote some columns for *The Cats' Pause* and was frequently on the radio as sort of the inside man on the Pitino beat. Like few others, he had seen the coach up-close, disheveled, and dog-tired. "He never sleeps before a game," Ford said. "He stays up all night thinking about it, comes to the office, does the walk-through with the team, gets on the treadmill and does five miles watching tape, then gets in the sauna. I really believe that's where he devises his final game plan. Then he goes to the blackboard to do forty-five minutes of chalk work by himself. He dresses, gives his last remarks to the team, comes through that tunnel, and you've heard the ovation. He gets two, maybe two and a half hours of sleep a night. I swear sometimes he's got a twin brother stashed somewhere. You'll see him all fatigued, run down, not looking too good, then he'll take a shower, put on one of those Armani suits, smile that sparkly smile, and you'd swear it was a different person. He's got this whole thing about fighting through fatigue.

"Rick's the ultimate competitor, whether it's the NCAA tournament or gin, and he's also the single most organized person you will meet in your lifetime. I'll tell you how organized he is. We were at a junior college tournament in Las Vegas one summer and we go over to Nieman Marcus. This is July. He picks up this tie that's got a little blue in it, and he says the next time you see this tie will be New Year's Eve in Louisville. And New Year's Eve, Kentucky's playing Louisville in Louisville, and I happen to notice that Rick is wearing that tie he picked up at Nieman Marcus."

Pitino's attention to sartorial detail—he kept his dozens of shirts hanging in order by color and style—was an item well noted and more than occasionally emulated around Kentucky. Following his lead, more Kentucky men began getting their hair styled. Kentucky women studied him even more closely; some of them who had not been basketball fans before Pitino arrived changed their ways. Children and pets were named after him. By the time Laettner's shot went down, there was no doubt that the coach had become the most recognizable and popular personality in the state.

There were some, suspicious of Yankees in general and silky ones in particular, who felt deep-down that Pitino had become too big for the good of the program, but it was hard to sell that point of view as long as he won. The most important qualification for a Kentucky basketball coach is that he be the best there is, and the general feeling around the commonwealth was that theirs qualified.

For his part, it was important for Pitino to be in a place where people thought that of him. In the analysis of why he ultimately turned down New Jersey's humongous offer, it might be well to point out that staying at Kentucky allowed him, for the first time ever, to coach in a place where he had won a championship. The word "bask" would be a pertinent one. Kentucky lavished Pitino with praise and attention, and if he thought it was silly at times, it flattered him nonetheless. But he was not so insecure as to prioritize the approval ahead of his agenda; he wanted it on his terms. He wanted Kentucky basketball to conform to him, not vice versa. That was why, in part, he changed the team's uniform styles so often; why, in part, he made a stage show out of Big Blue Madness (he once roared onto the court on a motorcycle); why, in part, he didn't recruit Kentucky kids just because they were Kentucky kids. The reason that Pitino was up to the Kentucky task was that his ego was equal to it. He thought enough of himself as a coach that he didn't care about the way Adolph Rupp did things; he didn't even want to know.

"I'm a historian of basketball," he said one early-winter afternoon at a round table in his Memorial Coliseum office. "I wouldn't know Kentucky basketball history like somebody who was born in Kentucky and has studied it religiously, but the fact is, I've kind of distanced myself from all of that for a variety of reasons. I have great respect for what Coach Rupp accomplished as a basketball coach, but he's so much different than me. Joe Hall's so much different than me. Coach Hall had a lot of pressure on him here, and one of the reasons, in addition to the fact that he followed Coach Rupp, is that he's from Cynthiana, Kentucky. Every little article in the paper his mom's gonna read. I'm from New York. Most of my adult life has been spent in New England. I don't really care what people think. I try to do my job and not let the outside pressures come into my life. I want to know about the history of Kentucky basketball, but in another way I don't want to know. I don't want to know, did Adolph Rupp go to this town and do this? Now, if it meant recruiting to me, I'd do it in a second . . . "

Distancing himself from Rupp was a practical matter for Pitino. If he didn't know that intrinsically, he found it out soon enough, when Jason Osborne's grandparents advised him that their Mister Basketball would be having no part of Rupp U. Until Derek Anderson transferred from Ohio State, it had been eight years since a black player from Louisville had come to Kentucky.

But there was more than one legacy to be cleared away as Pitino set about carving a New Kentucky out of the rich bluegrass soil. While Rupp's successors and Pitino's predecessors, Joe Hall and Eddie Sutton, had weaned the UK program from its segregationist beginnings, its sullied tradition had been perpetuated under their administrations. For his part, Sutton had succeeded in purging the Kentucky locker room of magnanimous partisans, but the gold stars he won for that effort seemed of little consequence when a thousand bucks spilled out in Los Angeles. Obviously, Pitino had to go another mile. If he was not buddy-buddy enough for the alumni and boosters, there was an explanation: he wanted to keep them as far as possible from easily tempted young athletes.

The result was that Pitino was able to maintain the only unsullied compliance record of any Kentucky coach since Johnny Mauer, the man Rupp replaced in 1930. That's not to say that his watch avoided the hint of impropriety—there were pesky questions about Anderson's transfer procedure and Mercer's recruitment—but he went by the book, for the most part, and the official record will show that Pitino raised the standard of Kentucky's integrity to a level that it hadn't seen in a long, long time.

With the space that he felt compelled to keep between himself and his kingdom, it was unlikely that Pitino would ever completely understand what he, as the man who restored the honor to the name of Kentucky, meant to the people there. He could try, of course. It helped that he could identify with their passion for basketball, and with the deep need that the game satisfied for both of them. For both of them, it was a way to win the respect they craved. For Pitino and Kentucky, basketball and self-esteem were all mixed up together. "I didn't at first fully comprehend the depth of the way people here feel about basketball," he said that day in the office. The part that he didn't get was feeling that way about a team that you didn't coach or play for. "But I think I have a full appreciation of it now. It's taken eight years."

If it took that long to appreciate what UK basketball meant to Kentucky, it would take forever for Pitino to understand that he, the gym rat from Queens, the youngest son of a super, the guy who talked and ate and dressed so differently than the people who paid his salary . . . that he, because he was the coach—because he was *the coach*, the chosen one, the one who led Kentucky out of the wilderness—had come to mean much the same thing. For the time being, he was the personification of Kentucky basketball. In the state where they called basketball a religion, they called Rick Pitino a savior.

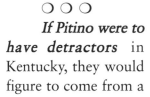

If Pitino were to have detractors in Kentucky, they would figure to come from a place like The Coffee

The man in the Italian suit: Even Pitino's clothes said he wasn't another Rupp.

Club in Danville, whose mostly retired members were of distinctly Ruppian vintage. Some of them even predated the Baron. One, an 87-year-old unbasketball fan, former mayor, and tobacco warehouser named Roy Arnold who wore a bow tie and drove a 1964 Chevy Bel Air with 53,000 miles on it, claimed that the last UK game he attended was at the old Alumni Gym. "Georgia Tech beat the shit out of 'em," he said. That would have been the 35-31 game in 1928.

Danville was one of the historic towns of Kentucky's Bluegrass region and The Coffee Club was a private concern on Main Street—across from the Farmer's Bank and two doors down from the pool hall—where local men of varying backgrounds, retired and otherwise, gathered at all hours of the day to settle the affairs of world and state. There was no television at The Coffee Club, and no card-playing allowed. There was merely a bathroom, a coffee pot, and a round table at which the opinionated members came and went, discussing issues of widely ranging import and solemnity, Kentucky basketball naturally but not obsessively among them.

The club had been established after Grider's Pharmacy closed a few years before. For twenty-five years, the amiable friends had gathered for coffee and conversation at George Grider's Main Street drugstore, referring to themselves as the Old Goats. Grider, an Old Goat himself and a local historian who had strayed briefly to Princeton, New Jersey, where he watched Albert Einstein walk down the street at the same time every day, shoes untied, coat unbuttoned, hands behind his back, was eventually compelled to sell his pharmacy to Kroger's. Kroger's wasn't an option for the Old Goats. Nor was McDonald's or one of the spacious breakfast-bar establishments; this was much too august and traditional a congregation for that.

Given the long-toothed range of its perspective, the club's frame of reference for basketball affairs was of course the man who overdeveloped the sport in the world of Kentucky. One of the Old Goats, a local institution named Clemens Caldwell, attended summer basketball camps that Rupp held at Barbourville in the thirties. Caldwell also had a brother-in-law who used to sell cattle to the Baron. The cattlemen teased the great coach about buying a full-bred herd the year Kentucky players were caught shaving points. Caldwell still raised livestock and walking horses on his old place at the edge of town, but he was better known for the other things he had out there. He was renowned for his gamecocks, which fought famously all over the world, and had gathered one of the country's most extensive collections of Native American artifacts. For what it was worth, he also kept a pet sparrow at the house. Caldwell, who commonly showed up at The Coffee Club with a flannel shirt half hanging out, a soiled farmer's cap, crooked glasses, and a curio or two from his collection—a Paleo Indian pipe, perhaps, or a random dinosaur tooth—had found many of the precious pieces on the property his family had owned for six generations. It was no ordinary farm. Caldwell's thick-walled old house was held together with hog hair in the cement, and even the fences had historic value, made of indigenous Ordovician limestone and constructed by a great half-black, half-Shawnee fence builder. Except for Caldwell's digging around, the homestead was practically untouched since before the Civil War, which came so close that the family hid the horses.

Danville itself had been torn by the war; the First Presbyterian Church supported the South and Second Presbyterian the North. There was no such division over contemporary basketball, however—it was the thing that brought Kentuckians together, after all—except for the one between the diehards and the die-easys. For a town only thirty miles from Lexington, there was a surprising number of the latter, chief among them being Arnold and Bill Kemper, a gentleman engineer and lumber company proprietor who devoutly avoided conversation about basketball but spoke encyclopedically about everything else. "After living here for thirty-six years, I've finally gotten to where I listen for the scores," Kemper conceded, willing to budge no further. On mornings after Kentucky games, Kemper preferred to sleep late and give the other Goats an hour or so to banter about basketball before he arrived. He would then fill his cup, pull up to the round table, and steer the conversation toward such items as the eight-foot zinnias at Wolf Creek Dam, German scientists, Cleopatra's method of birth control ("a crocodile turd soaked in lemon juice and honey"), the evolution of English, figure skaters' rear ends, bird counts (he once calculated five million in a single roost), Kentucky towns no longer on the map (including Chicken Bristle, Nonesuch, and Monkey's Eyebrow, which actually remained on a few), the demographic shift occasioned by the Battle of Hastings, and cheap catfish at the pay lake.

Despite his concerted efforts, however, there was no chance of circumventing basketball chatter entirely. Pitino was naturally a regular topic, and the tone was far more accommodating than one might expect from the accumulated point of view seated around the table. The other thing was, Charlie Hazelrigg wouldn't permit anyone to say a bad word about the Kentucky coach.

Hazelrigg had been a professor at Danville's Centre College for so long that he didn't just have tenure, he said, he *invented* it. (Centre's sporting claim to fame, incidentally, was a 6-0 victory over Harvard in

1921, which still prompted a chemistry professor to ask his students every year if they could identify the significance of C6H0.) He was also a first-order basketball fan and unabashedly loyal to Pitino for what the coach had done in the wake of Hazelrigg's greatest tragedy. His son, a husband and father of three and a Kentucky season-ticket holder, had been killed when a tornado picked up and crashed his car. A sportswriter at the Danville newspaper informed Pitino of what had happened and Pitino promptly sent off a letter to Tab Hazelrigg's three children, sharing his own experience of losing a young son and encouraging them to take care of their mother. Since the day the letter arrived, Charlie Hazelrigg had not tolerated even the most incidental criticism of Pitino. (On the other hand, he hadn't said a nice thing about Dean Smith since the Carolina coach called the Cats' Rick Robey a son of a bitch twenty years before.)

Of course, Hazelrigg came and went like everybody else at The Coffee Club, and behind his back the others were able to sneak in at least a cynical word or two about the Yankee coach. Throughout the fall of 1996, for instance, there was much yammering around the state about an on-campus basketball facility that Pitino championed as a replacement for the 23,000 seats at Rupp Arena. The Central Kentucky Skeptical Society, as the Danville gents might have been called, viewed the arena business in terms that were not as civic in nature as arena business is generally supposed to be. "I think the whole thing is Pitino," submitted Raymond Miller, a dapper 83-year-old former financier. "This arena thing is a reflection of how big he has become and thinks he is. It's a perfect opportunity for him to throw his weight around."

At The Coffee Club, however, a good theory never stood alone. It was evidently a rule. "I'll tell you why they think they need that new arena," countered Al Mead, a former hardware man who was known as the first merchant around to display inventory on the sidewalk. (Subsequently, when his friends drove through the country and saw stoves and refrigerators left out in the yard, they would remark that Al must be franchising.) "The only reason they need a new arena is because Tennessee's is bigger."

"That's probably the best explanation yet," replied dairy farmer Oliver Payne, who was more than locally renowned for using artificial insemination to raise a rich Holstein bloodline from a famous bull named

Posh, the Abraham of Holsteins. "They can't let that happen."

Bill Kemper looked hard at Payne and shook his head. "I don't know," he said. "What do you make of a man that gets a bull to ejaculate like that?"

Danville was a long way from cornering the market on Kentucky skepticism, and there were plenty around the state who surmised that Pitino coveted a new arena as his enduring monument. Having fun with the coach's East Coast accent, some were calling it "Pitiner Arener." Of course, Pitino was quick to quash that kind of talk.

"Let me set the record straight," he had said publicly. "This is not something that I wanted. How many games would I actually coach in this new arena? You won't even have my name on a door at that arena. Do I want to be part of it? Of course I would. But my longevity . . . I certainly want to end my coaching career here at the University of Kentucky, but I can't coach as long as Adolph Rupp. We all know that.

"But if they do a feasibility study and then say that it's in the best interest of the university, we'll raise that money in a shorter period of time than you can imagine. I will say this: I will be involved if it does happen and I guarantee you it will be the finest arena built. I think we're looking at more than a hundred million dollars. That's a lot of money." Pitino suppressed a mischievous grin. " . . . It's gonna take us at least two and a half weeks to do that.

"Look, if The Unforgettables can reach the Elite Eight, this team can build an arena," he added seriously. "Believe me, it can be done. I got a check the other day for ten dollars from a guy in Western Kentucky who said he wanted to be the first to contribute to the new arena."

If anybody was still wondering why a conspicuously ambitious guy from New York would turn down thirty million New Jersey dollars in order to continue coaching college kids in Kentucky, they should have listened hard to what the man said in the fall of 1996 about a new arena. He said that he had no doubt whatsoever that he—all right, that *Kentucky*; same thing—could, at the virtual snap of a finger, raise a hundred million bucks or whatever it took to build the best basketball facility in the world, which would then be filled with what he considered to be the world's finest basketball fans. He could coach in that environment. Sure he could.

○ ○ ○

When Sports Illustrated published a controversial profile of Rick Pitino in its last February edition of 1996, at least one Lexington store sold the magazine under the counter with *Penthouse* and *Hustler*. One might reasonably conclude from this that, in Kentucky, the only difference between pornography and criticism of the Cats is the number of people who indulge. The article, entitled "A Man Possessed," was preoccupied perhaps to a fault with Pitino's ambitious side, which was obviously much of him, but on the whole it wasn't all that severe except for the ill-chosen illustration of Pitino pulling a wagon carrying his wife strapped to a basketball goal and another of the coach's face separated by a hoop, the left side of him polished and perfect, the right side featuring his drifting eye and thick, maniacally swept hair.

In the end, the commentary that came out of the entire thing said more about Kentucky than its basketball coach. While Pitino was embittered toward the magazine, refusing further interviews with it until he received an apology—which more than a year later was still not forthcoming—citizens of the commonwealth viewed the episode as another case of the Eastern press screwing with the best thing they had. The timing of the article confirmed that in their minds, coming as it did just as Pitino took his team into the postseason tournaments. Once again, as the case had been so many times over so many years—possibly with justification—Kentuckians had a hard time making the distinction between criticism and persecution.

The thing is, Pitino was supposed to be the one who got them past all of that. Rupp's country-Kansas ways were easily mistaken for Southern and Joe B. Hall was Kentucky to the core, but Pitino was as Eastern as *Sports Illustrated* or the *New York Times* or any of the media about whose judgments the state was so infamously defensive. He was Kentucky's compromise, its surrender to the metropolitan influences that set the tone for contemporary basketball. While keeping the program above board, he was also expanding its geographic and socio-economic base. That was his complicated task, and by all previous accounts he was doing it remarkably well; so why, all of a sudden, this?

The commonwealth's outrage was based on reflex and general principle, but it also reflected an ardent approval of what Pitino stood for. They heartily endorsed his record, of course, but there was much more to his administration, and Kentucky's acceptance of the outsider's reforms was an indication of its eagerness to change the way it was thought of, if not the way it thought. The people's collective attitude represented a good-riddance not of Rupp, but of the reputation that Rupp rightly or wrongly had taken on.

If Pitino erred at all in his endeavor to redefine Kentucky, it was in his subtle repudiation of the Baron. While professing no particular interest in Rupp's precedents, claiming that they had no bearing on his time or task, he knew all the while that they did: it was important for him to do things differently. In his book, he wrote that "Adolph might not agree [with] what we're trying to do at Kentucky." There was little doubt that he was referring mainly to the recruitment of black players. He called it "the one area where we still need to make great strides." Few could disagree, but Kentucky old-timers, even while acknowledging the strides that had to be made, preferred that the coach make them without stepping on their man Rupp along the way. Herky Rupp was so upset by the remarks in Pitino's book that he thought about calling a press conference to refute them.

All of that notwithstanding, there was no disputing that Pitino, as the antithesis of Rupp, had gone the extra mile to ingratiate Kentucky's black community. And, unlike Rupp, he also had the active support of Kentucky's athletic director and department. In 1992, UK brought in Wes Unseld, the very symbol of the program's failures in recruiting black players, to coach his Washington Bullets in an exhibition game at Rupp Arena. Less than a month later, the Cats held an intrasquad scrimmage dedicated to the Lexington chapter of the Urban League. In 1994, Pitino found a place on his coaching staff for Winston Bennett, the only black player Louisville had sent to UK in the twenty-five years before Derek Anderson arrived. Meanwhile, at Louisville's Dirt Bowl, an inner-city summer basketball league, Pitino was sighted more frequently than U of L's Denny Crum.

Even as he went far afield for his top recruits—after spiriting Mashburn out of New York, he went back for Rodrick Rhodes—Pitino understood the importance of cultivating Louisville. From the sixties to the nineties, Louisville's black community had produced ten Mister Basketballs. Six of them (Unseld, Wesley Cox, Darrell Griffith, Tony Kimbro, Dwayne Morton, and Jason Osborne) had attended the University of Louisville. Only one—Winston Bennett—had attended the University of Kentucky.

Therein lay at least some of the importance of both Rick Pitino and Derek Anderson to the Kentucky basketball program. And therein lay the problem for the country players and good ol' Kentucky boys—the next generation of Farmers and Pelphreys and Coxes and Hagans and Ramseys and Joneses and Beards—who, in another time, would have worn the blue and white shirt with such pride and distinction.

There were still plenty of folks who held on to the idea that Kentucky was special enough to once again be the kind of team it used to be; to win at the national level with a squad made up mostly (some argued that it should be entirely, although not even Rupp went that far) of Kentucky boys, many of whom would necessarily—and fortuitously, of course—be white. Rick Pitino was not one of them.

He was asked about that one afternoon in his office. He was specifically asked whether it was feasible, given the development of rural white players as they compete increasingly against city players at basketball camps and pattern their games after the mostly African-American superstars whom they watch on television, for a program of Kentucky's magnitude to ever again put together a first-rate, nationally competitive roster with homegrown talent; or whether that was a pipe dream.

"I think it's a pipe dream," he replied without hesitating. "I'm not even sure I see any Kentucky players coming here in the next two years."

5

Mountain Ball

The easy way to explain the phenomenon of Kentucky basketball is to say that the man in the brown suit is responsible; that Adolph Rupp took a little team that didn't amount to much and built it into a colossal thing that meant the world. And there is surely much to that, although the outfit he inherited in 1930 wasn't so bad; the previous coach, John Mauer, had been 40-14 in three seasons and was referred to in local reports as Kentucky's Moses. He left without a Southern Conference championship, however, and while Rupp, Kentucky's Joshua, never actually won one of those either, in his third year the conference became the Southeastern, the Wildcats beat Mississippi State in the tournament final, and off they went. It was a fine thing for Kentucky to be the best in the South—to be the best in anything anywhere—and the citizens were highly pleased with the unfamiliar prestige brought to their state by the swaggering Kansas man. For his part, Rupp was highly pleased with the prestige that came *his* way in the deal. When the Northern newspapers were not as readily impressed, the Baron, seeing about that, began playing in New York and Chicago, where ol' Kentucky showed 'em for sure. The Yankees could say what they wanted about who was ignorant and who was backward, but the scoreboard had a different opinion. And that's why basketball became a religion in Kentucky: It allowed people to come to terms with themselves; it connected them to something that was large and good and really truly *something*.

It's all a fine theory, but the thing is, basketball had done that for Kentucky even before Rupp arrived. Not long before; just a couple of

◀ *Carr Creek: Along the school's path to the 1956 state championship, Freddie Maggard was twice carried off the court for winning tournament games with last-second shots.*

years. In 1928, Carr Creek and Ashland—especially Carr Creek—made the people of the entire commonwealth and the eastern part in particular awfully proud to be who they were and from where they were from, for a change.

Nobody had ever heard of Carr Creek until 1928; there was no such place. In Knott County, near Carr Creek, the creek, there was a board stuck to a log and somebody had painted "Dirk" on it, and that was what the place was called until two ladies from Boston built the Carr Creek Community Center on the side of a mountain and started teaching school there. At tournament time in 1928, the local folks had to take down the Dirk sign to avoid confusion because suddenly everybody was talking about Carr Creek and wanting to know where it was.

The graduating class of 1927, consisting of four boys and three girls, had been Carr Creek's first. There were eighteen boys in high school for the year of 1927-28, and eight of them, all cousins, made up the basketball team, which was coached by Oscar Morgan, who was called into service on the basis of being the school's only male teacher. Most of the students rode mule wagons to school as far as the roads went, then walked the rest of the way. During basketball season, it was too dark and too late after practice for the cousins to make it home, so they stayed in a two-room cottage near the school and stole the neighbors' chickens for dinner. There were basketball goals in an auditorium built for Bible-reading, but the ceiling was only twelve feet high so the boys practiced mainly on the wagon-tire hoops nailed onto a couple of tree trunks they had cut down and strategically placed so as to minimize the number of times the ball rolled five hundred yards down the mountain.

When Carr Creek won the regional tournament in Richmond that year, the fans were so charmed they bought the fellows real uniforms to replace the cut-off khaki pants and white T-shirts that had been doing the job. Observers were captivated not only by the Creekers' story, but also by their full-court press, the likes of which hadn't been seen before, and the extraordinary ball-handling skills that the mountainside had persuaded them to master. Carr Creek's game was much more than dazzle and showmanship, however. That was demonstrated during the state tournament at UK's Alumni Gym, where the relatives took apart three better-known opponents to reach the championship match against undefeated Ashland and future Kentucky All-American Ellis Johnson.

By this time, Carr Creek had won over most of Kentucky, courtesy of a disbelieving press corps. Nine of the first ten state championships had been claimed by the big Lexington and Louisville schools, which led to the assumption that it would always turn out that way; for a little thing like Carr Creek to play in the title game was unheard of. *Carr Creek* was unheard of. And at halftime, it led Ashland 4-3. Even after Ashland prevailed in four practically Biblical overtimes, Carr Creek's performance was so celebrated that it was invited along with Ashland to the national high school tournament in Chicago.

As might be expected, the Creekers were a sight in Chicago, a story unlike any the city had witnessed. Will Rogers even wrote about them. And Carr Creek was equal to the prose, its second victory coming against a team from Austin, Texas, that many had picked to win the tournament. When the boys beat Bristol, Connecticut, and sang out the school cheer afterwards, the Chicago crowd—which included an Illinois high school coach named Rupp—was on its feet singing with them. The *Chicago Tribune* said that it was the most emotional scene in the history of the tournament. As Carr Creek played the game it finally lost to a team from Vienna, Georgia, three thousand people crowded around the outside of the gymnasium to hear minute-by-minute reports. Meanwhile, Ashland never did lose, carrying the national championship trophy back home to Eastern Kentucky, where both teams were given the heroes' welcome.

Ashland and Carr Creek had brought respect to the mountains at a time when nothing else did. In the Northern cities and their national media, the image of Appalachian Kentucky had been restricted mostly to moonshine, banjos, and families shooting at each other; to speak of hillbillies was to choose between pity and ridicule. What's more, the outside world made little distinction between Eastern Kentucky and the rest of the state; it was cruel to all of Kentucky. But at last, the mountains had been able to answer. Through the game of basketball, Kentucky had found a way to lash back.

That was the lay of the land that spread before Adolph Rupp when he strode so grandly upon the scene in 1930. Kentucky had been mobilized in its war against the world and needed only the right general to lead it into glorious battle. The smoke is still clearing, but it can be seen now that Rupp and Carr Creek played complementary roles in the military buildup that became Kentucky basketball, the difference being that he won more, lasted longer, and talked a much better game.

Carr Creek, however, had more than fifteen minutes of fame. It built its own gym, maintained its own tradition, and actually won the Sweet Sixteen twenty-eight years after coming so incredibly close. And all the while, it inspired any number of similar Kentucky hamlets, some of which carved out their own historical niches by bringing state championships home to places, mapped and unmapped, like Inez, Hazel Green, Midway, Hindman, Heath, Earlington, Corinth, Brewers (undefeated in '48), and Cuba (unforgettable in '52).

Because it recognized the cultural wisdom of allowing schools of all sizes to compete for one state championship, Kentucky was able to keep alive the underdog theme that first Carr Creek and then the state itself thrived on. The state tournament crowds in Lexington or Louisville would invariably adopt one of the small-town, big-dream schools that came out of either Eastern or Western Kentucky, many of which had risen above their circumstances by virtue of efficacious closeness and uncommon style. And no team ever brought more style to the Sweet Sixteen than Cuba, an obscure far-Western Kentucky outpost whose boys took the floor passing and dribbling to the strains of *Sweet Georgia Brown*.

Cuba's coach, Jack Story, had shown his country players film clips of the Harlem Globetrotters and instructed each to pick out one Globetrotter to copy. The challenge was eagerly undertaken by the team's two stars, Howard Crittenden and Doodles Floyd, who had grown up playing one-on-one with a rubber ball that they shot into a tin can nailed to the side of a smoke house. Crittenden picked out Marcus Haynes, the great dribbler, and Floyd went for a bigger, funnier man, Goose Tatum. Before long, Floyd was cracking jokes as he banked in hook shots and Crittenden was dribbling between his legs, behind his back, and around and around Kentucky schoolboys who had never seen such a thing. In the first state tournament held at Memorial Coliseum, Cuba made it to the 1951 finals before losing to Clark County and its legendary coach, Letcher Norton, an entertaining but rugged competitor who once beat the tar out of a gambler he found in his locker room at halftime. The next year, Crittenden and Floyd were back, more popular than ever, and danced off with the big prize. The people stuck at home—somebody had to feed the cows—met the team on the highway with a fourteen-mile motorcade.

Rupp had made the long trip three times to recruit Crittenden, who declined the scholarship in a decision that he later said was the dumbest of his life, instead accepting the safe offer from nearby Murray State. It was a familiar story for rural stars to whom Lexington was a distant and frightening city. The result for Crittenden was that he became a high school principal rather than a legend. The legend, in this case, is Cuba, which provided yet another patch for the colorful basketball quilt in which the entire commonwealth is wrapped up.

Howie Crittenden: Cuba's dribbling whiz tried to emulate Marcus Haynes of the Harlem Globetrotters.

In Kentucky, the towns and their high schools bundle together with the state university like too many kids in a one-blanket house, warming themselves with each other's body heat. It's a familial, uniquely exclusive arrangement. In Indiana, where the high school basketball tradition might exceed Kentucky's and Indiana University has maintained a commanding regional presence, the state makes room in its bed for Purdue, Notre Dame, and Indianapolis's professional franchises. North Carolina is a virtual basketball dormitory, accommodating numerous major colleges and Charlotte's new pro teams. The cultural pervasiveness of Alabama football is defined by the fierce cover-tugging between Auburn and the Crimson Tide. Nebraska has only the Cornhusker football team between its crisp white sheets, but they remain unwrinkled by domestic tradition and uncolored by generational history. To best understand the singularly symbiotic relationship between the places of Kentucky and the University of Kentucky, think of Richie Farmer. Where else would an unexceptional college player have a street named for him?

Farmer's legend came from the hills of Eastern Kentucky and the thrills of the Sweet Sixteen, but it helped that The Unforgettables were so important to the commonwealth. The greater the glory attained by UK over the years, the stronger the pride felt by every little town that delivered a boy there. And if towns from opposite corners of the state sent their boys to Lexington at the same time, all the better. There has never been much else to bring Kentucky together. The horsemen have little in common with the miners, who don't have much to do with the farmers, who keep their distance from the city folks. In Kentucky, even neighbors—*especially* neighbors—are notorious for the staunch ways in which they do not get along. But let somebody take a swipe at the Cats, and Kentucky becomes a single blue cell of defense.

"I can only speak about Eastern Kentucky," said James Goode, an associate director at the UK Appalachian Center, "but there's a very distinct rivalry mentality there. If you look at the history of Eastern Kentucky, you see that just after the Civil War came a lot of lumber companies, then the coal companies came around the turn of the century. They formed very distinct lumber camps and coal camps with distinct identities. Huge rivalries developed between the coal company communities. The coal companies had their own baseball teams with elaborate stadiums, and they traveled throughout the coal fields competing. The rivalries were a way of life. The town of Lynch had six different sections of its population, which were basically ethnic nations within the town—Hungarian, black, whatever. The coal companies kept them apart not because they [the companies] were prejudiced, but because these people could not get along; they'd kill each other. My dad told me that they once found a body on the garbage dump in Lynch for thirty straight days. The trouble could be over card games, women, feuds—whatever.

"I served four terms on city council in Benham, which shared borders with Lynch and Cumberland. Benham and Lynch no longer had company schools—they had consolidated with Cumberland—and I would propose merging fire departments or the like. There would be fierce opposition. You know, the Redskins can't mix with the Tigers—the Cumberland Redskins and the Benham Tigers—even though the schools were already consolidated. There was always that underlying rivalry that had been created through sports. And I think it had more to do with poverty than place. I think poor people have chips on their shoulders, and maybe with good reason."

It was inevitable that the drama created by economically and ancestrally contentious communities would be played out through the local high schools. In many small-town settings, especially, the high school represented not only the community's young people, but its independence; i.e., its success as a place. "The idea in Kentucky," said Dr. Alan DeYoung, a UK professor of education and sociology and author of *The Life and Death of a Rural American High School*, "was to let the local people run the schools, and the state would subsidize whatever the local groups would do. Middle-class citizens of the community invariably decided that having a visible school was the mark of progress and enlightenment, and somebody would start up a one-room schoolhouse. Those were usually through the eighth grade. For the most part, only in the towns did the schools go all the way to high school. The high school symbolically came to represent your community.

"In effect, it was a matter of using state money to subsidize civic pride. The other town has a school, so you have to have a school. It was a marker of your community versus the other community. Those schools were not just famous for basketball but for bands, theatrical productions, all kinds of things. Basketball was not just a question of athletic talent, but of how much time and energy and belief there was in what was going on there. Basketball was the way the town was represented, the symbol of its pride." While the Kentucky High School Athletic Association has served the state well by continuing to include the small schools in its basketball championship (only Hawaii and Delaware do the same, Indiana having played its last one-class tournament in 1997), state lawmakers have been singing from a different hymnal. Their role has been to set curriculum standards that have effectively put most of the small schools out of business. Since the 1930s, the total number of schools in Kentucky has been reduced from 8,500 to around 1,400, and 800 high schools have been consolidated into fewer than 300. While the academic benefits of these mergers have been difficult to discern, the cultural effects are more visible—chief among them being a tangible decline in the rural sense of community.

"School laws don't give a shit about communities," said DeYoung.

"They don't take into account the importance of the school to the community. The state forces consolidation by telling the small school that it has to have stuff in its curriculum that it can't afford. With the better roads and availability of gasoline after World War II, a lot of communities saw consolidation as the answer. All the books and reports were saying that you had to have four hundred kids in a school because the only way to provide a decent education was to have a big curriculum. The school bus became the symbol of mid-century education. The kids up in the holler need an opportunity for advanced biology—send the bus up there. Meanwhile, the kids who don't take biology have just lost their school. Now, in the last few years, a lot of people have decided that schools are too big. Some urban areas are trying to deconsolidate. Never has anyone proven that consolidating schools always has a positive impact. Part of the problem is that we didn't have standardized tests in the fifties like we do now. We can't compare."

We do have these records from the fifties, though: We have Cuba winning the Kentucky state basketball championship in 1952. We have Inez winning in '54 and Carr Creek in '56. "Those places," observed DeYoung, "were bastions of civic-minded people proud of their accomplishment and wanting to showcase them by beating the shit out of you in basketball. The attitude was: We've got this game down and we're gonna show you guys next week."

The Cuba school system has since vanished into the Graves County consolidation. The Inez kids go to consolidated Sheldon Clark High School. Carr Creek is part of Knott County Central. The proud country ballplayers from those once-famous places all heard the same cheers when they took the floor in their new colors: "Two, four, six, eight . . . You had to consolidate!" In the years since, the humiliation has only worsened: Not one of the three conglomerated institutions has played in a state semifinal game. The remote mountain schools of Eastern Kentucky—the neglected, one-room affairs that Jesse Stuart immortalized in his regional writings— did more consolidating than anybody, and of all the big county schools they made, none but Richie Farmer's Clay County has won the Sweet Sixteen.

There is, however, an *unconsolidated* school from Eastern Kentucky that has won a contemporary state championship. When Paintsville High School brought home the trophy in 1996 behind J.R. VanHoose, a six-foot-nine-inch sophomore, it was the first small mountain school to achieve such glory since Carr Creek forty years earlier.

○ ○ ○
Loretta Lynn, the coal miner's daughter, grew up a few miles east of Paintsville. Larry Flynt, the porn king, was raised not far in the other direction. Between them, they represent pretty much the gamut of Appalachian clichés— barefoot poverty, coal-dusted faces, porch music, plaintive women, reckless men, and an uncensored, vice-inclined culture. There's truth in those images, but there is also this: Between the singer's Butcher

Sweetest Day: Paintsville's Sweet Sixteen championship defied modern history.

Hollow and the hustler's Magoffin County also lies a tightly packed, mountain-walled town that is anything but an Appalachian cliché.

That's not to say that Paintsville has no Appalachian *color*. It's not without its stereotypical aspects—such as the way it pronounces itself, like a half-quart and some calves' meat: *Pints-veal*. It's also a kinfolk kind of place: In a population of 4,655, there are sixty VanHooses to keep the Butchers, Burchetts, Castles, Wards, Ratliffs, and Tacketts company. And then there's the traditional mountain commerce: A former mayor says that when he took office a half century ago, there were fifty taxi drivers in town and forty-five of them were bootleggers. The abundance of cabs, of course, should not suggest that Paintsville was otherwise citified: When the government built a ten-story apartment building in 1982, locally known as "the high rise," it took months to fill the place beyond the second floor because the country folks were afraid to use the elevator; when they finally dared higher, they were assigned elevator partners. (Afterwards, one grateful resident approached the local director and told him it was the first winter in which she hadn't looked through her kitchen floor and seen the ground.) Their Appalachian peculiarities are a source of amusement for even themselves, and the local folks, consequently, have a way of commenting upon their own customs with native humor: The new fishing regulations at Paintsville Lake, they say, require that you throw back anything under six cylinders.

Paintsville sits in the heart of the Eastern Kentucky coal fields, ten thousand square miles and nineteen counties of low mountains and narrow valleys known as the Cumberland Plateau. It is a region rich in minerals and natural splendor, which, for the first half of the century, was left mostly undisturbed by the auger-mining industry that tunneled deep into the Earth for its black bounty. The crowded little towns that developed in the Cumberlands were either coal camps or mercantile and professional enclaves whose dollars were as figuratively sooty as the miners' faces. Outside of the towns, tucked into the sheltered hollows that have accommodated the same families for generations and sometimes centuries, country folks lived self-reliantly in faded wooden homes not always accessible by car or truck. Many still do; the only way to the front door is across one of the swinging pedestrian bridges that span the creeks, each leaving a half-dozen or more vehicles parked along the side of the winding road. Even the poverty in the area once held a simple beauty, but that was largely lost when strip-mining began to systematically disfigure the mountains by cutting off their tops, felling their trees, and polluting their streams. The relative ease of strip-mining turned some of the technologically emboldened local folk into sudden millionaires whose Bel-Air mansions loom incongruously amidst the rusting cars and gray-sided dwellings of their less (or more?) fortunate neighbors. In the early sixties, the national media—the *New York Times*, *Life* and CBS, among

The victory bus: Their triumphant return to Paintsville was a moment the 1996 state champions will never forget.

others—documented Eastern Kentucky's Appalachian depression with reports that revealed miners working for six or eight dollars a day and children who ate the dried mud that held together the rocks of their chimneys. Kentucky's poverty was so publicly disgraceful that *Pravda* carried a front-page picture of an unwashed Appalachian mother standing with her dirtier children in front of their sagging shanty.

The photographs and films in those stories became the Appalachian cliché. Unlike the Rocky Mountains, the Appalachians were settled in pioneer times by European hill people and industrialized by profiteers who reconfigured the region's rural destiny. Except for the unsightly shaving administered by the strip miners, however, the mountains themselves could not be reconfigured, and the difficulties in traversing them accounted for an isolation that continues to define Eastern Kentucky. Independence, resourcefulness, and family strength were the best products of this topographical remoteness; violence and illiteracy were the worst.

As the anti-cliché, however, Paintsville stands as an eminent exception to the Appalachian myth that is perhaps the most institutionalized and damning of them all: the one about ignorance. Its basis in truth has to do with the fact that the old mountain schools were crude affairs, open maybe half the year, in which an eighteen-year-old teacher could be beaten bloody by a nineteen-year-old second grader. In 1963, forty percent of all the one- and two-room schoolhouses in the United States were located in Kentucky, with a disproportionate number of those in the mountains. Nearly a quarter of Kentucky adults were illiterate. Some of them might have been teachers. The teaching position was fiercely coveted in many of the job-depleted hollows, and the one who got it was often the one who could deliver the most votes to the school board. Kentucky had a slogan ready for when the national education ratings came out every year: Thank God for Arkansas.

Paintsville, on the other hand, sends ninety percent of its high school graduates to college. School, in fact, appears to be what Paintsville is largely all about. The city high school sits back comfortably in a mountain shadow on Second Street, a block from Main, with the elementary school, the Catholic school, and the vocational school just down the sidewalk. Johnson Central, the much larger county high school into which the neighboring rural districts consolidated in 1969, is situated across Paint Creek, less than a mile distant, on the fast-food, discount-center highway strip, facing the bluff that marks the town's western boundary. The Paintsville kids would go there except that the town keeps passing bond issues to keep its own school, defying the trend that restructured so many Kentucky districts in the sixties and seventies. The people of Paintsville—many of them bankers, lawyers, doctors, merchants, and insurance agents brought together by the mines of Johnson, Floyd, Magoffin, and nearby counties—figure that consolidation is for those who need it, and they don't.

The results are fundamental to Paintsville's way of life. As a school town, it is consequently a family town, its big and small houses arranged in such a neighborly fashion that one like J.R. VanHoose's historic old home on Fourth Street will have as many as eight hundred kids on its porch at Halloween, many of them in from the surrounding hills. Paintsville's main residential area is so accessible to the high school that the school doesn't even serve lunch—the students who don't pack are able to walk home or to one of the mom-and-pop restaurants close by.

Moreover, its stubborn independence has made the Paintsville school district one of the remaining few in rural Kentucky with a significant tradition; and, at that, a tradition that encompasses considerably more than basketball. The legacy is principally scholastic—Paintsville's test scores rank consistently among the top ten in the state—but even in the context of athletics, Paintsville has deeper traditions in baseball and football than it does in basketball. The baseball team has an extensive state-tournament history, going often and winning once, and it has sent more than sixty players to college or pro ball. (The local baseball tradition also includes the Paintsville Yankees, which played at Johnson County High School as late as 1982, at which time Paintsville was the smallest town in America with a minor-league franchise.) Meanwhile, the former PHS football coach, Walter Brugh, still holds Kentucky's record for victories.

Basketball was such an unconventionally low priority in Paintsville for so long that the only way for school officials to get the high school gym built was to promote it as an auditorium. On the other hand, a school board member was once elected on a platform of putting lights on the football field. Paintsville was proud of its football field—Belfry's, by contrast, had a creek bed running through at about the 3-yard line—and prouder of its fine teams, whose mettle often prompted local opponents to engage in extreme defensive measures. There was the game at Hazard in the late thirties, for instance, when the Hazard police chief stood in the end zone and announced that he would shoot any Paintsville player who dared to cross the goal line. Fortunately, one of the Paintsville parents was comparably equipped, and a standoff ensued. At Prestonsburg, a similarly threatened Paintsville player named Eck Chandler is said to have run all the way home after scoring the winning touchdown, sprinting out the gate and never looking back. At Elkhorn City, Paintsville was about to win a playoff game when a lady from the home side walked out on the field and sat on the ball. Jack Pelphrey, John's dad, whom the Elkhorn City folks recognized as the one who had been making noise all night with a piece of an old air horn from his truck, went down to congratulate the Paintsville players and suddenly found himself looking up at the stadium lights. A later inspection revealed a buckshot scar on his forehead.

Many of the rural schools in Paintsville's vicinity were unable to field a football team (too few boys, too much harvesting), and the local basketball tradition was concentrated primarily among them. In the next county, just twenty miles down the crooked road, a little place named Inez was as well known for basketball as nearly any in Kentucky, winning state championships in 1941—the year the school's first gym was built—and 1954, after which the town of Paintsville turned out to meet and fete its neighbors on their triumphant journey home. The mid-fifties were salad days for hillbilly basketball. King Kelly Coleman played in Wayland, one county to the south of Paintsville, and the county after that was the proud home of Carr Creek. The state championship between Inez's in 1954 and Carr Creek's in 1956 was won by Johnny Cox and Hazard, which is situated just a couple mountains west of Carr Creek and fifty miles from the Johnson County line. In Johnson County alone, Meade Memorial, which practiced outside for many years, had Donnis Butcher, who later played for the New York Knicks and coached the Detroit Pistons, and an even better player (according to some) named Junior White, who worked in the mines year-round, scored forty-nine points after walking twelve miles to a road game, and after high school disappeared back into the coal tunnels; Flat Gap, which once beat the Morehead State freshmen, boasted Carroll Burchett, who would succeed at Kentucky, and Charlie Osborne, who would set records at Western Kentucky; Oil Springs was so talented that it once split the squad in half and won two holiday tournaments on the same day; and Van Lear, where the coal miner's daughter lived, might have been the best of the lot. Any of those schools could put a licking on Paintsville.

When they all consolidated into Johnson County High School at the end of the sixties, there was a feeling that it was essentially over for the rest of the state. It didn't work out that way. Johnson County's basketball tradition has not been the equal of any *one* of the tiny mountain schools that it was created from.

Paintsville, meanwhile, was certainly not thinking about the basketball implications when it refused to consolidate. It would have been easy to go along with the trend; Paintsville's two hundred and fifty high school kids, unlike those from the country, wouldn't have had to deal with new and difficult transportation concerns or worry about acclimating themselves to a new town. The only thing Paintsville had to lose was its identity as a community. It chose, at considerable cost, to hang on to that, never dreaming that a state basketball championship would one day result; never realizing that one could have so much to do with the other.

The little school's rise in basketball didn't occur right away. Until John Pelphrey and his crowd came along in the eighties, Paintsville had never been even a scrub pine on Kentucky's basketball landscape. But a player like Pelphrey goes a long way in a town like Paintsville. He and his able high school teammates, Joey Couch (who would later captain UK's football team at the same time Pelphrey captained the basketball squad) and Keith Adkins (who played college basketball at Notre Dame), quickened the pulses of the home folks by taking Paintsville to three straight Sweet Sixteens. As they did, it became evident around town that there were suddenly a lot more young boys bouncing basketballs in the schoolyard and signing up for the youth teams whose winter leagues are closely chronicled in the sports section of the local weekly. When Pelphrey was named Mister Basketball and became regionally immortalized as a leading member of The Unforgettables, this trend escalated into a craze. Paintsville had become connected to something much larger and ostensibly grander than itself. Through Pelphrey, it had acquired a redefining oneness with Kentucky basketball.

Among the local boys who aspired to be another Pelphrey was a rapidly growing grade-schooler named Jonathan Robert VanHoose whose mother had to accompany him to the local movie theater to assure the ticket seller that he did, indeed, qualify for the child's rate. Like many of his friends in the close, amiable community, J.R. lived within two blocks of the school, a pleasant happenstance that produced some lively asphalt ballgames. The youngster's size served him well in these games and on other occasions when he chose to put it to use, such as the time in fourth grade when another boy was making fun of a girl with hearing aids. "Look," J.R. said to the boy, "I'm bigger than both of you. So if you want to pick on somebody, why don't you pick on me for being tall?" Then he took the girl by the hand and walked her out to recess, where, for a change, he opted out of the customary basketball game.

Due to his height and conspicuous aptitude, J.R. was already being associated with basketball. He was in the gym a lot because his father, Bob, a land agent for a nearby coal company, had agreed to help out his childhood friend Bill Mike Runyon, head coach of the Paintsville Tigers. As a boy, Bob VanHoose had moved to Marion, Indiana, when his father took a job there with General Motors, but his parents and the Runyons maintained their ties by playing Rook together in Paintsville every summer. Bob VanHoose was enough of a basketball player to eventually letter at the small-college level (St. Francis of Fort Wayne, Indiana) and Bill Mike, who would have been his high school teammate if the VanHooses hadn't moved, accused his friend of costing Paintsville a trip to the Sweet

Sixteen. So when Bob brought his young family back to where his roots were, Runyon prevailed upon him to make amends by keeping stats and being somebody to talk to on the Paintsville bench.

Four years later, J.R. joined his father there as a strapping 6-foot-4 1/2-inch eighth grader, occasionally even starting. Runyon had meatier boys and better shooters available, but he admired J.R.'s soft hands and his bottomless appetite for rebounds. By ninth grade, VanHoose received his first piece of recruiting mail. It was from Pelphrey, who had taken a job as an assistant coach at Marshall University in West Virginia.

The next year, as a 6-9 sophomore (he was listed as 6-10) VanHoose made his indelible entry into Kentucky folklore. Following the traditional pattern, it happened at the state tournament. Paintsville had arrived at the Sweet Sixteen following a highly anticipated but disappointing regular season which ended in a blowout loss to Lexington Catholic High School. But the Tigers, long on talent and size, had collected themselves for the district and regional tournaments and earned a first-round match with Owensboro in the Sweet Sixteen. The Owensboro game went into overtime, during which only two points were scored. They came in the final seconds, when a shot by VanHoose's gifted classmate, guard Todd Tackett, descended short and J.R. won the game by fielding it in the air and placing it in the hoop. The points gave VanHoose twenty-five for the game and the rebound was his twentieth. Tackett said later that he had not undershot on purpose, but he had been playing with VanHoose since the fourth grade and knew that a short miss stood an excellent chance of landing in the big fellow's hungry hands.

The next night against Allen County-Scottsville, the finish came down once again to the mutually trained reflexes of Paintsville's sophomores. Scottsville tied the game on a difficult 3-pointer with six seconds remaining, and as its players, expecting a timeout, turned toward each other to indulge in the moment, Tackett took off down the floor. VanHoose, knowing his friend would do this—he had been doing it in similar circumstances for six years—caught the ball as it came out of the basket, stepped over the baseline with his right foot, and Marinoed a pass to the other end of the court, where he calculated his speedy receiver would be. Tackett's layup dropped through a second or so before the buzzer sounded.

The Saturday morning semifinal game was against Paintsville's nemesis, Lexington Catholic, whose reserves included a coach's son named Mike Pitino. The young man's father should have been there. Those who were saw a performance that the *Lexington Herald-Leader* later ranked as the greatest in the history of the Sweet Sixteen. As Paintsville turned the tables with an astonishing 79-55 upset, VanHoose scored twenty-nine points and outrebounded the entire Lexington Catholic team, 27-25. At the time, the twenty-seven rebounds were reported as a tournament record; only months later was it discovered that King Kelly Coleman had pulled down twenty-eight against Carr Creek in the 1956 semifinals. Had he known, Runyon—who was told that VanHoose had broken a record held by Wes Unseld—would have kept his center on the floor for a couple of the six minutes he spent on the bench; he was going at a rate of more than a rebound a minute.

VanHoose was named the Sweet Sixteen's Most Valuable Player after a title game—the first between Eastern Kentucky teams since 1928—in which the Tigers dominated four-time state champion Ashland, a large school located sixty miles up the Country Music Highway from Paintsville. He had taken the fast track to folk status, arriving ahead of the schedules established by Farmer, Pelphrey, Chapman, Cox, Hagan, and Jones. The term they use in Kentucky for a storybook high school player is "schoolboy legend;" as a sophomore, VanHoose was practically that already. But he still had a ways to go before he would be an all-out Kentucky legend, and it wouldn't happen, couldn't happen, unless and until he had worn the name across his chest in block letters.

The concept naturally appealed to him. VanHoose was a Kentuckian, after all, and besides that a history buff well-known to the Paintsville librarians; he spent virtually every Saturday morning in their stacks unless the Tigers lost the night before and Runyon called a special practice. His special interests were the Civil War and family ancestry, which, with the help of about fifty letters he had collected from various VanHooses and Van Hausens around the country, he had traced back to Germany in 1514. "My ancestors have been here since the late 1700s," J.R. explained in his thick, ingenuous mountain accent. "I had a bunch of ancestors in the American Revolution and a bunch in the Civil War, too. My fourth or fifth great-grandfather was sixty-eight years old and he joined up with the Confederacy. He was riding back home after he enlisted and he encountered three regiments of Union infantry who were wanting to take over his home town, West Liberty, Kentucky [in the county west of Paintsville]. He rode out into the middle of the road and told them to stop, then started blasting at them with his old squirrel shotgun. They thought he was a crazy old man and I guess they were too stunned to do anything right away. He shot one, then he loaded up and shot another one, and then he loaded up and shot a third. Finally the Union captain called out his company of a hundred men, and as they rode by they shot and killed him in the road. They say he was the first Eastern Kentucky soldier killed in the Civil War. James Davis. His daughter married into the VanHoose family.

"I just feel like Kentucky is home," the handsome teenager said. "No matter where I go, I'm going to be a Kentuckian, and an Eastern Kentuckian. It kind of makes me mad the way people talk about Eastern Kentucky. They call us rednecks and hicks and stuff and pick on this part of the country because we have a funny accent. Everybody thinks we have dirt roads and marry our sisters and eat dogs."

The fact was, VanHoose *liked* his funny accent and wasn't too interested in going away to have it ridiculed. Besides that, he was a homebody. It was only after he hooked up with Amy Stricklin, a neighbor girl two years older than he, that J.R. began venturing out now and then to dances and social settings. Still, his idea of a good time was leafing through Civil War records or officiating an elementary school basketball game: The little guys were awed when they looked straight up into the pleasant, youthful face of their towering hero; one of them refused to take off a shoe that J.R. had tied for him.

Because it was home, VanHoose wanted very much to play basketball at the University of Kentucky—almost as much as Paintsville, Eastern Kentucky, and the rest of the commonwealth wanted it for him. But as the nets came down at Rupp Arena, there was plenty of time for all of that to play out, and hopefully another state championship or two to bring back to the mountains. Meanwhile, the story was rich and the glory was great. Before the team had finished celebrating on the floor, Bill Mike Runyon felt a tap on the shoulder. "I want you to know," said the school district's former longtime superintendent, Oran Teater, "I can now die a happy man." The sentiments were largely in that vein. When the Tigers crossed the Johnson County line on their way home, they were met by screaming fire engines and all four of Paintsville's police cruisers.

Everybody headed to the center of town, to the gym that had seen nothing like this since it was built in 1950.

Paintsville's accomplishment carried with it the spirit of an Appalachian renaissance. With the MVP and the rest of the Tigers huddled around him, Runyon held up the trophy to share with his friends and neighbors—men he hunted with and women whose voices filled the high school gym when his boys played the game in the best tradition of mountain basketball. "We were able to achieve this with a bunch of mountain boys from Eastern Kentucky," he said proudly, "and if you want to call us hillbillies, call us hillbillies—because we are the state champs."

◯◯◯

Most of Kentucky's full-blown basketball legends were folk heroes before they even arrived at the state university. That's not to say that the UK uniform had nothing to do with history's cataloging; it assuredly did and does. The prep hero who strays, in fact, is a sort of lapsed Kentuckian to whom no measure of achievement can restore the surrendered birthright. Along those lines, the most celebrated high school player in Kentucky history, mid-fifties sensation "King" Kelly Coleman, has seen his legend diminish over time to an esoteric, half-blown

The king: Kelly Coleman was Kentucky's most famous prep player.

level for the simple fact that he didn't play for the Cats. Wes Unseld's place in the state's historical pecking order is similarly compromised. It works both ways: The Big Blue superstar who does not carry a Kentucky pedigree must be a rare All-American indeed to rate a place in the pantheon of genuine Bluegrass legends. Kyle Macy overcame his Indiana roots to become the most popular Wildcat of all and Dan Issel of Illinois makes the legend list as the school's all-time leading scorer, but Cotton Nash, a three-time All-American from Louisiana, doesn't.

Legend status in Kentucky is not an empirical reckoning; it is the product of an unofficial but deep-seated dynamic that is simply understood in the regional scheme, on the order of a social structure. The imported UK stars, with few exceptions, are as the nouveau riche, temporarily enjoying the privileges of the legend class although, for them, it can never be quite the same as it is for the native-born. That leaves a proper and loyal few, a culturally correct roll call of basketball immortals who have brought honor to the Bluegrass. It leaves Cliff Hagan, who was a man among boys when he led Owensboro to the state high school championship and a dashing idol when he brought home a collegiate crown for Kentucky; Wah Wah Jones, who dominated Kentucky at Harlan High and then helped Kentucky do the same to the rest of the country; and Rex Chapman, who left the program two years early but made his permanent mark when he came out of Hagan's hometown in 1986 carrying the banner for those who feared that the Kentucky program had left behind the Kentucky player. Special places in the Kentucky heart are also reserved for the likes of Ralph Beard, Frank Ramsey, Johnny Cox, Vernon Hatton, and Jack Givens, each a Kentucky high school great and a UK All-American.

Given Kentucky's profound appreciation for its own, it is possible, even, to gain admission into this gallery without achieving collegiate greatness. The classic example is Richie Farmer, a full-fledged Kentucky legend in spite of the fact that he started only rarely for the Wildcats, and then only after every third Appalachia Kentuckian from Carbon Glow to Jamboree and Crummies to Paw Paw, including Greasy, Frozen, Dice, Dwarf, Wax, Rowdy, Co-Operative, Quicksand, Shoulderblade, Pippa Passes, Hi Hat, and Hell For Certain, had phoned into the talk shows pleading for and demanding it. Although not tall nor fleet nor especially creative, Farmer was a fantastic high school player with two other things going for him: he hailed from the mountains of Clay County, which endeared him to the look-after-their-own folks of Eastern Kentucky; and he saved his best basketball for the Kentucky state tournament.

Traditionally, Bluegrass legends have been born in the Sweet Sixteen, as it is called—also known to citizens of the commonwealth as "The

Greatest Show on Earth." When Adolph Rupp coached UK, it was his custom to grant a virtually automatic scholarship to the most valuable player of the Sweet Sixteen. In a time when many mountain schools were isolated by virtue of road conditions, many Western Kentucky schools were isolated by virtue of distance, and the media was not nearly as electronic or nimble as we know it today, countless other Kentucky stars were undiscovered until the state tournament. The Sweet Sixteen is the state's annual festival of basketball, and the acclaim bestowed upon its heroes can last a Kentucky lifetime.

So it was with Richie Farmer. He was an eighth grader in 1984, when he appeared in his first state tournament, and made the all-tournament team as a freshman the year Clay County lost the championship game by a point to Hopkinsville. After he shot and passed his mountain school to the big prize two years later, the pressure was on Kentucky coach Eddie Sutton to bring Farmer to Lexington. But Sutton had a history of coaching greyhound guards, and Farmer wasn't his type. He was, however, Kentucky's type. By the time Clay County reached the championship game again in his senior season, Farmer had already broken Wah Wah Jones's career tournament scoring record. He added a remarkable fifty-one points in the state final against Louisville Ballard. Clay County lost the game, but Kentucky gained a legend. Richie Farmer had become the most popular prep star in Kentucky history.

He was not, however, the state's best or even its most famous schoolboy player. The best would have been Hagan or Jones or Unseld or the one who was, without a doubt, the most famous—the king of high school basketball.

Kelly Coleman came along at the same time coal was giving up its reign as king of the mountains, so the title was transferred to the most phenomenal high school basketball player the Cumberlands had ever seen. The son of a miner who lived between Paintsville and Carr Creek in the Floyd County community of Wayland, in a house on the Right Fork of Beaver Creek that rented for fifteen dollars, Coleman was a man-child of Ruthian proportions. He ate thirty hamburgers a week, put away a beer and a milkshake for every hamburger, and played basketball with the same sort of gluttony. He once had seventy-five points and forty-one rebounds on a night he was alleged to be drunk. When the Hindman coach boasted before a big game that his team would hold Coleman to twenty-one points, the king's reply was, "Which quarter?" As a senior, he broke the Kentucky scoring record he set as a junior by fifteen points a game, averaging nearly forty-seven. Publicly, Adolph Rupp called him "the greatest high school player who ever lived . . . a combination of Cliff Hagan, Frank Ramsey, and all the other great stars who have played at Kentucky." Privately, he told Coleman that he was the best offensive player the coach had seen at any level. At 6-4, 215, Coleman was an enormous guard with range, power, instincts, ball control, and a mean streak.

When Coleman arrived at the 1956 state tournament with the Wayland Wasps, helium balloons were passed out with his name on them and an airplane dropped leaflets over Lexington proclaiming him "the greatest prep basketeer in history." His fame and his mountain origin would have made him fantastically popular under unconflicted conditions, but there was a small matter of what some perceived as questionable citizenship on his part—drinking and arrogance being among the issues—and a larger matter of the scholarship Coleman had accepted to West Virginia, where he would be a freshman teammate of Jerry West. Kentuckians could excuse a number of vices, but treason was not among them. When Coleman scored fifty points in the first round of the Sweet Sixteen, he was purposefully booed.

And when he was booed, he was ticked. Coleman was angry for the rest of the tournament, taking it out on the field by littering it with his scoring and rebounding records. His basketball ambition had always been to carry Wayland to a state championship, and the rude treatment he received only made him more determined. But when the Wasps lost their semifinal game to Carr Creek on Freddie Maggard's last-second shot—despite Coleman's tournament-record twenty-eight rebounds—the king adjusted his sights. There was still a consolation game to play, and he told Lexington sportswriter Billy Thompson that he was going to give the fans the greatest exhibition of basketball they had ever seen: He was going to score sixty points. "And then, Billy," he said, "you tell 'em for me to drop dead." But Coleman missed his mark. He scored sixty-eight. Then he left the premises. His sister accepted his awards for him, explaining that the king was shy. Various rumors had him in a tavern getting bombed and in his hotel room reading comic books. Actually, the truth was in between: he was in his hotel room drinking bourbon and telling the state of Kentucky to go to hell.

Coalminer's son: Coleman was considered a better prospect than Oscar Robertson or Jerry West.

Coleman's grudge against Kentucky went deeper than the booing. It was a complicated tale that involved the things Kentucky people did to sabotage his deal with West Virginia. When, largely through their efforts, the West Virginia scholarship was denied because of recruiting violations, Coleman went ahead and accepted one to Kentucky. But he never intended to go there; it was just a way for him to get even. He ended up playing college ball at Kentucky Wesleyan and a little bit of pro ball after that, then moved to Michigan. He worked in the circulation department of the *Detroit News*, but the job wasn't the reason he went to Michigan. He went there because it wasn't Kentucky.

As he approached his sixties, Coleman had begun to mellow about Kentucky. He visited his mother and sister in Wayland on occasion and played golf with friends at Green Meadow Country Club in Pikeville when he was there, but he still steered clear of testimonials and all-time teams and anything that would place him once again in the context of Kentucky basketball. Privately, he was just getting to the point where he could talk about it freely.

"I'd rather wait till I was eighty to say these things," he said from his home in suburban Detroit, as snow fell in the late winter of 1997. "But yes, there was a lot of pressure from Kentucky when I was a senior. People were calling me, writing me, coming by the house. The governor, Happy Chandler, called. John Y. Brown Sr., the lawyer, came to my house trying everything he could try to get me to come to Kentucky. A lot of people were telling me things I could have. Anything that I would want would be made available to me.

"At the time, I planned on going to West Virginia. They came in when I was a junior and started giving me cars. A lot of Kentucky people got mad when they found out about that. That's what caused the NCAA investigation. Of course, the Kentucky people said they weren't trying to punish me, but West Virginia was put on probation for a year and the NCAA wouldn't allow me to go there. After that, there was no way possible I would go to Kentucky. But at the time, my father was working in Cleveland and people in Kentucky said they would find him a job near home. They found him a job with a coal company in David, Kentucky. He had to be in that job thirty days before they couldn't lay him off, so I kept stringing them along until I knew they couldn't do anything about it. When school started in September, I just didn't show up. A year later, my father was killed in an automobile accident."

The arrangement with West Virginia had been an elaborate and compelling one for a poor mountain miner's kid. The car was a 1954 Dodge and it was complemented by a gas card, shoes, watches, coats, and assorted goodies. To protect their interest in Coleman, the Mountaineers enrolled him in a West Virginia military academy for his senior year of high school. The king, however, was not a military-academy kind of guy, and within a week had picked up enough demerits to earn a trip back to Wayland, where, in the absence of his stern father, he spent the winter drinking bourbon, breaking records, playing pool, and filling his pockets. Fans from around the state and country sent money to the famous boy's house for no apparent reason. Others bet on how many points he would score and shared their profits with him. On many occasions after a game, Coleman would shake hands with a gauntlet of winning gamblers outside the gym and pull his hand back twenty dollars richer for each shake. Meanwhile, University of Kentucky boosters were making generous suggestions of their own, offering scholarships for Coleman and each of his three sisters. They also presented him with a twenty-foot petition signed by thousands of Kentucky fans who thought it would be best for the young man to continue his education at the state university.

Were it not for basketball and what was expected of him as the king of it, Coleman would have probably married his high school sweetheart and found some work around Wayland. But his life wasn't that simple, so he married his high school sweetheart—and was still married to her forty-one years later—got his revenge on UK, and took a scholarship to Eastern Kentucky University. He left there after six weeks, unable to get along with the coach, Paul McBrayer, and worked for a while at a steel mill in Ohio before enrolling at Kentucky Wesleyan, where he averaged twenty-seven points as a freshman and eventually set the school's career scoring record, all the while contributing heavily to the rest of his reputation. The New York Knicks made him the ninth player taken in the NBA draft but didn't find his lifestyle to be compatible with professional basketball. He turned down a chance at pro baseball to play a couple of years for Chicago in the American Basketball League, leading the team in rebounding once and in scoring twice before the league folded. Many of the ABL players went on to the NBA, but, despite the obvious fact that Coleman was among the best in the league, the NBA had no place for his baggage. He caught on with the U.S. Stars, who traveled with the Harlem Globetrotters, bounced around, had a family, owned a gas station, ran a motel, went back to college for his degree, taught some school, and moved to Michigan.

"Hindsight is kind of easy now," Coleman said in his fifty-eighth year, "but if I had to do it all over, I probably would have gone ahead to Kentucky. Rupp promised me that if I went to Kentucky we would be national champions and he would take our team to the Olympics in 1960. Whether or not I would have lasted that long, I don't know. Lincoln Collinsworth told me that Rupp and I might have had trouble getting along. Rupp wanted anything that was worthwhile to be his happening. He didn't want anybody to outshine him. I was pretty sure I was going to be the focal point at Kentucky, and I don't know if he would have liked that. I don't know if *I* would have liked that. I don't think there's any doubt that I would have set scoring records at Kentucky, but I really wanted to be on a team where I didn't have to do all of the scoring.

"The number one thing that drove me away, though, was all the booing at the state tournament. It started with the first tipoff, and from then on, every time the ball hit my hands the people would boo. When I got rid of the ball, they would stop. I'd get the ball again, they'd boo. They finally came over to my side in the consolation game, after I'd scored about sixty points, but by then it was a day late and a penny short. The whole thing destroyed me. After that, I can say in all honesty that I probably never played at more than seventy-five percent of my capacity. I lost my desire and wasn't in good enough physical condition to play the game right. My sort of lifestyle just led to that. The Knicks cut me the day before the season started, and there was only one guard on that team who could have carried my shoes. That was Richie Guerin, and he might have carried one of them. The other guards were jokes.

"You know, when I was a senior in high school, I was Mister Basketball in Kentucky, Jerry West was Mister Basketball in West Virginia, and Oscar Robertson was Mister Basketball in Indiana. And I was considered the best prospect of the three. You'd never know it now, would you? I could shoot and rebound with Oscar, but he had better foot movement and I'm sure he played better defense. I thought I was better than West, and I still think I was."

For most of his adult life, Coleman had been tormented by the idea that somehow the excesses of Kentucky had deprived him of his destiny. "It took me at least twenty-five years, a quarter of a century, to get over it," the king said. "But it feels better now. I just think everybody takes athletics too seriously, and Kentucky is probably the leader of the pack. We make heroes out of people that shouldn't be heroes. I probably didn't deserve it." After Coleman had finally made peace with himself and his homeland, his golf friends in Pikeville were still telling him that he should have gone to Kentucky. He had learned to laugh, as long as they said it the right way.

By that time, Wayland High School didn't exist anymore—it was consolidated into Allen Central—but in 1995 a Wayland man bought the old building at auction for $65,000 and cleaned up the gym. Then he went into business. For thirty-six bucks, people came from miles around to play two hours of basketball on the floor that King Kelly Coleman played on.

○○○

Billy Ray Cassady was six years old when Inez High School built a gym and won the 1941 state championship. With that, his childhood was all mapped out.

Cassady had a first cousin on that team and a father who was all-region when there was a jump ball after every basket. When the '41 boys

Billy Ray Cassady (left, with Omar Fannin and the state championship trophy from 1954): "Basketball is what put Inez on the map."

practiced in the new gym—before that, they just used the dirt court—
Billy Ray and his buddies would wait for a break in the action, then dash
out and take a quick shot or two before the varsity started up again.
"That's all we had to do," he said, except for the summer, when they
played fox-and-dog, chased each other on bicycles, fished for creek bass,
and hunted rabbits, squirrels, and birds on the mountainsides. The basketball goals were not centrally located, so when one wasn't handy they
shot tennis balls into coffee cans nailed to sheds or whatever. Once, they
put up a goal, tamped down the court, had a whale of a game, got into a
fight, tore down the goal, and sent it home with the boy who brought it.

The ball was Billy Ray's, and he knew what to do with it. So did his
pals. By the time they were in high school, "We knew two plays ahead of
time what so and so would do." Inez had a state-tournament tradition,
nine trips in all, but when Cassady's 1954 crew lost its season opener to
Phelps, well, "Everybody said we'd be the sorriest outfit Inez ever had,"
he recalled. The team didn't lose again until it got caught in a scheduling
predicament, finding itself in the prestigious Louisville Invitational Tournament the same day it was supposed to be playing Henry Clay High
School in Lexington. It couldn't be said that Inez ever backed out of a
basketball game, so the boys did it all, playing four times in twenty-four
hours. They lost to Henry Clay but won the LIT, prompting the *Louisville Courier-Journal* to refer to them in its headline as "Ironmen From
Mountains . . ."

"The richest basketball tradition there is is right here in Inez. Basketball is what put Inez on the map," said Cassady one winter afternoon
in the mountains. He was living at the edge of his inconspicuous hometown, just off the Russell Williamson Bypass, named for his old principal
and basketball coach. The new bypass provided a smoother route to
Paintsville than the asphalt pretzel they called Highway 40, but otherwise there hadn't been much improvement thereabouts. The proud old
school building, used now as a community center, didn't look so good.
The school itself had consolidated into Sheldon Clark in 1972. Cassady's
heart still hadn't mended. Sheldon Clark is situated just outside town and
Cassady was connected to it by virtue of having been the athletic director
there for a while, but it just wasn't the same as having the little old school
right there in the middle of things. "Back when they had small schools,"
he said wistfully, "that's when they played basketball. It was somethin'

else. When you played teams in the fifteenth region and went into their gyms, buddy, listen . . .

"You know, people said that when Inez and Warfield combined, good Lord, what a team it would be. But now the kids are scattered all over the county. When school's out, you just don't see 'em. It was different when everybody was a community. After a ballgame, all the men in town would meet at the drugstore to talk about it. Basketball was about all there was in our community. If I went outside for a bar of candy and somebody saw me, or saw me drinking pop, they'd tell on me. My brother told on me once for smoking a cigarette while we were rabbit hunting. He called up the coach and said, 'Mr. Williamson, you know what Bill did?' The next day at practice, Coach said, 'Anybody who's been smoking, hit the stairway.' I was the first one up, but the rest of the team was right behind me."

Not in the least discouraged by the fact that it had only fifty-something kids in the senior class, Inez made it back to the state tournament in 1954. With Cassady leading the way, the mountain boys won, won, and won, arriving in the Memorial Coliseum finals against Newport, a city school from Northern Kentucky. "When we walked out onto the floor and they saw that big 'I' on our warmups," Cassady reminisced forty-something years later, "there was a roar from the crowd and I felt like I was floating on air. We went out into our layup line and I went up first to put up a little crip shot. When I took off, it seemed like I went up and up and just never stopped. I remember as I was going up thinking, 'When am I gonna stop?' The ball hit that backboard and went flying off to the other side and the rim hit me around my elbow. I had never jumped that high in my life." Cassady settled down sufficiently to win Most Valuable Player honors as Inez carried home its second state championship. Back in the mountains, Paintsville sent out its fire truck to meet the victors and other surrounding towns invited the team over for community suppers.

Four boys from that Inez lineup went on to play college basketball—two of them at Morehead State and one at Eastern Kentucky. Cassady was the fourth. "I got a charley horse during the state tournament," he recollected, "and they took me in to see the UK team trainer. I was afraid to get in that whirlpool they had at Memorial Coliseum—I'd never seen anything like that—so Coach Williamson came with me. I was sittin' in that thing when all of a sudden this fella walked in and said,

'Hello, Russ.' Coach said, 'Hello, Coach Rupp.' I thought, 'Coach Rupp?!' I'd never seen him before. It shocked me that he would be in there. But he looked at me and said, 'Son, we've got a scholarship for you if you want to come to the University of Kentucky. I said, 'Well, I don't know.' I don't know why I said that. If they wanted me at Kentucky, I was going to Kentucky."

Eastern Kentuckians were plentiful on the Wildcat teams back then. Earl Adkins of Ashland and Jerry Bird of Corbin were there when Cassady arrived. "I remember one day Coach Rupp asked Jerry Bird, 'Son, you've seen the movie *The Ten Commandments*, haven't you? Tell me, what's the tenth commandment?' Jerry couldn't think of what to say, so Coach Rupp said, 'I'll tell you. Thou shalt not be stupid.' We all broke up laughing, and when we did that, he made us all run the stairs. We didn't ever laugh again at practice."

Accompanying Cassady to Kentucky was a fine player from neighboring Johnson County, Meade Memorial's Donnis Butcher. They rode back and forth to Lexington together, and after Christmas break Cassady twisted down Highway 40 to pick up his teammate. But when he got there, Butcher's mother said that Donnis was over at the gym and he wasn't going back to UK. Cassady found Butcher involved in a game of three-on-three and asked him what was going on. Butcher confirmed that he wasn't going back to Kentucky, explaining that he hadn't attended any classes the first semester. He subsequently enrolled at nearby Pikeville College and went on to an NBA career as both a player and coach.

Cassady turned out to be a part-time player at Kentucky, sixth man on the Fiddlin' Five, the 1958 national championship squad that beat Elgin Baylor and Seattle in the finals. "We had four mountain boys on that '58 team," he said. "That'll never happen again." In addition to the lefthander from Inez, there were Adkins, Abraham Lincoln Collinsworth of Salyersville (father of Cris, the broadcaster and former Cincinnati Bengals football star), and All-American Johnny Cox of Hazard. Talent was rolling out of the mountains; there would have been a couple more Eastern Kentuckians on the Fiddlin' roster if Bobby Shepherd and E.A. Couch of Carr Creek's 1956 state champions had seen fit to stay.

Shepherd had transferred to Carr Creek as a tall, clumsy kid from the community of Kingdom Come. But when a boy went to Carr Creek he became a basketball player, and the resourceful ones who played in

1956 were somehow able to surmount King Kelly Coleman in the Sweet Sixteen semifinals, the game ending on Freddie Maggard's dramatic field goal. Maggard had also beaten Central City the day before with a last-second shot in the second overtime after Couch [number 33 in the photo on page 122] had tied the game with two free throws after time expired in regulation. [Couch's eventual brother-in-law, Jim Calhoun, who later played on two national championship teams at the University of Cincinnati, wears the black eye and number 29 in the photo.] Thus inspired, Carr Creek beat Henderson by four points in the championship match, provoking another round of mountain celebration when Maggard, Couch, Shepherd and the others returned to the hollows of Knott County, which was still four decades away from its first stoplight (one finally went up around Christmas, 1996, at the intersections of State Routes 80 and 160 in Hindman). Gracious Wayland even threw a banquet for the Creekers, and in Hazard, a county over, Dawahare's clothing store outfitted every Carr Creek player with a new suit. Before he went off to the University of Kentucky, E.A. Couch had married the captain of the cheerleaders in his.

"I ended up with a family, and that was great, but getting married shot my career," reflected Couch forty years later from his home south of Paintsville, where he moved when his children were young. "Coach Rupp didn't like married players. He had some over the years, but he didn't like it. The situation was bad for me as a player—being away from my teammates, not getting enough food to eat. UK gave us books and a thousand dollars a year to live on. That was it.

"It was hard all the way around. The experience of the Eastern Kentucky player in general was that Rupp didn't like 'em. Everybody always thought he did, and he recruited a lot of 'em, but when we got there he talked about our area in a bad manner. It destroyed the confidence of the Eastern Kentucky boy. He even did that with Johnny Cox, but Johnny overcame it. Rupp was a great coach, but only for a certain type of boy. Some of the players who maybe weren't close to their coaches in high school got along okay, but I was used to having a good relationship with my coach. Our coach and assistant coach lived right next to the school, and I lived ten miles away, so the coaches were always there and took care of us. At Carr Creek, I knew my coaches loved me." For Couch, athletics seemed to carry with it family connotations. It started with his father, one of nine Couch brothers who made up the Bluegrass Coal Company baseball team. The elder Couch was offered a contract with the Cincinnati Reds, but the mine paid more—especially for a baseball player—and there weren't any other Couches on the Reds. Perpetuating the Couch tradition of sports and family, E.A. Couch would send a couple of his own sons to college on athletic scholarships, Joey (John Pelphrey's Paintsville teammate) to Kentucky for football and David to Army for basketball. Couch, in fact, is a sports name all over the Cumberlands, the latest in the line being mountain legend and UK quarterback Tim Couch of Leslie County, a distant relative to the Paintsville Couches.

"A lot of the mountain players had trouble making the adjustment at Kentucky," Couch went on. "Bobby Shepherd left his freshman year, and he wasn't the only one. So many players left that year, they had to call off the freshman season. I only stayed two years. I just wasn't the same player I had been in high school. The only time I ever did any good was when Coach Rupp and Coach Lancaster weren't there and they had this fella from Hazard who ran practice. When the fella from Hazard ran practice, I'd be the best player out there. Then Rupp and Lancaster would come back, and nothing. They didn't even take me on road trips. They made a referee out of me for practice."

Rupp used to wax Biblical about mountain players—"I will lift up mine eyes to the hills, from whence cometh my help," he would quote— but he preached a different sermon in practice, and the chorus of amens from the Eastern Kentucky players was not nearly unanimous. If they are the ones to whom the most pride has been attached over the years, they are also the ones by whom the most has been swallowed. Couch and Shepherd were two more entries on a long list of relationships that failed to measure up to their romantic expectations. The reasons for this checkered history are speculative and numerous—among the suspects are homesickness, academic shock, Rupp's attitude, demographics, lifestyle, the competition, pressure, prejudice, jobs back home, and girls back home— but most of them amount to the fact that the Appalachian boys felt alienated in Lexington. That was understandable. To them, a mountain was a place where nobody was around but family; a campus was a place where everybody was around but family.

And so Johnny Cox of Hazard was a star for the Fiddlin' Five but Mickey Gibson of Hazard, who would have been a star for Rupp's Runts, had an argument with the trainer and didn't stay. Billy Ray Cassady of

Inez played for a national champion but Bob Tallent of Maytown had an argument with Rupp and didn't stay. Carroll Burchett of Flat Gap (Johnson County) had a solid career at Kentucky but Donnis Butcher of Meade Memorial (Johnson County) neglected to go to class. Jerry Bird of Corbin and Lincoln Collinsworth of Salyersville stuck it out, but E.A. Couch and Bobby Shepherd of Carr Creek elected not to. Larry Pursiful of Lone Jack, a wonderful shooter, flourished at UK but Bobby Slusher of Lone Jack, who once scored eighty-three points in a high school game, transferred to Cumberland College. Farmer of Manchester and Pelphrey of Paintsville, both Mister Basketballs, made names for themselves in Lexington, but Mister Basketball Todd May of Virgie transferred to Pikeville College and Mister Basketball Kelly Coleman of Wayland never showed up. Wah Wah Jones and Dicky Parsons of Harlan and Little Bill Davis and big Marion Cluggish of Hazard will forever be associated with Kentucky basketball, but Dan Hall and John Lee Butcher and countless other mountain names have been lost in a litany of transfers, walkouts, flunkouts, and personal considerations.

Many of the mountain players recognized this pattern in advance and over the years went elsewhere to play ball. Grady Wallace of Betsy Layne repaired to South Carolina and led the nation in scoring. Frank Selvy and Darrell Floyd of Corbin both went to Furman and each led the nation in scoring twice. (Between the three of them, Eastern Kentuckians were the major-college scoring leaders for five consecutive seasons in the fifties.) Phil Cox of Cawood made all-conference at Vanderbilt three times. Danny Schultz of Middlesboro made all-conference twice at Tennessee and, like some other mountain fellows, managed to beat Kentucky while he was away.

As he entered his junior year at Paintsville High School, J.R. VanHoose was well aware that he, too, could find significant, even satisfying success at a university that wasn't Kentucky. It was an option. *For him*, anyway, it was an option; a lot of people in Eastern Kentucky didn't see it that way. It was like Tucker Daniel, the president of Paintsville's tourism bureau, had said in late fall, just before the annual Apple Festival (when fifty thousand people packed the town for clogging, dog and auto shows, a gospel sing-along, a quilting contest, a square dance, a country music act, and the Apple Bowl doubleheader featuring the football teams of Paintsville and Johnson County high schools). "Everybody here thinks there's only one program," said Daniel, who had sent two sons to other colleges on athletic scholarships. "They see Kentucky as the best program in the country and they figure, why the hell wouldn't he go there? J.R. is gonna hear this over and over. It's a mantra."

Tim Couch, who was recruited by virtually every major football school in the country after setting national passing records at Leslie County, had heard this mantra everywhere he went and ultimately signed with Kentucky, an event that the *Herald-Leader* trumpeted with a front-page, banner headline. And that was only *football*. Bob VanHoose knew the Couches, and knew what Tim had gone through. He also knew—everybody did—that in J.R.'s case, the mantra would be repeated early, often, and at full volume, because the mountains had not produced a basketball prospect like him since King Kelly Coleman. Within the state, he had already been identified as the top player in the junior class—an exceptional class—and a coaches' poll had named him the best player in Kentucky, the first junior to receive that recognition since Darrell Griffith in 1974. Some of the recruiting services had rated him among the top five juniors in the nation and the best of the big men.

The hubbub over VanHoose naturally reached Pitino's ears, and while the Kentucky coach was not likely to let public opinion do his recruiting, he was less likely to overlook a good big man a hundred miles down the road. He had been happy to chat with VanHoose when the prospect made an informal visit to Lexington, where he found a locker at Memorial Coliseum with his name on it and his number-40 jersey hanging inside. The arrangements were for assistant coach Winston Bennett to entertain VanHoose at a UK football game, but according to NCAA regulations J.R. wasn't allowed to ride with Bennett to the game; they made a two-car caravan and met in the parking lot. The game itself was typically mediocre, and as Kentucky aligned itself to punt yet again, an intoxicated fan shouted over to Bennett, "What are you bringing him to a *football* game for? He'll never want to come to Kentucky!"

Subsequently, Pitino had invited both VanHoose and his teammate, Todd Tackett, to be guests of the university at Big Blue Madness along with two other highly rated Kentucky juniors, guard J.P. Blevins of Metcalfe County and power forward Harold Swanagan of University Heights in Hopkinsville. There are very few secrets around the Kentucky basketball program; when VanHoose and Tackett entered Memorial Coliseum through a side door, Wildcat fans clustered around noisily and made a point of hollering out their names, informing the Paintsville pair in no uncertain terms that Kentucky was where they belonged.

Having already met VanHoose and knowing that he and Tackett were coming to Big Blue Madness, Pitino had not made a concerted effort to see the two of them work out during September's open recruiting period. The Paintsville players had met at the school three days a week for pickup games that allowed the recruiters to watch (but not talk to) VanHoose, Tackett, and Josh McKenzie, a six-six blacksmith forward who was also a college prospect, and Pitino had scheduled a visit for one of those days, but something came up. Meanwhile, other head coaches and assistants made longer trips to Paintsville. Indiana, Marquette, and Florida had all been there on the same day, Florida with head coach Billy Donovan and an assistant who was highly appropriate for the occasion, John Pelphrey. (Pelphrey, whose in-laws lived about a block from the VanHooses, was jogging by one day while home for a family visit and had paused momentarily to talk to Bob VanHoose over the back-yard fence when J.R. innocently wandered out the door, causing Pelphrey to mutter a nervous good-bye and take off down the street.) Kevin O'Neill, Tennessee's head coach, had personally represented his interest in VanHoose—he saw the big guy make four out of four three-pointers one afternoon, an unusual occurrence—and Louisville head coach Denny Crum had brought along assistant Scooter McCray. Indiana's Bobby Knight had sent his top assistant and recruiter, Dan Dakich, but the VanHooses were still looking for Dakich's boss.

Having played high school and college basketball in Indiana, Bob VanHoose was a long-time admirer of Bobby Knight. Throughout the fall, he had steadily insisted that the family ties to Indiana, among other things, made J.R.'s field of vision a little broader than that of most Kentucky prep stars. "Most of the recruiters feel that Kentucky players are going to go to Kentucky," he said on the day after his visit to Big Blue Madness, the afternoon before the evening of Paintsville's own version of it. The elder VanHoose was in charge of the Tiger Madness program, and as he spent his Saturday running errands in J.R.'s white Blazer, he found himself doing the thing he had done virtually every day for the past several months—talking about the recruitment of his seventeen-year-old son. "Everybody seems to be recruiting against Kentucky. Indiana and Tennessee are always asking about UK, and they both have dropped subtle hints about UK not having its own arena. A lot of recruiters are afraid that he's the typical Kentucky boy, and if he has a chance to go to Kentucky he won't really consider anywhere else. We've stressed that he's not typical. One, his parents are from Indiana. Two, one of his best friends is John Pelphrey. I know of some players who have gone to Kentucky because they were afraid of the fallout if they didn't. I'm already getting some of that at work: 'So you went to see Bobby Knight. They're gonna run you out of town . . . ' But that sort of thing doesn't have much effect on J.R."

While waiting for Knight to come to Paintsville, the VanHooses had driven the four hours to Bloomington, Indiana, for an informal visit. Knight was impressed when J.R.'s first question was about the library—that was always his first question—and J.R. was impressed when The General started quizzing him on Civil War history and Kentucky's role in it. The two of them had a fine time, but the VanHooses were drawing no conclusions on that basis. They were looking for a clearer sign.

"Bobby Knight has only visited two Kentucky kids since he's been there," Bob VanHoose said, steering the Blazer around the slanting mountain curves and past a buck hanging upside-down from a tree in somebody's front yard. (He had made a point of giving the truck to J.R. for his seventeenth birthday, before it would arouse the suspicions of those who might view it as a recruiting enticement.) "He has never visited a junior in Kentucky. I don't think it's my place to tell him this, but if Coach Knight would visit J.R., I think that would have a big impact. It would be very significant."

On his weekly radio show, *Cats' Pause* editor Oscar Combs had said that VanHoose's recruitment would mark the first Kentucky-Indiana showdown since both schools pursued Delray Brooks, an Indiana native who chose IU but transferred to Providence, where he played for Pitino, and was now one of Pitino's assistants at UK. "Oscar also said Kansas is in the picture and Roy Williams [the Kansas head coach] was down here, which he wasn't," noted the elder VanHoose. "But Kansas does like him.

"Oscar may yet be right about Indiana and Kentucky, but Tennessee is awfully strong in there, too. They started writing to Bill Mike a couple years ago. Tennessee just covers you up in mail. Since September first [a month earlier, when colleges could begin sending mail to recruits],

J.R. has probably received about five or six hundred pieces of mail, and I'd say that a hundred and fifty of them have been from Tennessee. Tennessee will write you one page and send it express mail. Yesterday O'Neill sent two overnight letters, knowing that we'd be going to Big Blue Madness. They both reminded J.R. that he's still number one on their list. Sometimes, they'll send you an overnight and several more letters in the regular mail the same day.

"If it was me, with everything that's happening with J.R., I wouldn't be able to get my head through the door. A light day will be four or five pieces of mail. Yesterday he had twelve at the house and four sent to school. He keeps every letter and files them all. Beth [J.R.'s mother] types the labels for the folders and J.R. staples the envelope to the letter and puts it in the folder as soon as he reads it. The letters are from everywhere. He's already heard from most of the schools in the Big Ten and several in the ACC—Duke, North Carolina, North Carolina State, Wake Forest, Clemson. He gets mail from UCLA, USC, Texas, Texas A&M, Rice, Hawaii. Right now the bulk of it, other than Tennessee, is Indiana, Vandy, Kentucky, Florida, Michigan, and Michigan State. He got four today from Cincinnati—they're starting to kick it in. He's gotten a few from Arkansas, but other than Kentucky, Tennessee, Vandy, and Florida, he's not hearing much from the SEC schools. They all pretty much figure he's locked up for Kentucky."

In truth, VanHoose was much taken with Kentucky but locked up only for Paintsville, which in turn would be attempting in 1996-97 to lock up a second straight state high school championship. One of the national preseason magazines had ranked the Tigers nineteenth in the country. The recognition itself was heady enough, but among the ranked, Paintsville was surely the only public school with graduating classes typically under seventy. As Bob VanHoose pulled up at Tony & Terry's Furniture in Salyersville on his final errand of the day before hustling back home and over to the gym, Tony Burkett couldn't resist a comment on Paintsville's lofty rating. "Number nineteen in the country," he said to VanHoose. "It's like deer season just opened and you've got orange fur."

The people of Paintsville were understandably eager to get their first glimpse of the nationally ranked, orange-furred team that would defend the Kentucky state title, and at five o'clock Saturday night parents began dropping off cheerleaders and student volunteers at the back door of the little high school. Bob VanHoose had already been there for more than two hours, making sure everything was in place: There was a large new photograph of the state champions over the scorer's table and a sign over the stage recognizing the 1996 Class A Cheerleading Champs (unlike basketball, the cheerleading competition was conducted in classes).

An hour later, the Paintsville gym, like Memorial Coliseum the night before, was entirely blue, and the two Kentucky prospects, in the spirit that had evidently rubbed off from Big Blue Madness, were putting on a show in the layup line. VanHoose dunked with his shirt pulled over his head. Tackett tried in vain to stuff the ball after passing it to himself off the back wall; he had better luck jamming left-handed. Meanwhile, the state-champion varsity cheerleaders were hand-springing down the freshly painted floor and the grade-school girls were polishing their round-offs. Then the house stood for the pledge of allegiance, two thousand Eastern Kentucky voices blending in a chorus of patriotism that could come from nowhere else: " . . . one ni-tion, under God, indiveesible . . . "

The scrimmage itself meandered along and was tied with ten seconds to go when VanHoose rebounded on the defensive end, passed off, trailed the play, and slammed home the game-winning dunk. He seemed to be the only one on the court who had even noticed that the score was tied. Apparently it mattered to him; the job done, he raised his arm halfway in an understated celebration and jogged contentedly off the floor.

It was the kind of moment that a college recruiter should have seen—the six-nine superstar competing hard to the last second in an intrasquad scrimmage that nobody else really cared about. Pitino, in particular, should have seen it. Despite all the ranking and hoopla, word was beginning to get out that Pitino was growing skeptical about the chances of a mountain kid—at least this particular mountain kid, the best one in a long time—being able to make a difference at Kentucky.

A few weeks later, in his office at Memorial Coliseum, the coach's voice turned soft when he answered a question about VanHoose's prospects. "I'm not real sure he can play here," Pitino said. "We haven't made up our minds about him as a staff. I'm not sure he has the athletic ability to play the kind of style we play. And I also don't think he's any six-ten [the height he had been listed]. When he was here, he stood next to Winston Bennett, and he looked about the same height to me. I asked Winston how tall he was, and he said six-seven. But I don't know. I haven't seen him play. He apparently has good basketball instincts, and that's important in our system. John Pelphrey was a guy who had great instincts and played very well that way . . . I just don't know yet."

It was a tough call for the Kentucky coach. He didn't doubt that VanHoose was talented and technically sound enough to be a good major-college player, and he was well aware, having coached Farmer and Pelphrey, of what it meant for Kentucky—especially Eastern Kentucky—to see its own in a Wildcat uniform. He understood how important it was, for both the state and the basketball program, to maintain the sacred bond between the school and the mountains, and how much this special player, the best the Cumberlands had produced in a long time, might mean to that venerable relationship. But the mountains had always been there for Kentucky. The cities hadn't. Rupp had given Kentucky the mountains; Pitino would give Kentucky the cities. That would be his breakthrough and his legacy.

For Pitino, Paintsville was charming but Louisville was critical; Louisville was a mission. Since arriving from New York, he had been intently, specifically collecting athletes who would allow him to play creative, tenacious, cutting-edge basketball while, at the same time, putting behind the stigmas that attached themselves to the old Kentucky. J.R. VanHoose was Old Kentucky's kind of player, but Pitino was the New Kentucky, which would be built around all the Derek Andersons he could come up with. The only question, really, was whether the New left any room at all for the Old.

6

Careers

For twenty-four years, Kentucky and Louisville never even played. It was Kentucky's fault. Adolph Rupp had basically two rules about scheduling teams within the state: The game would be held in Lexington and the winner would be the home team. Under those parameters, Louisville wasn't a good fit. But not even the Baron could dictate the NCAA tournament pairings, and thus it happened that in 1959 the Wildcats were ingloriously upset by the U of L in the Mideast Regional.

It was the last time the two Kentucky teams played until the same occasion in 1983. By then, UK's aversion to Louisville was common knowledge and much lamented, so the NCAA intervened on behalf of the basketball public, doing what it could to arrange a postseason showdown. It would have happened in 1982 had the Wildcats not been upset in the first round by something called Middle Tennessee. A year later in Knoxville, Tennessee, in what was referred to as The Dream Game, the Cardinals scored the first fourteen points of overtime to agitate Kentucky again, 80-68.

Louisville, and in particular its coach, Denny Crum, had for years been challenging UK to an annual confrontation. When he failed to get a response from Memorial Coliseum, Crum began lightly slap-punching the Kentucky program, saying that his recruiting class was better than Kentucky's or that he wouldn't trade one of his starters for two of UK's—things like that. This infuriated the Wildcat camp, which saw no advantages in a Louisville game and resented the impudence of what it considered to be a precocious upstart. The Cardinals had competed on Kentucky's

◀ *Rupp Arena: Family members have gone to court over custody of season tickets.*

level throughout the sixties and seventies and won a national championship in 1980, but they weren't Kentucky. UK still owned the state, and that uncompromised support was its nest egg. In the Wildcats' view, playing Louisville would amount to putting up their nest egg as a prize for the winner; there was no need to take that risk. It would also seem strangely disorienting to compete as the bad guy in Freedom Hall, where the Cats were accustomed to hosting a game every year for their Louisville fans.

The original Dream Game, however, brought in a tide that the Kentucky coaches could no longer stem. Joe Hall and his athletic director, Cliff Hagan, were ordered by the UK Athletics Association Board to immediately undertake negotiations for a series with Louisville that would commence the next year. Hall objected formally, reading from a written text which alluded to Kentucky's "unique border-to-border support . . . The one thing that is the most unifying force in this state is Kentucky basketball," the coach said. "I inherited a tradition here in Kentucky basketball of not scheduling in-state schools during the regular season. I think this tradition has served us well."

Nonetheless, the tradition was about to surrender. The following November, UK opened its season with a determined 21-point victory over Louisville in Rupp Arena and the rivalry was on. Two years later, after the Cardinals had won their second national championship of the decade, it was threatened again when new Kentucky coach Eddie Sutton complained that he had a scheduling problem and spoke as if Louisville should accommodate him in whatever way he required. "Kentucky is a bigger program than Louisville," Sutton said unadvisedly. "Even though they won two national titles in the 1980s, Louisville is like the little brother fighting for recognition from the big brother . . . Kentucky is bigger than the Yankees or the Cowboys. No other program is as loved and supported like Kentucky basketball." The scheduling conflict was resolved, but the sniping between the two parties carried on mutually.

The principal agitator in those years was a radio commentator named Jock Sutherland who had attended UK, coached high school basketball in Lexington, been an assistant to C.M. Newton at Alabama, and scouted Kentucky opponents for Joe B. Hall. From his 1979 state-championship Lafayette team, Sutherland had sent point guard Dirk Minniefield to Hall, perhaps anticipating an assistant's job out of the deal. Although he denied having designs on a job, thereafter Sutherland openly brandished his contempt for Hall's bang-it-in coaching style, in particular the restraints it placed upon Minniefield. It startled the UK community when the ex-coach broadcast his pointed criticisms over WVLK in Lexington. The station asked him to exercise a little moderation, and when Sutherland resisted it took him off the air. He ended up at WHAS, the 50,000-watt powerhouse in Louisville, where he was free and in many ways encouraged to bash Kentucky at every opportunity.

Before the December 1991 Dream Game in Rupp Arena, Sutherland was doing his radio schtick on the edge of the floor, where the Kentucky players were warming up, when the UK equipment manager, Bill Keightley, walked out from the locker room to attend to various things. As he came around the grandstand, Mr. Wildcat caught a glimpse of the Cardinal incarnate and stopped in his tracks. Every few moments he would poke his head around the grandstand, but seeing Sutherland still there he would retreat back to safety, refusing to walk onto the same floor that the anti-Cat already occupied.

For the most part, Mr. Wildcat's game face was no respecter of opponents. He had taken his duties seriously since 1962, when he started washing sweat socks for Adolph Rupp, who worked a few paces down the narrow lower corridor of Memorial Coliseum. "Before I was connected with Kentucky basketball, I would be all charged up before a game," said Keightley, who was a mailman then. "My hands would perspire, and if they lost, I couldn't go to sleep that night. I still get nervous, but after being here so long, I know how you're supposed to be on game days. You're totally focused. You really don't want to see anybody. You don't want to be bothered. Coaches are the same way. On game days, don't ask me anything that's not necessary. As Coach Rupp used to say, don't speak unless you can improve upon silence."

Keightley had just about mastered his pregame anxieties when they threw him a curve called Louisville. For days before the Cats played Louisville every year, he was a wreck. "Of course, everybody knows I get excited about the Louisville game," Keightley said early one morning before the showdown in late 1996, holding forth in the equipment room—the cage, they call it—that bears his name. "I like the people at Louisville, but unless you're my age you probably don't understand that for many years Louisville was what would now be known as virtually an NAIA

Mr. Wildcat: Equipment manager Bill Keightley gives Kentucky fans a presence in the UK locker room.

school. They were not at our level. And they can beat you now. They're worthy of that now. But early on it was like some new kid on the block saying, hey, look at me, look how great I am, when they hadn't hardly done a thing. When you've been there and done what we've done, you've got the right maybe to run around and beat on your chest a little. But until that time, just settle down."

Keightley's loathing of Louisville was one of the things that endeared him to so many of the people of Kentucky. In ways just like that, Mr. Wildcat was them. He was them because two generations ago his dad strung an antenna from a big tree to an insulator in their Lawrenceburg home and took the radio battery to a garage to have it charged every couple of weeks so they could listen to the Cats and the Grand Ole Opry. He was them because his cousin was the great Aggie Sale, Coach Rupp's first All-American. He was them because he played basketball under legendary coach Ralph Carlisle (who once ran a player out of the gym for taking a one-handed shot) at Kavanaugh High School, whose founder, the estimable Rhoda Kavanaugh, patrolled the baseline carrying an umbrella which she often used to smack the boys who weren't rebounding or playing defense to her satisfaction. He was them because he got really nervous before ballgames. He was them because he hated Louisville. He was them because he was Mr. Wildcat. On the other hand, Rick Pitino was certainly not them: He was New York; he was designer; he was rich; he talked funny; and unlike Mr. Wildcat, he didn't consider it part of his job description to sit back in his office and talk basketball with the Kentucky folks who wandered in off the street.

Although he, too, placed great emphasis on the Dream Game, Pitino was amused by Keightley's intensity over Louisville. To Pitino, the game was not a holy war; it was a way to make some inroads in the commonwealth's biggest city. In him, the series had found an influential champion. "We want to continue it as long as we're breathing," he had said. "I don't think we'd ever not want to play Louisville. This is something written in stone." Given the historical difficulty Kentucky had experienced in recruiting Louisville players and the urgency to begin doing so, it was incomprehensible to Pitino that a Kentucky coach would choose in any fashion to disassociate himself with the city. The math was too simple to see it any other way: All the while Kentucky was refusing to play Louisville, Louisville players were refusing to play at Kentucky. In the same vein, it may or may not have been a coincidence that Crum's teams were among the first in the country to play up-tempo, urban basketball, engaging the very type of player who was avoiding Kentucky. Either way, there was no doubt that the U of L was benefiting enormously from Kentucky's stodgy old customs.

With Pitino's New Kentucky, of course, stodgy was out and Louisville was very in. Pitino had not yet hit the mother lode of Louisville talent, but he had already made a big strike. He had persuaded Derek Anderson to come over, and that move alone was doing wonders for the season at hand.

As the last days of 1996 were played out, Anderson was moving up a notch in the national consciousness with every passing game. When the season began, he had not been touted as even an all-conference player. Six weeks later, he was being projected as the SEC Player of the Year, a first-team All-American, and a lottery pick in the NBA draft.

Not coincidentally, Anderson's roll coincided with his team's. For the next month after the Wildcats' eye-opener with Indiana, there was not a hotter team in America. Remarkably, in the absence of the four NBA draft choices, Kentucky's numbers were nearly identical to the championship season's; once again, the Cats were leading the country in margin of victory. In the weeks following the Indiana massacre, they blew away Wright State by twenty-eight, Notre Dame by twenty-four, Georgia

167

Tech by twenty-nine, and poor UNC-Asheville by fifty-four before Ohio State played them a comparatively close one—well, sixteen points—in Cleveland.

The Ohio State game was the warmup for undefeated Louisville on the last day of 1996, back in Derek Anderson's hometown. For Anderson, the occasion stirred memories of the days when he literally dreamed of being a Cardinal. On the very night before the New Year's Eve showdown at Freedom Hall, in fact, he dreamed again of racing down the floor in a red uniform next to his neighborhood buddy, DeJuan Wheat, Louisville's star point guard. Wheat had grown up across the street from the projects where Derek's great-grandmother lived, and the two of them— along with Boo Ferguson (Anderson's half-brother), Terence Stewart (his *real* cousin) and Jason Osborne (*not* his real cousin)—played with and against each other in the Dirt Bowl and on the playgrounds and in the high school gyms when they were full and when they were empty. DeJuan and Derek had visited the University of Louisville together, and they had even visited the University of South Carolina together. They wanted to be together. Mostly, they talked about the day when they would both be Cardinals. But one thing led to another, and now here was Anderson, home for the holiday in blue and white.

Even in a Kentucky uniform, Anderson still seemed to play his best basketball back at home. It was probably the showman in him. For his second and last Dream Game, he worked the crowd from the moment the TV cameras began to swivel at courtside, scoring UK's first three baskets on show-stopping dunks. It was enough to make Bill Keightley swoon, though not enough to relieve his Louisville anxiety. The Cardinals were not Indiana; they were a quick, smart team with a veteran backcourt, and they led by one at halftime.

It wasn't until the last ten minutes or so that the Cats did their usual thing, following Anderson and Mercer to an eventual twenty-point victory that left observers wondering if they would ever be seriously threatened again. It was more than Anderson and Mercer: Mohammed and Magloire were performing far in excess of expectations; Scott Padgett, a versatile 6-8 forward from one of Louisville's Catholic high schools (St. Xavier), had regained his eligibility and was making a significant difference; and Pitino's press was leaving befuddled ball-handlers in its wake. Kentucky's effort had become such a team thing that even the fans were producing. Capt. Dan Armstrong figured he won the Louisville game by discovering at just the right moment that his cable carrier had added ESPN2; the Cats went on their run as soon as his popcorn stopped popping and the fizz settled on his Mountain Dew. Dave Byrd, meanwhile, was convinced that the turning point was when he switched from his old UK sweatshirt to the new Ron Mercer denim jersey. Bob Bratcher was just as certain that the game had been clinched when he ripped off his jeans and went with the Big Blue shorts.

It was all working for Kentucky. Magloire and Mohammed, playing at all-conference level as a two-headed center, combined for twenty-five points and thirteen rebounds as the Cats routed Tennessee, advancing their winning streak to twelve. There wasn't a close game among the dozen. By January, Kentucky's domination had become so routine and so complete that a small part of the Rupp Arena crowd actually booed during the second half of the Mississippi State game, when the visitors began to solve the press with floor-length passes. The Wildcats' lead was ten at the time. Most in attendance were stunned at the scattered but unmistakable rebuke. For their part, the Kentucky players were taken aback and simultaneously stimulated, charging off on a 22-1 run that resulted in a 29-point victory. A few days later, as most of the Kentucky community continued to disavow the rude few who were apparently impossible to please, athletic director C.M. Newton wondered out loud whether the booers might have been motivated by their investments in the game. An accessory to this theory was the fact that the point spread was thirty.

Two games later, Kentucky's collective attention was refocused when Mississippi unexpectedly stopped the winning streak at fourteen. Ole Miss was a worthy and highly motivated opponent, seizing a chance to earn a Top Twenty-Five ranking for the first time in school history, but few doubted that the four-point outcome was largely attributable to the pulled back muscle that limited Anderson to ten minutes and no points. Pitino, however, was not interested in using his star's injury as an excuse—at least not publicly—and he resented the fact that a Kentucky defeat seemed to require one. When the second loss of the season provoked what he perceived to be an alarmist line of questioning—What's wrong with Kentucky?—Pitino lashed back irritably. "That is such bullshit," he said, addressing a TV reporter specifically and the Kentucky mentality in general. "Why can't you give Ole Miss credit? They played a great game.

What, all of a sudden are we the Chicago Bulls, that we can't lose a game? I think sometimes we're a little arrogant."

By any analysis, the Mississippi loss revealed Anderson's value to the Kentucky cause. It was around that time that the likable senior, whose court sense and high spirit were as vital to the Cats' game as his deadly quickness, was selected by the *Chicago Tribune* as the top player in the country for the first half of the season. He verified the choice in Kentucky's next outing, lighting up Georgia for twenty-four points in a surprisingly easy road win that had the reporters at his locker again, charmed by his waggish smile and easygoing confidence.

The only impediment in Anderson's game was the foul trouble that his competitive exuberance often got him into. Against Auburn on January 18, however, it was not foul trouble that bounced him in and out of the lineup. Anderson slipped turning upcourt in the second half and appeared to bruise his right knee when it hit the floor. After leaving the game for a spell, he came back and played three more minutes before finally checking out with twelve points and the victory well in hand.

Despite the down time, the Kentucky star was still leading the SEC in scoring, and on Monday he was named conference Player of the Week. That morning, though, he went to the gym to work out and was surprised that he was unable to spring off his right leg. The UK trainer, Fast Eddie Jamiel, told him to brace for the possibility that his anterior cruciate ligament was torn.

Jamiel took Anderson to the UK Sports Medicine Clinic for an X-ray, and a short while later appeared at Wildcat Lodge with the photo and the team physician, Dr. David Caborn. They found the player in his room and showed him the tear.

Anderson couldn't believe what he saw. "It took me about an hour to get over it," he said. "I don't think I could have gotten over it like that if I hadn't accepted the Christ. I'd have been asking myself, 'Why me? Why now, when I'm having such a good season?' But I knew I couldn't think that way. I thought, 'Maybe this is what He wants. Maybe He doesn't want me to go to the league. Maybe He wants me to be a schoolteacher.'"

○ ○ ○

By Monday afternoon, all of Kentucky had heard that Anderson's collegiate career was over. In Williamstown, Jason Ryan considered checking out of work a little early to go home and grieve. In Danville, the Old Goats at the Coffee Club expressed their sympathies on behalf of a fine young man. And on Cat Chat, Jason Puckett, who had walked the same halls as Anderson back at Doss High School in Louisville, broke the news to his far-flung friends.

I can't believe what I just heard. Pitino announced that Derek Anderson is out for the year with a torn ACL. Oh Lord . . .

The worst possible thing that could have happened did. This is an incomprehensible blow to the team and could all but dash any title hopes we have. As Coach Rupp would say, "We are in big trouble NOW."

I'm still in total shock.

The injury supplied another reminder that a UK basketball player—especially a preeminent and personable one like Derek Anderson—occupies an uncommon place in the worlds of sports and Kentucky. He is substantially more than an athlete admired for his skill and contribution to the team; not unlike a family member, he is a special figure to whom prominent emotions are attached. For days after Anderson went down, Kentucky fans from around the country poured out their feelings, sympathies, and revised forecasts for the rest of the season.

David Morgan e-mailed his Kentucky colleagues from Alabama:

The news about Anderson hit me like a ton of bricks. I'm about as down as one person could be. I dared think that we could repeat. It would have been possible with Anderson, but now it is unlikely. We have been taken down a notch.

Frank Dudley Berry chimed in from California:

I firmly resolve
(1) to keep in mind always that DA has been damaged infinitely

more than anyone else by this disaster;

(2) not to mourn too much for the titanic Kansas-Kentucky struggle that was shaping up;

(3) not to give up hope, but at the same time to lower expectations; and finally,

(4) in case the bitter cup must be drunk to the very last dregs, i.e., Kentucky is ousted by some hated rival (UNC, Duke, Louisville, or Indiana), not to engage in any debate on the Internet about the effect of this.

And from North Carolina, Rick Suffridge summarized his sentiments and those of many:

This is really tragic for Derek, who was finally having his moment to shine. Derek's enthusiasm, hustle, talent, and love of the game make him a joy to watch—one of my all-time favorite UK players. I'll be pulling for you Derek!

As for the team, this is simply devastating. We can talk about other players stepping up, but there is nobody else who can match DA's offensive explosiveness or his defensive energy. While at this point I have a hard time seeing UK getting past the Sweet 16, I have faith that if anyone can pull this team through, it is Pitino. It is time for Pitino to do some coaching!

Unlike the Big Blue public, Pitino wasn't afforded the luxury of saying what he really felt after Anderson's injury. It was important that his reaction—especially in front of the team—be couched in the manner that he thought would have the most salutary effect on the Kentucky players. To the opportunistic coach, there was a bright side: The worst moment of the year was the best possible time to request more effort. Knowing that they couldn't refuse him, Pitino told his men that each of them had to give the team another twenty percent in addition to what he was already giving. "Step up" was the operative phrase. The Cats were not only without their best man; they were left with just nine active scholarship players. Jeff Sheppard, the talented senior redshirt, would not be available unless a hard decision were made to activate him, and forward Oliver Simmons had left the team. Two of the remaining nine, Cameron Mills and Anthony Epps, had come to the Kentucky program

The bad news: "I can't believe what I just heard. Oh Lord..."

as walk-ons. Some basketball critics might have been cynical when Pitino spoke early in the season about the relative scarcity of talent available to him, but now the shortage was genuine. As a result, every one of the nine had to step up. Allen Edwards had to step up on the wing. Wayne Turner had to step up as an offensive player. Scott Padgett had to step up as a defensive player. Mohammed and Magloire had to play like the veterans they weren't. Jared Prickett had to assume some leadership. Epps had to show the others how to win. Even Cameron Mills, whose previous minutes had been token, would have to step up. And, of course, Ron Mercer. Mercer had to leap up, which was what he was essentially known for.

It was a rough few days for Pitino, who had brought his team so far so fast, all the while relying so heavily on the senior who did more things well, and with more enthusiasm and charisma, than any player he had ever sent out to the floor. On Tuesday, the day before Kentucky was scheduled to play Vanderbilt in Cincinnati, the coach went forward grudgingly with his regularly scheduled press conference at Memorial Coliseum. There was none of the usual bantering, the good-humored insult. When somebody inevitably asked him what he thought of the team's chances without Anderson, Pitino turned uncharacteristically surly. "What do you think our chances would be?" he snapped. "I think it's obvious, isn't it? . . . I guess we'll just pack in the season right now and quit." He also stated

unequivocally that Sheppard would not be taken off the redshirt list "because it'd be terrible for Jeff Sheppard."

That night, to hype the game in Cincinnati and stay in touch with
the rabid fans on the southern bank of the Ohio River, the exhausted
coach arrived with a small entourage and four state troopers at Florence
Mall in Northern Kentucky, where more than two thousand blue-cov-
ered friendlies squeezed in to watch him air his weekly radio show. Many
of them had been there since the early afternoon. Front and center, having pulled chairs up to the makeshift stage at 12:30, were Howard and
Margie Buckley, an amiable Kentucky couple who fed scrambled eggs to
the raccoons in their backyard in Elsmere. The Buckleys had missed only
a handful of Kentucky games on radio or television since the end of
World War II. They were unable to get tickets to the games—their only
hope was a new arena—and had to be content instead with the season
tickets to Cincinnati Bengals football games that Howard won back in
1967 for successfully naming the team in a public contest. Howard still
carried a clip about the contest, but there was another sporting memory
from the late sixties that the Buckleys held more dearly. That was Dan
Issel's time at UK. For more than twenty-five years, they had been waiting to meet Issel so they could give him the scrapbook they had compiled
on his UK career.

At the mall, the Buckleys found themselves happily surrounded by
Kentucky soul mates. Directly behind them were Dolly Barnes and her
married daughter, Michelle Leach, whose mother-in-law was a cousin of
Joe B. Hall, and next to the Buckleys was Marsha Jones, whose baby
daughter was dressed the way she had come home from the hospital, in
a Kentucky cheerleader's outfit. (She was not the only baby in the house
wearing a cheerleader sweater, another being an infant girl whose mother
was convinced that she would marry one of Pitino's sons.) As the afternoon passed and the mall turned increasingly blue, Jones talked about
how she and her husband had turned their house into a virtual Kentucky
museum; it was almost done except that they still needed to tear up the
family room floor and remake it like Rupp Arena's. The Joneses' Kentucky collection included autographed shoes, knives engraved with important dates and scores, and game tapes going back to the day they
bought their VCR.

And on the other side of Marsha Jones, having punched out early to arrive at Florence in time to secure the front-row seat that he couldn't do without, was Jason Ryan. Ryan knew this particular mall very well, having sat down on the floor of its Foot Action store when the Cats lost an NCAA tournament game to Marquette in 1994. As he wiled away the hours waiting for the show to begin, he clutched a basketball he had brought for Pitino to sign and a smaller ball belonging to a friend who said he would trade Ryan two tickets for the coach's autograph on it.

The fans were not without diversions until Pitino arrived. His warmup act was a sports talk show put on by WLW in Cincinnati, hosted for the night by a high-volume Kentucky admirer named Bill Cunningham. A half-serious sensationalist who made his living through hyperbole, Cunningham was fond of referring to Pitino with deific terms, jangling on in evangelistic language about the coming of the Kentucky coach being prophesied in the Book of Revelation. After UK's national championship the year before, the host and entrepreneur had arranged for the trophy to be escorted like the Holy Grail to Cincinnati, after which it naturally put in an appearance at his Northern Kentucky restaurant. Cunningham placed a life-sized cutout of Pitino next to the trophy and charged customers ten dollars to stand by the two items and have their picture taken. More than seven hundred people lined up.

"Who here," he bellowed to the Florence Mall crowd, "would give up a knee right now to Derek Anderson?" Two thousand hands went up.

Respectful silence came over the mall at seven o'clock, when Pitino seated himself across from radiant faces. Before speaking, he looked up and saw a homemade sign hanging from the railing of the second level: *Good Luck Derek. We Love You.*

"This is one of the most disappointing days of my life," the Kentucky coach said softly. "Seeing Derek, probably two months away from being a lottery pick [in the NBA draft] . . . to see this young man's dream fall apart, at least for the present . . . it's difficult to swallow."

Pitino tried to be positive. He said that, unlike the occasion of Anderson's back injury before the Ole Miss game, there was time now to adjust the team for the end of the season. He said that there were still good athletes on the roster, and he had been to the Final Four (Providence) with less talent. But it was a cheerless moment. When he paused, it was so quiet in the mall you could hear a national ranking drop.

○○○

The public ad-
dress announcer some-
how got confused before
the Vanderbilt game and
called out six Kentucky
starters. Pitino had an
explanation: "Without
Derek," he said later,
"we need all the help we
can get."

Actually, Pitino
needed help, all right,
but to get it he turned
to an old friend: the
three-point shot. As an
overachieving young
coach at Providence,
Pitino had brought
three-pointers into
vogue by instructing his

Happier days: Smiles returned to the faces of Anthony Epps and Ron Mercer
when the Wildcats found a way to win without Anderson.

smallish, slowish club—principally Delray Brooks, his assistant at Kentucky, and Billy Donovan, his former assistant who had become head
coach at Florida—to heave them up in leading-edge numbers. At Kentucky, his first team had come honestly by the nickname of "Pitino's
Bombinos." He remained a champion of the long shot, but as his talent
base expanded over the years—as he began to recruit athletes with more
mobility and less touch—Pitino, still the trend-setter, had shifted his
emphasis to defending the three-point shot. So when the Wildcats stepped
back and fired thirty-two threes against Vanderbilt, it was a sign that
their accommodating coach was no longer playing to an advantage in
talent but resorting again to tactics. The reality of his new game plan was
underscored when he put Cameron Mills onto the floor in the first half.
Mills, the former walk-on whose scholarship was not won with speed or
defense, had banged his head so hard it knocked him out a few practices

earlier and was not expected to be ready for Vanderbilt. But it was an anxious game and Pitino wanted another shooter in it. His choice was a walk-on with a concussion averaging 1.7 points a game. Mills gave him oh-for-three.

The coach had better luck with his other tactic, which was getting his guys to play harder. When Mercer belly-slid into the Kentucky bench going after a loose ball, Pitino was so tickled that he rushed over to his marquee sophomore and gave him five fast spanks on the end facing up. ("I think that's the first time since he's been here that he's dived after the ball," Anthony Epps observed afterwards. "That can really get a team going, when somebody like Ron Mercer takes off his tuxedo and starts diving for the ball.") Hustling got Kentucky a 17-point lead and a 58-46 victory that Epps celebrated at the buzzer by flinging the ball to the ceiling of Riverfront Coliseum.

"It's been a great day," remarked Pitino as he pulled up a chair for the post-game press conference, his eyes bright again with the twinkle that had been missing the night before at Florence Mall. "First, Derek had highly successful surgery. And we played defense as if we had not eaten in seven days. This game pleases me more than any we've had this season. That's the kind of effort it's going to take for us to win after losing maybe the best player in the country. Statistically, this is like the Magic losing Penny Hardaway.

"But we're still Kentucky. It's not like we're David and Vanderbilt is Goliath. We still have players on scholarship."

It was a fine line Pitino was walking—assuring his players that they were still Kentucky while persuading them that they could no longer expect to win simply because of it. Whatever comments he made to the press were made with that end in mind. At the age of forty-four, Pitino had become a master of the motivational sound bite, taking liberal advantage of the fact that, as the Kentucky coach, whatever he said for the record would resonate throughout the state. When he opened his mouth, he was like E.F. Hutton in a really big room. For Pitino, the press conference was a medium, a commercial, and a coaching opportunity all at once. His media strategy, in general, was to look the questioner in the eye, to be as selectively informative as possible, and to be mindful that every word he uttered could potentially reach the ears of 1) his players, 2) recruits, and 3) any number of other people who could be important to him down the line. The artistry was in his ability to walk this tightrope in Italian shoes.

Pitino's best piece of persuasive craftsmanship may have come in the previous year, when he had to sell a team of high draft choices on the concept that they should donate their stardom to the common cause. Seldom, if ever, had a college basketball team spent so much talent (Mercer *didn't start*) so magnanimously. For all their individual acclaim, the best thing about the '96 national champions might have been their *passing*. The mental conditioning for '96-'97 started out as an easier sell, what with the pro guys long gone, but when Anderson was lost, the man in the never-brown suit had an entirely different bill of goods to peddle. It wasn't about sacrificing scoring averages; Mercer was the only remaining player who had much of one. Somehow, he had to get his men to buy into the business of the extra twenty percent . . . and this from a team whose endless pressing already demanded that the players be in fifteen-round shape. As fortune would have it, Pitino was most of the way through the motivational book he was writing: *Success Is A Choice: Ten Steps to Overachieving in Business & Life.* For this challenge, he couldn't afford to let any of the steps go untested.

Whatever the coach was doing in the locker room, it worked on Cameron Mills. The inauspicious Lexington native, whose previous efforts had scarcely been sufficient to provide a scouting report, made his first tangible contribution as a Kentucky player in the following game, scoring twelve points in a ten-point triumph at Arkansas. The key figure, though—the star of Kentucky's latest victory and many to come—was widely acknowledged to be Rick Pitino, whose part in keeping the Cats on course prompted gratuitous praise from a colleague, Georgia Tech's Bobby Cremins, who described him as "The Man" among current college coaches. Cremins's public remark was gratuitously refuted by CBS commentator Billy Packer, an elite figure on the Kentucky fans' enemies list (whose ranks were led by writer-commentator John Feinstein and included, among others, analyst Digger Phelps, Jock Sutherland, Denny Crum, and Bobby Knight), who shot back, "On what basis would you make that comment? I think he is certainly one of the outstanding coaches in any era, but to say that he is The Man would be, I think, an overstatement." Packer's point had to do with the fact that Dean Smith was at that moment bearing down on Adolph Rupp's record for lifetime victories. There was merit to that opinion, but Pitino was putting together a body of work that was hard to match in the short term, at least, first building a national champion from the wreckage of probation, continuing to win after most of the championship starters had departed, and still continuing to win after the heart and soul of the remaining team was sent to the sidelines at midseason.

The Cats proceeded to thrash Florida next and by the time they returned to Lexington to play Georgia, expectations had returned to a more accustomed level. It was a Saturday game, starting at one o'clock, and by ten, shopper-fans in endless ensembles of blue and white were crowding the Kentucky Korner store in the mall of the Lexington Center, which houses Rupp Arena. The souvenir shop offered sixty-five different styles of Kentucky hats and as many jackets. "I've thought about starting a coat check service," cracked the manager. "Can you imagine if somebody lost their ticket, and they walked up and said, 'I've got the Kentucky jacket . . . ? ' "

On the concourse, the gentlemen of the Committee of 101 were stacking programs while ticket scalpers skulked about with their treasures. Lower level seats, originally marked at eighteen dollars, were trading for seventy-five, but a perch in the upper level could be had for considerably less. Both levels were filled by the time Derek Anderson, two weeks removed from his ACL tear, trotted onto the floor to hug his teammates and slap hands as they warmed up. Rumors had gotten around that his recovery was going so well he would be playing again before the end of the season, but there was no precedent for such a thing and no rationale for believing it. Pitino would only go so far as to say that maybe, sometime down the line, Anderson could shoot a technical free throw when the moment was right.

For a few minutes of the Georgia game, it looked as though Pitino might be tempted to accelerate his shooting guard's rehabilitation by quite a bit. As the visitors squared up for open shots, a couple of irrepressible Kentucky women in section 230, row Z, were reduced to "Oh oh ohs" and "Ooh ooh oohs," building up to an "Oh foo" when the Bulldogs beat the press and climaxing in an "Oh shit" when their lead reached ten. It was very early, but patience had been thrown to the wind the first time Jared Prickett tossed a ball out of bounds. "Well, I swear . . . " said one of the nice ladies. "Never in my life . . . " countered the other.

Georgia was coached by a former Pitino assistant, Tubby Smith, who had worked wonders at Tulsa and was doing the same in the Southeastern Conference over the two years he had been in Athens. The Bulldogs were positioning themselves for an NCAA tournament seed, but despite their early advantage they quite apparently were not yet in Kentucky's class. By halftime, the Cats had already reversed the score and established a 16-point lead. The highlight of the afternoon, however, was halftime itself, when the cheerleaders made themselves into K-E-N-T-U-C-K and Derek Anderson strolled out to be the "Y." The ladies in row Z weren't the only ones with tissues in their eyes.

The game was won easily, and by the second half the issue had become whether this would be the right moment for Anderson to shoot a free throw and whether, thinking wishfully, the NCAA tournament would be the right moment for him to play again. Those were fanciful notions, however. For the time being, the more reasonable dialogue had to do with the ripple effects of Anderson's injury—specifically, whether it would persuade Ron Mercer to turn pro at the end of the season. Pitino's position was that the stellar Tennessean was better suited to another year or two of the college game but readiness was in the eye of the NBA: If he were drafted high enough, the time would be right. Since he had arrived at UK, Mercer, a mature young man who looked deep into people's eyes and spoke softly, had given every impression that he would finish college. That was certainly his mother's preference, and he also appreciated the educational opportunity before him, but Anderson's cruel fate had stirred the debate in his mind, even as it tumbled about in the heads of countless Kentucky fans.

And while the folks were at it, Mercer wasn't the only one about whom the possibility of a premature departure was much discussed. A couple days after the Georgia game, the latest Pitino rumor was introduced to Cat Chat by a California Kentuckian named Terry Branham:

This is not intended to start rumors about Pitino leaving UK. I was just curious what anybody else closely associated with the team might have heard. I heard this rumor from an NBA player. That last year Pitino talked with Boston, but did not want to leave because they did not have the talent to win immediately. He felt UK had a chance to repeat.

He has an arrangement with Boston which is not definite but is likely if certain scenarios can be met. The first was Boston drafting UK's Walker. If the other things were to happen, he would then negotiate with the Celtics to be their coach.

Although Pitino had never categorically quashed the NBA rumors—particularly the annual buzz concerning the Celtics—too many of them had already vaporized to put any credibility in another. The fact was, the coach was feeling good once more about the task at hand. He stated after the Georgia game that, despite his uneasiness after the Clemson loss and again after Anderson's injury, he now thought that the Wildcats, reconfigured and pleasing him increasingly, had the capability to win another championship for Kentucky.

"The national championship?" he was asked.

"Well," he replied, "we're not going to get any parades for winning the SEC."

○ ○ ○

On the early February morning of Kentucky's important game with South Carolina, ESPN reported that Pitino had flown to Boston the night before to talk with the Celtics.

Ron Mercer: Stepping up, and up.

Not much of a fuss was made. The people back home in Kentucky, having become jaded concerning Pitino rumors but titillated over the possibility of a conference race, concerned themselves mainly with the duel for first place in the SEC.

South Carolina had a perfect conference record, but in the SEC that never counted for much until you played Kentucky. The game was billed as the biggest in Columbia since the Gamecocks were ranked number one in 1970, and Kentucky came into it short-handed, having temporarily lost Prickett to an ankle injury. In the end, however, Prickett's absence wasn't the problem as much as South Carolina's penetrating guards. The Gamecocks had three of them, and the Cats didn't have the speed or depth to keep up. The result was a five-point overtime loss that suggested a reordering of both the SEC and the mindset of Kentucky folks. The latter's expectations had been adjusted when Anderson went down, but the reality of defeat was something different to deal with.

Anderson's presence would have no doubt made an enormous difference in a game like that one—his quickness alone would have mitigated much of the guard disparity—but it wasn't only his production that Kentucky missed. It was also what he did for Ron Mercer. In his second season at Kentucky, Mercer's star was not yet equipped with a wagon hitch. His talent was indisputably of the first order, but he had been content to let it flow from Anderson's source of energy and tempo. Uneasy with the attention he was receiving from both the public and the defense, Mercer hadn't had a breakout game since his older teammate had gone down. He scored eighteen points against South Carolina, but on that tense evening the Cats needed a few more than eighteen. The tough defeat convinced Pitino that it was time for his remaining superstar to start playing like one.

Most of the scuttlebutt had Mercer still projected anywhere from the second to the fifth pick in the next NBA draft if he declared himself eligible for it—a proposition whose likelihood was endlessly debated around the state of Kentucky—but his unspectacular post-Anderson games made him vulnerable to all manner of skepticism, including his coach's. Never one to pass up a good motivational opportunity, Pitino addressed that topic before the Cats' nationally televised game with Villanova the following Sunday. Specifically, he told Mercer that Villanova's highly touted 6-9 freshman, Tim Thomas, was overtaking him in the opinion of the pro scouts.

His message to the Wildcats as a whole was similarly challenging. Villanova, the Big East Conference favorite, had been one of the top-rated teams in the country at the beginning of the season and the February 9 matchup loomed as perhaps the most formidable on Kentucky's regular-season schedule. 'Nova's front line was the very personification of formidable, averaging 6-10, 240, and featuring a couple of bearish seniors alongside Thomas. To dramatize the size and strength his guys would be up against, Pitino and his assistants put together a creatively edited highlight tape of the Big Easterners rebounding, making them look like Chamberlain, Russell, and Rodman. Rebounding was not Kentucky's strong suit, but Pitino felt that it had to be against Villanova.

And when Sunday arrived, somehow it was. As Kentucky fans watched nervously from around the state and country (in North Carolina, the four-year-old son of Cat Chatter Rick Suffridge had a birthday party to go to, so Suffridge dropped him off and watched the game from the electronics department of the nearby K-Mart), the Big Blue put on the sort of exhibition that hadn't seemed possible three weeks earlier. Villanova could make no sense of the Kentucky press, and when the visitors hurried up a shot, the Cats licked up rebound after rebound. Mercer seemed particularly inspired, scoring twenty-three points to Thomas's nine and outrebounding the bigger freshman eleven to one. The rout was so overwhelming that Cameron Mills scored in double figures and the freshman walk-on, Steve Masiello, made the first three-pointer of his career. The halftime margin was twenty; victory came by thirty-seven. Even more impressively, Kentucky, goaded into a rebounding frenzy by its scheming coach, dominated its meatier opponent on the backboards by an unbelievable 42-17. Pitino had also asked of his men that they shut out Villanova from the three-point line; they did.

The game was such a mismatch that CBS cut away from it in many markets around the country, eschewing the second half in favor of a much closer contest between top-ranked Kansas and Iowa State. This provoked a predictable outcry from out-of-pocket Kentucky fans, who inundated the switchboards in Kentucky-border towns like Nashville; Cincinnati; Huntington, West Virginia (where the station manager said there might have been some death threats in his e-mail); Evansville, Indiana; and Cape Girardeau, Missouri. Darrell Bailey of Ohio was so determined to straighten out the network that he supplied Cat Chat subscribers with a comprehensive list of all the pressure points: phone numbers, mailing addresses, and e-mail addresses for sponsors—including Budweiser, Goodyear, and Chevrolet—and other parties that might have been interested in a viewer rebellion. Over the next few days, spokesmen from CBS affiliates all around the Ohio Valley vowed that they would never, ever switch off from a UK broadcast again.

For the Kentucky fans, CBS's repentance was a consolation that couldn't replace the afternoon of hardcourt splendor that had been irretrievably snatched from their lives. For all their victories over all the years—the most in college basketball—it wasn't often that the Wildcats actually outdid themselves. On the basis of what occurred at Rupp Arena on February 9, it was safe to say that Pitino was getting the extra twenty percent he had asked for.

"Coach is a good motivator," Mercer said afterwards. "He says things that you don't realize until after the game he said just to motivate you. He was saying to me, 'You know, this Tim Thomas is definitely number two in the draft right now.' A person like me listens to that kind of thing. It's all a matter of how we listen. That's what we're all doing right now. Our team is paying attention to Coach."

The Villanova game put Pitino in a light mood. As he strode in to meet the press, a swarm of electronic newsmen simultaneously raised their microphones and dropped to their knees so the view of other reporters behind them wouldn't be blocked. "We kneel before you, O Mighty One," joked a radio guy.

"This is what I've been waiting for," replied Pitino, who then went on to praise Mercer's effort as his best at Kentucky and to tease about making medical history by bringing Anderson back for the end of the season.

"Derek tells me he's gonna play," he said. "When Cameron Mills was out there shooting the ball, Derek leaned over to me and said, 'Tell Cameron to enjoy his minutes. I'm coming back.' To tell the truth, I want him to think he can come back so he can work himself into playing condition quickly enough to be a first-round draft pick. Really, though, I think any talk of Derek coming back is foolish and idle chatter. I think he's done everything he could for the University of Kentucky. Now it's time for us to help him."

After the Cats bid farewell to retiring LSU coach Dale Brown by presenting him with a little ceremony and a 36-point defeat, Anderson was in the layup line for the mid-February Florida game at Rupp Arena. It was one of those special Kentucky occasions, the jerseys of three more players (Kyle Macy, Johnny Cox, and Frenchy DeMoisey) being retired along with something or other from Mr. Wildcat, who was most definitely not retiring as equipment manager. Keightley's honor was a surprise to him, and the old Marine nearly lost it.

In the ensuing forty minutes, however, Kentucky was never in that kind of danger. Florida was beaten within a few, the Wildcats scooting to a 30-8 lead on their way to a 29-point victory. As the score mounted, Pitino was half-hoping that Billy Donovan, his former player and coaching protégé, would offer up a technical foul to get Anderson into the game; anything to keep the guys interested. Anticipating an easy afternoon and forever fearing a letup, Pitino had promised a series of penalties for players who didn't meet his standards defensively against the Gators. "I haven't figured out yet what the penalties will be," he said, "Just running. Pain. Something demented."

Meanwhile, Anderson wasn't much interested in becoming a motivational tool or in making token appearances for the crowd's sake. He was getting serious about playing some real minutes. Although there was no scientific data to suggest that he would be ready to play anytime before summer, there were indications that he might anyway. As he was about to leave the locker room after the Florida game, Joanne Pitino sidled up, gave him a hug, and said, "I was hoping it would be today. March, right?"

Inevitably, the whispers began to make their way around the state. On February 17, a day short of a month after Anderson's injury, Jim Parks, a UK employee, filed an intriguing Cat Chat report from the campus.

I am sure it has been discussed but here goes my information for everyone. First, DA was going one on one with Mercer in practice on Friday. He even dunked the ball a couple times, until Pitino stopped it. Pitino said, "I don't want any of that" over the microphone he uses. DA smiled that grin we all know. He looked really sharp doing layups. He was playing horse with Mercer and he hit two threes just clowning around. Mercer missed both shots. Someone at practice (don't know who he was, but he is connected with the team in some way) said DA wouldn't be able to stop or cut with 2 G's of force on that knee. I don't know what 2 G's is, but he looked damn sharp for a Jan 18th injury.

Pitino, whose public statements concerning Anderson seemed to reflect mood swings, stopped making jokes about his star's return when he saw that people were taking the possibility to heart. "Derek is the most optimistic young man I've ever come across," he said during his regularly scheduled press conference the day before the Wildcats played at Alabama. "The other day I asked him what percentage short is his knee from the other one, and he said ten to fifteen percent. I asked the doctor the same question and he said forty percent. I don't think it's in Derek's best interest to come back. I think it's in his best interest to strengthen his knee for the NBA draft. I've been hearing NBA people say that if he's available late in the first round they'll still take him. But they don't think he'll be available late in the first."

If Anderson did become a first-round draft choice, it was beginning to look pretty certain that he wouldn't be the only one from UK. Mercer's breakout game against Villanova had boded splendidly for the ongoing season but not so well for Kentucky's next. "Since the Villanova game I've noticed a significant change in Ron Mercer," Pitino told the Wildcat media. "You're covering him for the last time, so enjoy it. That is, if he continues to play the way he has lately."

Mercer's ability to provide highlight tape had never been doubted—his angular dunks were regularly featured on ESPN's Sportscenter show—but for the first time in his two-year collegiate career he was beginning to show some consistency. The bottom line was that he had become the main man on the third-ranked team in the country. The Alabama game would mark the third time in four outings that Mercer scored twenty-three points, which were more than enough for a double-digit victory.

At Vanderbilt four days later, the Wildcats were joined on the bench by actress Ashley Judd of the Naomi-Wynona country-music Judds, a UK graduate whose knowledge of basketball, like her rooting interest, was vintage Kentucky. Judd, who once refused an offer of a sweatshirt on a chilly movie set because it said North Carolina on it, took the opportunity to ask Pitino if he was still recruiting Los Angeles point guard Baron Davis; if so, she would make sure to check him out when she was back on the coast. Meanwhile, to make good use of her time as long as she was in God's country, she hoped to catch VanHoose and Metcalfe County's J.P. Blevins.

Kentucky's trips to Nashville had invariably involved subplots of one sort or another. Vanderbilt's Memorial Gymnasium was a notoriously difficult place for the Wildcats to play in, and aside from the state universities such as Eastern or Western Kentucky, Vandy had historically been the most popular major-college destination for Kentucky-raised players who didn't have or care to accept the opportunity to represent the Big Blue. Seldom had the pipeline flowed the other way, but Ron Mercer—the latest subplot in the long rivalry—went a long way toward balancing the trade deficit.

For Mercer, the Vandy game was a visit home to play against the school at which he originally intended to enroll. With his pride on the line again, and in serious jeopardy as the Commodores sprinted out to a 22-point lead, the quiet forward carried the Cats with seventeen of his twenty-three points in the second half. The wrenching three-point defeat was especially tough on the home folks, who had once counted Mercer among their own, but it would be the last time they would have to suffer that way: While the Cats were in Nashville, Pitino made a point of calling on Ron's mother, Birdie Mercer, to hash out the pros and cons of her son turning professional after the season. From the moment his immense talent had become apparent as a high schooler, Mrs. Mercer had steadfastly maintained that Ron would stay in school until he earned his college degree. The difference now was the terrible injury to his soul mate; if it could happen to Derek, it could happen to him.

The decision was made at that meeting, but Pitino wanted no distractions for the Cats' next game at Tennessee. So nothing was said until the ten-point victory was in hand—Padgett scored twenty-four and Mercer was booed every time he touched the ball by yet another home-state crowd that had once thought he was theirs—advancing Kentucky's overall record to 28-2 and setting up another conference showdown with South Carolina. The next day, to get it out of the way so that he wouldn't have to answer the same questions throughout the SEC and NCAA tournaments, Mercer put on a white suit, draped a gold medallion around his neck, and ended the speculation by announcing that he was indeed submitting his name for the NBA draft at the end of the season.

As a professional spin doctor, Pitino was a heck of a basketball coach. Somehow, he managed to make the loss of his All-American sound like a long-term gain for Kentucky. He recognized that as more and more underclassmen left their studies behind for the crazy money the NBA was offering them, college recruiting had taken on a paradox: In order to attract the best players, you had to have a history of losing them. "It's a tremendous thing," he said of Mercer's jump. "ESPN had [a graphic listing] Mashburn, Walker, Mercer. I mean, that's awfully impressive. They [the top prospects] see they [Kentucky players] are ready and being drafted in the top five or six players. To me, that's one of the greatest recruiting tools you can have. Any time Ron Mercer steps onto the court in the NBA, they will announce him from the University of Kentucky."

It was all part of the New Kentucky he was building. Pitino *wanted* NBA players in the Kentucky program; he had to have them. If that meant saying some premature good-byes along the way—if, in fact, those good-byes actually worked better than a home visit—well, he was a good-bye kind of guy.

7

Commitments

Pitino showed up at Paintsville's practice on December 4, his first
day back home after a week and a half in Alaska and Chicago. He called
Bill Mike Runyon late in the morning to tell the Paintsville coach that he
would be there in the afternoon to check out VanHoose and, while he
was at it, Todd Tackett, and he arrived with Bill Keightley around 3:30,
just after the players finished stretching. Runyon locked the door to the
gym, but when practice ended at 5:10 there were three hundred people
hanging around outside. With Runyon's help, the Kentucky savior made
an uneventful getaway, mentioning as he left that he was impressed with
the way the Paintsville prospects passed the ball.

Paintsville, meanwhile, was impressed that the coach made the trip.
The little mountain town had seen him only once before, on the occasion
of Paintsville Country Club's K-Day outing for Kentucky lettermen and
boosters, an annual golf extravaganza at which the local Big Blue backers
had been accustomed to seeing Joe B. Hall frequently and Adolph Rupp
practically every year. Rupp was partial not only to mountain guards, for
which he backed up the truck, but to the crab claws, burgoo, and barbecue sandwiches that were served alongside the various tees. The Baron
was a K-Day institution, placing a chair "up the long holler"—the front
nine—in close proximity to the crab claws. When everybody there had
heard his stories, he would pick up the chair and move over to the chicken
livers. His successor, Joe Hall, was a Kentucky country boy who also
chose not to bring his clubs on K-Day, opting instead for his fishing rod
and throwing a line into the creek on the back nine, under the swinging

◀ *J.R. VanHoose: The best high school player in Kentucky*

bridge that bears the sign, Two Carts at a Time. (The locals will tell you that a Tennessee football player once waited there an hour and a half for another cart to come along.)

With the futures of VanHoose and Tackett on the line, Paintsville was hopeful that Pitino would make another K-Day appearance the following summer. The players were doing their part. Two days before the coach's visit, as Perry County Central dedicated its new gymnasium in Hazard, the Tigers had come from fifteen points behind to beat one of the top-ranked teams in the state on VanHoose's last-second basket. The big guy scored twenty points in the first half and Tackett scored twenty in the second. Later that week, VanHoose had nineteen points and twenty-one rebounds in a victory over Allen Central, but he came up gimpy afterwards with a sprained ankle.

Without VanHoose, and with Tackett suffering from preliminary work on a root canal, the Tigers struggled at home against neighboring Magoffin County, their difficulties keeping the PHS students, whose custom was to never sit down during a ballgame, on their feet through overtime. Despite the eventual victory, it steamed Runyon to see Magoffin score repeatedly on putbacks that would have been Paintsville fast breaks with VanHoose in the lineup. But it didn't surprise him. "Every day in practice," he said later, "everybody stands around and watches J.R. VanHoose rebound." Nor did it surprise him that, with VanHoose still out, Paintsville lost its next game at Prestonsburg, a bitter rival whom the Tigers had not played since the police were called six years before to break up a fight that involved two hundred people on the playing floor; the game was finished with only the coaches and cheerleaders in the gym.

While VanHoose found it painful to sit and watch his state-champion teammates lose in the next town over, something else was nagging him even more as 1996 wound down. For weeks after Pitino's visit to Paintsville, J.R. had received only one letter from Winston Bennett, his main UK contact. None of the Kentucky coaches had called Runyon about him. "He's wondering about Kentucky, showing some concern about it," his father said from his office at Addington Mining one morning just before Christmas. "They're showing nowhere near the interest of Indiana or Tennessee, those people. I'm trying to let him realize that Kentucky is not the only college out there. Notre Dame just offered him a scholarship. Indiana, Tennessee, Kansas, Florida, Michigan State, North Carolina State, Ohio State, Louisville, Marquette, Cincinnati—they've all made it known that a scholarship is available for him. Kentucky has not done that.

"On the other hand, I think Todd's chances of going to UK are much improved. Pitino has written him once since he was here, and they like his athleticism. Of course, they hadn't shown much interest in him at all before, so they had to do that. But it's hard to tell with J.R. When Pitino was here, he asked Bill Mike if he thought J.R. could adapt to Kentucky's style. Bill Mike's answer was that a basketball player's a basketball player. All of this uncertainty makes it really hard, because J.R. would probably like to make an early commitment by the end of the season.

"There are just so many things to consider," the elder VanHoose went on. "Another thing you have to think about is that Bobby Knight has five big men leaving next year. The only big guy they have now who would still be there when J.R. is a freshman is Jason Collier. Collier's a great kid. I think his personality and J.R.'s are very similar; they'd be two peas in a pod. But Collier wears number forty [VanHoose's number]. That was the first thing J.R. noticed. He said, 'He's gonna have to change his number.' I said, 'Don't count on it.' I think eventually it's gonna come down to Kentucky and Indiana. Tennessee's still in there, and he's got some genuine interest in Kansas, but I think the two hovering around the top will continue to be there."

For the people of Paintsville, that wasn't quite good enough. Paintsville was such a Big Blue town that even the high school wore Kentucky colors. It was the owner of Paintsville's McDonald's franchise, a fan of Pelphrey's spirit and Pitino's management style, who paid $6,500 at a charity auction for two tickets to the Tennessee game five years earlier. It was a Paintsville man, dying of cancer and refusing his morphine on the days the Cats played—it made him too drowsy to concentrate on the game, he said—who prevailed upon Pelphrey to get a card signed by the Kentucky players and then requested that it be buried with him. Kentucky fever was passed along in Paintsville's schools and stores and door-to-door on its amiable streets.

The VanHooses' neighbors, for instance, Sid and Jann Garland, were commuting season-ticket holders who seldom missed a home game under

193

any circumstances. It was a commitment that required more than casual maintenance. To wit, they had a decision to make concerning Notre Dame's December visit to Lexington because the daughters of former San Francisco Giants shortstop Johnnie ("Peanut" to them) LeMaster, a lifelong neighbor who once made a basket in the Garlands' driveway hoop by shooting the ball over the porch roof, had the bad sense to schedule their double wedding for the same night. "I imagine we'll go to the game," Jann said. "Peanut never checked the schedule. He should have known better." There was a road game the year before that the Garlands might have missed on television because an ice storm knocked out electricity on their side of town, but the wife of a local attorney, who lived on the other side of town, drove around picking up people in her four-wheel drive utility vehicle and took them all to her house to watch.

The Garlands would still be proud of J.R. if he went to school somewhere else—after all, they maintained a high regard for their four sons who attended Vanderbilt—but it irritated Sid that, as a Kentucky booster, he wasn't allowed to put in a good word for UK or treat the boy to lunch, as he often had in the past. That went against the Paintsville way of life: It was a neighborly kind of place in which a strapping young-ster like VanHoose would shovel the snow up and down Fourth Street without being asked. (The Garlands and the VanHooses lived next door to each other until the VanHooses bought the big house around the cor-ner. The black family that moved into their old place, the Joneses, was the only one in Paintsville. They happened to arrive early in 1996, just as the high school basketball team was making history in the state tourna-ment. Noting that they were practically the only people left in town on the weekend of the Sweet Sixteen, Ken Jones, a surgeon, saw Garland outside the next day and said, "See, I told you everybody would leave as soon as we moved in.")

Sid Garland enjoyed a particularly close relationship with J.R., in part because when good things happened to Bob and Beth's boy, he liked to share them. The night after Paintsville won the state championship, the MVP was pounding on the Garlands' door holding the big trophy. He also had his picture taken in front of their house wearing his state championship jacket; Garland would have had his picture taken in it, too, but the jacket would have wrapped up the ex-Marine like a com-forter. Now Sid and J.R. had to wonder about NCAA regulations with every hello and how-you-doin': Did they have to stop sharing things just because the Garlands were partial to the state university's athletic teams? J.R. sometimes came over to borrow one of his friend's military history books; did they have to be careful about that? Garland kept treats in his freezer to pass out to neighborhood kids who happened by in the summer; would the NCAA bust them over a popsicle? The retired colonel wasn't inclined to withhold popsicles and history books, but he had stopped paying J.R. fifteen dollars to mow his grass, even though the teenager had been doing it since the fifth grade.

In the final analysis, it really wasn't necessary for Sid and Jann Garland to convey to J.R. their feelings about UK; he knew. He pretty much knew how everybody in Paintsville felt about Kentucky. While Paintsville eluded the regional stereotype in most respects, when it came to sports, the town was about as Kentucky as it got. E.A. Couch, the father of former Paintsville star (and UK football captain) Joey Couch and a standout on Carr Creek's 1956 state championship team, spoke from his Big Blue heart when he sat at his kitchen table outside of town and said, "If Kentucky doesn't get J.R. VanHoose, they're gonna live to regret it. It's sure not gonna help the popularity of Kentucky basketball in the mountains. To turn him down would be devastating to this area."

○ ○ ○

A low murmur passed through the crowd at Lexington Catholic High School. It was the night after Christmas and the Paintsville Tigers were about to take the floor against Shelby County in a holiday tournament that included some of the best players in the United States. The top three names from out of the state, Kenny Gregory of Ohio and New Yorkers Elton Brand and Karim Shabazz, had all been short-list Kentucky prospects when their teams consented to come to Lexington, but since then Gregory had committed to Kansas, Brand to Duke, and Shabazz to Florida State. That unexpected turn of events had removed some of the dazzle from the tournament, but it was left with a sufficient amount of intrigue in the matchups. For instance, VanHoose would find himself jumping center with the seven-something Shabazz if the Tigers managed to get past Shelby County in the first round. And the Shelby County game itself was compelling enough to attract Rick Pitino, who prompted a tenor hum and considerable finger-pointing as he strode into the gym with Bill Keightley and assistant coach Jim O'Brien, choosing a seat near the end of the lower level. Pitino, who knew the way there because his son had played for Lexington Catholic the year before, was easy to spot; he was the only one in the place wearing a suit.

As the Kentucky coach signed autographs for the youngsters bold enough to approach him, on the other side of the gym Shabazz's Woodmere Academy teammates applauded enthusiastically for the Paintsville cheerleaders as the bouncy girls warmed up with handsprings and flips; Kentucky cheerleading is an art form, and the New Yorkers' comments indicated that they had never seen such a thing before. What the rest of the spectators had never seen before, however—in addition to Pitino in their midst—was a confrontation of underclassmen the size of VanHoose and Shelby County's Nathan Popp, a 7-1 sophomore who had been in the basketball news around Kentucky since growing to extraordinary height as a middle schooler. Over the years Popp and VanHoose had struck up a friendship through weekly telephone calls, but this was the first time they had squared off on the basketball court.

The difference in the two of them was significant enough to beget tough questions about their relative potential. Popp was considerably taller and thinner, VanHoose obviously more assertive, polished, and offensive-minded. Popp's athletic ability was limited to the extent that he didn't jump center, nor did he catch the first pass thrown in his direction. VanHoose picked it off. But when the Paintsville center missed on the next steal attempt, Popp snatched the ball out of the air and spun around for an easy layup. From high in the bleachers, a burly fan yelled out, "Dunk the ball, man! My lands, you're seven-one. You've got to dunk the ball!"

On the other end of the floor, Popp blocked VanHoose's shot and Pitino smiled at Mr. Wildcat. Any shot of VanHoose's that Popp didn't block, however, the former made, putting in ten of Paintsville's first thirteen. He was also having success of his own rejecting the lanky sophomore's attempts. But none of Paintsville's smaller players could seem to stop the three-point missiles of Shelby's crewcut guard, Lance Ashby, and the Tigers trailed by five at halftime. VanHoose got Popp into foul trouble in the second half and piled up points from the line, but Shelby County protected its lead until Tackett hit a three-pointer and then a driving leaner with two seconds left to send the game into Paintsville's third overtime of the young season. Tackett, a shooting guard with athleticism that would serve him well on the asphalt of a larger city, had begun to develop something of a reputation as a buzzer-beater. His favorite player was the Indiana Pacers' timely and trash-talking shooter, Reggie Miller. "He puts pressure on himself to where he's got to produce, and he does," the 6-2 junior said. "I love the way he's everybody's enemy when he's on the floor."

Paintsville scored the first eight points of overtime, after which VanHoose took it upon himself to venture out and shut down Ashby's three-pointers. He seemed to want to be in all places simultaneously, at one point hustling back from the perimeter to block Popp's shot, then getting blocked by Popp on the other end, falling down, scrambling up, and grabbing the rebound after Shelby

College boards: VanHoose's rebounding was his ticket to the next level.

County's miss on the ensuing fast break. It was the kind of exchange that might have made an impression upon Pitino, who wondered about VanHoose's foot speed and reaction in the open court. But it was hard to tell if he saw it; people had him surrounded.

At any rate, Pitino hung around afterwards outside the Paintsville locker room until he had seen whom he had to see and the rest had seen him. As long as he was there, the recruiters from the other schools weren't about to leave. Kansas was in the house, the smaller Kentucky schools were well represented, and the assistant coach from Syracuse was noticeably animated on the subject of VanHoose. "You know you'll be hearing from me," he told J.R.'s father, who was fair game only because he was a Paintsville assistant. Under ordinary circumstances, the recruiters weren't permitted to talk to the prospects or their families, but they made certain the right people knew they were there. It was an awkward, unnatural scene. When Tackett emerged from the locker room, he approached Pitino and said hello, then backed off self-consciously when he realized that the coach couldn't really answer. Off to the side, Mr. Wildcat glanced at an acquaintance, jerked his head toward Tackett, and said, "That kid's bona fide. He's a player."

Tackett, whose coaches had intimated that he could average forty points a game for a team on which he was the whole show, would be willing to give up a professional baseball contract—he was an outstanding shortstop—for a chance to play at Kentucky. "I probably have a better chance in baseball," he said, "but college basketball would be a dream come true." And there was no doubt about the color of his dreams. Tackett's first basketball camp was Kyle Macy's. There was a party at his house the night UK won the national championship. His sister was a freshman there.

Runyon appeared from the locker room close behind Tackett, and as he did, Pitino stepped up briskly and closed in for a private conversation. While they spoke, VanHoose, who had closed out the night with thirty-one points and seventeen rebounds, came through the door and lightly squeezed Pitino's arm on his way past, the coach responding with a glance and a mumble. The chat lingered on discreetly, with Pitino granting Runyon's request to bring VanHoose and Tackett to the Wildcats' practice the next day; the Paintsville coach wanted his junior prospects to see the weight training and workout routines that each of the Kentucky players underwent and to understand the amount of work involved in becoming a big-time basketball player.

After that lesson was learned Friday afternoon, VanHoose set out Friday night to further his basketball education. Listed even taller than Popp at 7-2, Karim Shabazz represented an entirely different challenge than the Kentucky youngster had been. He was a limber, creative type of

Todd Tackett: A country guard with a city game, even Pitino found him intriguing.

player, with quickness that the Paintsville star detected in warmups. Then and there, VanHoose made up his mind that he wasn't going to invite Shabazz to block his shots, as Popp had done so frequently the night before. Taking the offensive, Paintsville's big man won the opening tip and scored the first bucket of the night on a putback. Shabazz answered with an electrifying spin move. For most of the first quarter, the two nationally rated pivotmen traded baskets. VanHoose whirled under the rim to score on a reverse off the glass, then made the same move in the other direction the next time. He had made neither the night before: In twenty-four hours, J.R. had figured out that it was necessary to expand his repertoire against a seven-footer. Shabazz's repertoire, meanwhile, included a tight spin to avoid a defender at midcourt, followed by a behind-the-back pass to an open teammate under the basket. Woodmere led by a point at halftime.

In the end, the difference was that Shabazz didn't have a Tackett to work with—or even an ordinary guard with whom he had played since the fourth grade. The deep connectedness of the two Paintsville classmates (Bob VanHoose liked to say that when one of them had to go to the bathroom, the other one felt the pain) was evident in the fourth quarter when J.R. saved a ball headed out of bounds and fired it blindly to midcourt, where Tackett took it in for a bucket and a foul. Then the center intercepted a pass on the press and without hesitating fed it to his speedier classmate for a three-point jumper. In the absence of a fat lady to sing, a robust gentleman in the back row stood up at that point, stretched, and declared, "Those hillbilly boys sure can play ball." VanHoose finished with thirty-two points, Shabazz with twenty-seven, and Tackett with nineteen.

With Woodmere's ten-point defeat, all three out-of-state schools had fallen to their Kentucky opponents Friday night. In the first game, an unspectacular aggregation from Harrison County, which on Thursday night had turned back UK prospect Harold Swanagan and University Heights, plugged its way to a 13-point upset of two-time New York state champion Peekskill despite thirty-two points and twenty-two rebounds from Brand, Peekskill's 6-8 powerhouse forward. In the next game, Jaron Brown, a 6-3 junior guard from Lexington's Bryan Station, scored forty points and heroically outmaneuvered the super-gifted Gregory of Independence High School in Columbus, Ohio. The evening's other winner was the undefeated host school, Lexington Catholic, which had already won a Florida tournament and was way too much for Paintsville's overwhelmed next-door neighbor, Johnson Central, leading 23-2 after a few frightening minutes.

The tournament moved to UK's Memorial Coliseum on Saturday, and after Jaron Brown pulled off another one-man triumph, scoring more than half of Bryan Station's points in a narrow decision over Harrison County, Lexington Catholic completed its sweep of Johnson County, putting a gaudy 98-72 stamp on the reddened forehead of Paintsville. The last time the two Kentucky powers had met it was in the Sweet Sixteen semifinals of 1996, when the Tigers had won big and VanHoose had apparently set the tournament rebounding record. Nine months later, it looked as though little Paintsville's lack of numbers had finally caught up with it: the defending state champions didn't have the manpower to contend with Catholic's depth and full-court, Kentucky-clone press. At one point, Lexington Catholic led by forty-four. In the end, Tackett's twenty-eight points and VanHoose's twenty-one seemed almost incidental.

Paintsville worked hard to beat Harrison County on Sunday, and Lexington Catholic broke its first sweat of the weekend while holding off Jaron Brown and Bryan Station for the tournament championship that almost seemed predetermined. Catholic's acrobatic junior forward, Shawn Fields, was named the tournament MVP, but the most heads were turned by Brown, a strong, smooth, and previously unheralded player who proved in a remarkable few days that he could compete with the best in the country.

A few weeks after his auspicious performance in the Lexington tournament, Jaron Brown announced that he would be playing basketball at the University of Kentucky in two years. It was a proud moment for his coach, Bobby Washington, who hadn't been contacted or even considered by Kentucky after his stellar career at all-black Dunbar High School concluded in 1965. "If UK didn't want a guy like Julius Berry," Washington remarked, referring to the Lexington legend who preceded him, "they wouldn't want any of the rest of us." He had gone on to play guard for Eastern Kentucky University and the Cleveland Cavaliers, and as a high school coach he had dutifully moved beyond the point of holding grudges against the hometown university. "You can't constantly live in the sixties," said Washington. "This is the nineties. If a kid like Jaron has a chance to go to Kentucky, I'm gonna tell him the advantages and the disadvantages. We haven't talked about the reputation Kentucky had when I was his age. I didn't think that was an important issue. The issues were the magnitude of the program and the up-and-down style of ball, which Jaron likes to play. UK is the number-one program in the country, I don't care what anybody says. Rick Pitino went to Rome and the pope kissed him on the hand. I'm telling Jaron, that's the magnitude of Kentucky basketball."

Brown was the second member of the state's junior class to make such a surprise announcement, having been preceded by J.P. Blevins of Metcalfe County.

○ ○ ○

Edmonton, Kentucky, is a practical town: the florist's shop is next to the funeral home.

The county attorney, John Paul Blevins, keeps his office across the street, right on the town square, which is actually more of a circle; all the traffic goes in one direction around the courthouse, and when somebody gets to the turn they want, they take it. There's also a pool room on the circle-square, and a farmer selling produce out of his truck. A block down from the center of town, on a sharp slope

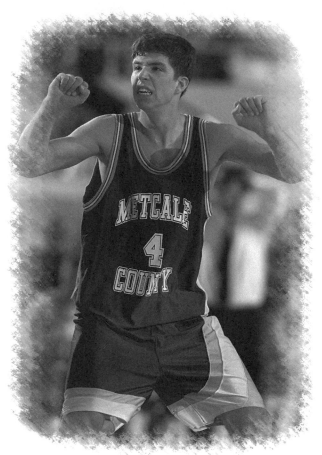

J.P. Blevins: The Kentucky dream comes true.

veering off Main Street behind the county attorney's office, smoke rises from the chimneys of Appalachian-style shacks all in a row. The mountains themselves, though, are nearly a hundred miles to the east; Edmonton sits closer to Western Kentucky University, and closer still, in all respects, to the neighboring towns of Wisdom, Marrowbone, Eighty Eight, Subtle, Summer Shade, Meshack, Breeding, Bear Wallow, and Black Gnat.

In Edmonton, as in most American places its size (population 1,500), prosperity has left the town square and relocated along the highway leading in and out. The Dairy Queen, the Pizza Hut, and Gene's Skating Rink and Recreation Center do their business out toward the actual hub of local activity, the top-of-the-hill Metcalfe County High School, popularized in January of 1997 as the place where the county attorney's son, J.P. Blevins, was playing basketball on his way to the University of Kentucky.

After he announced that he would cast his lot with UK, the state's two major newspapers, the *Lexington Herald-Leader* and the *Louisville Courier-Journal*, ran feature stories portraying the young Blevins as the quintessential Kentucky-boy basketball player. Already the most famous athlete ever to come out of Metcalfe County, a lightly developed farming region, Blevins had been dribbling with both hands since he was five and attending Pitino's UK basketball camp since he was nine. His most prized possession came from that first camp. It was a photograph of the boy and the coach, signed by the latter and inscribed by the former with the words that said it all: "Pitino's autograph to me more important than president's." J.P.'s bedroom was decorated with a poster of Rupp Arena, a Kentucky license plate (IM 4 UK), a picture of The Unforgettables, an autographed Rex Chapman poster, a Kentucky floor mat, a Kentucky beanbag chair, and a block-K flag, signed by Pitino, that the Metcalfe star said was the last thing he saw every night before going to bed.

While Blevins only had eyes for Kentucky, the assumption in the commonwealth all along had been that if an in-state junior were to declare for UK, it would naturally be VanHoose, the top-rated player in Kentucky and the franchise pivotman of the defending state champion. He and J.P., who played varsity ball in the seventh grade and averaged twenty points in the eighth, had bobbed back and forth in the prep ratings for a couple of years, but Blevins's stock had fallen off when he missed most of his sophomore season with mononucleosis. Consequently, Pitino surprised Blevins and everybody else with the scholarship offer. Blevins's answer, on the other hand, surprised nobody. "He took five or ten seconds to make up his mind," said his high school coach, Tim McMurtrey. "He considered it longer than I thought he would."

Metcalfe County had never before sent a boy to the state university on a basketball scholarship, and the occasion was met with bear hugs and misty-eyed emotion all around. Before Blevins made his wonderful announcement, the biggest thing to happen in that little slice of Kentucky was the Sunday morning Kyle Macy showed up at Edmonton Baptist with a local girl. "My daughter says J.P. can't even do his work at school anymore," said Virginia Edwards, a clerk at the Citgo gas station and store (which, on nights that UK played, did a brisk trade in chips and beverages until game time, then stood empty for two hours). "It's embarrassing to him."

Among the Metcalfe Countians giddy over one of their own was Virginia's daughter, Lisa, a ninth grader at the high school and a Kentucky fan from the start. "I was watching a game when she was born," said Mrs. Edwards, who as a child shot marbles with J.P.'s father. "She was hooked from that time on. My daughter lives and breathes Kentucky. Her bedroom is decorated with Wildcat stuff. For her birthday, she wanted to eat at Pitino's restaurant in Lexington. But that's okay. I'd rather she was interested in the Wildcats than rock bands."

At Pit's Barbecue, a man wearing a hat with a fish hook stuck in the side was spitting tobacco juice into a Coke can and talking about what everybody else in town was talking about. "J.P. might not be the best player we've had around here," said Leon White, "but he's the smartest [a 4.0 grade-point average]. The others weren't students like he is. One of 'em would get drunk on Friday and stay drunk till Sunday. Now, J.P.'s brother, he's brilliant. He's the smartest kid I ever saw."

The scholarship UK had promised J.P. would make him the second of the Blevins brothers to enter college as some kind of a first. Nobody from Metcalfe County had ever gone to Yale before John Forbes Blevins was accepted there. But while there was substantial hoopla on his account among the teachers in the district, John Forbes's breakthrough went pretty much undiscussed at the Dairy Queen and the Citgo station. Nobody drove over from a neighboring county to watch him take a test.

On the other hand, since J.P. announced for Kentucky it seemed as though Metcalfe County was the center of the basketball universe. "I knew it would be wild," the young point guard said as he polished off some chicken in the kitchen and made himself comfortable in the family room of the family's fashionable home on the residential hill across from the high school. "But I never thought it would be like it has been. At Monroe County, I had twenty-five kids come up to me before the game wanting autographs. I could see everybody else pointing at me. During the game the fans were yelling, 'Blevins . . . superstar . . . Blevins . . . superstar . . .' At Warren Central, there was a play that should have been a charge on me but they called a blocking foul instead. The guy from Warren Central that they called the foul on turned to the ref and said, 'There's a lot of UK fans here tonight, I see.'" Everywhere the Hornets played, they set attendance records. Back in Edmonton, where youth leaguers were fighting over who got to wear their hero's number four, the volume of mail had picked up noticeably. One letter arrived at the Blevins residence addressed "J.P. Blevins, Basketball Player, Edmonton, KY."

Every UK recruit within reach of Kentucky's fans is treated with some degree of celebrity, but Blevins's popularity was amplified by several factors: he was from a disenfranchised section of the state (basketball-wise) that longed desperately to feel like part of the Kentucky program; he was a polite, nice-looking, All-American kind of teenager whose enthusiasm for Kentucky was on the order of those who made him popular; and he was white. The latter was a seldom-said but inescapable

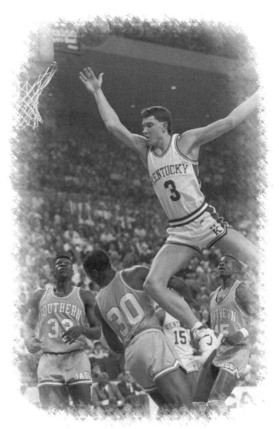

Rex Chapman: A generation of Kentucky kids pretended to be him.

consideration. The VanHooses knew, as well, that part of what made J.R. such a commodity was the fact that he was white. As a rule, Kentucky was not reluctant to embrace and genuinely care for its black basketball players, but there was no denying that it identified with and especially liked its white ones. And J.P. Blevins had freckles.

For their part, the Blevinses were of course just as proud of John Forbes and J.P.'s older half-brother, David Garmon, who, like the county attorney, had played basketball for both Western Kentucky University and Cumberland College. Garmon was something of a local hero himself, having led Metcalfe County to the Sweet Sixteen in 1985, but the credit and the glory were not entirely his. J.P. was a different case. His was a singular achievement. John Forbes's was, too, the difference being that his achievement had nothing to do with basketball or Kentucky. John Forbes didn't have his picture taken with a Yale professor when he was nine, and he didn't look at the Yale flag every night before he went to bed. Going to Yale was a remarkable thing for a rural Kentucky kid from a public school system, but it was not the thing that all his friends had dreamed about since they first saw their idols in the deep liquid voice of Cawood Ledford. What made J.P. different was that he was actually getting to do what Kentucky boys closed their eyes and wished for when they blew out birthday candles.

And he was one of those boys; he certainly was. When Joe Hall was the UK coach and J.P. was still crawling, he wore a T-shirt that said, "Hang On Joe, I'm On My Way." Shooting at the basket behind the house as a child, he said, "I would be Rex Chapman playing against Louisville or Indiana. Rex had career nights every night, and Kentucky never lost."

While it is generally presumed that, due to the influences of folklore and geography, the most ardent Big Blue fans are concentrated in the Bluegrass (central) and mountain (eastern) regions of the state, the fact is that Western Kentuckians have surmounted terrific distances—Paducah to Lexington is more than 250 miles—to sustain an uncompromised loyalty to the state university. And if there was a Kentucky fan in every Edmonton family, there was a bigger one in the Blevins family than most. "When I was growing up," said John Paul Blevins, "the state was economically deprived and there was one thing—basketball. Adolph Rupp put it there. We didn't have TV until I was in the fifth grade, but my granddaddy listened to all the games on the radio. That was before Cawood. He listened to Claude Sullivan. That was our entertainment; we listened to the Cats out of Louisville and to the Grand Ole Opry out of Nashville." Even while Blevins played for Western Kentucky and Cumberland, his heart was with the Cats. From a lifetime of studious devotion, his knowledge of UK basketball had become almost encyclopedic by the time his son was given the practically unthinkable opportunity to enlist in the tradition.

As the county attorney, tall, gray, droll, mustachioed, and deep-voiced, the elder Blevins retained such a torrid passion for Kentucky basketball that he had to watch the games in a room by himself. J.P. was usually alone in another room. "It's so tense when there's a game on," said Martha Blevins, who, reddish-haired and bubbly, was her husband's antithesis, "that we can't stand to hear each other. If it's a tournament game and Kentucky is trailing, John will have to get in his Bronco and drive around town for a while."

The recent years had consequently been anxious ones for both father and son. They knew that Pitino was interested in J.P. all along; the question was how much. Billy Donovan, the Florida coach who had been Pitino's assistant, first called Tim McMurtrey about the precocious kid when he was playing on the Metcalfe varsity in the seventh grade. The communication had been steadily maintained, but Blevins didn't talk about it. He knew that what mattered was not the early contact, but his improvement and physical growth; he didn't dare think seriously about Kentucky until he was over six feet tall. By the ninth grade, when he had grown and gained quickness at the same time, it was obvious that he was headed to Division I whether or not Kentucky came through. The Wildcats wrote him often—mostly personal stuff from assistants Winston Bennett and Jim O'Brien—and Tennessee, of course, wrote him more, wishing him Happy Birthday, Happy Thanksgiving, Merry Christmas, etc. Cincinnati was right behind Tennessee in the amount of mail. Wake Forest furnished Blevins with its "word of the week." The Western Kentucky coach, Matt Kilcullen, met J.P. on the No. 1 tee at a golf tournament in Bowling Green and said he wanted to be the first to officially offer him a scholarship. The attention was flattering and promising, but the fact was that if Kentucky was truly interested in him—he was never sure of that—the other schools were wasting their time. Blevins was averaging thirty points as a sophomore and had finally begun to think of UK as a real possibility when he became ill and had to sit out the greater part of the season. "It didn't look too promising a year ago when J.P. was lying on the couch," his mother said.

If nothing else, the setback took the pressure off. Blevins never gave up on the idea of a Kentucky scholarship, but the townspeople let it drop for a while. Even when he got off to a good start as a junior and continued to lead the state in scoring, not much was said about his UK prospects. "I didn't tell my friends that I was talking to Kentucky on the phone," said J.P. "Nobody really knew if Kentucky was interested. People first started to figure something was up when Pitino showed up at our game at Warren Central on January second. I came out of the dressing room and he was the first person I saw. He was headed up the steps and everybody was pointing and hitting their buddy on the arm."

Pitino's offer came that very night, and Blevins's announcement followed the next day. It was major news around the state—especially in Edmonton, of course, and also Paintsville, where J.R. VanHoose and Todd Tackett were both left wondering what it meant for them. The message to VanHoose was that he was not Pitino's number-one priority in the state or even in the state's junior class, and the complication for Tackett lay in the fact that he and Blevins were similar in size and style. VanHoose and Blevins, bonded by camps and rankings, had kept up an ongoing phone relationship, but after J.P.'s commitment it was Tackett who called. "He told me that J.R. didn't see how I was handling the pressure," Blevins recalled. "He said that everywhere you go, everybody is watching you thinking, 'Can he play or can't he play?'"

For both Blevins and VanHoose, the recruiting phase was a passage of native life complicated by the fact that the questions came from the inside as much as the outside. If there was anything that gave Blevins pause concerning the University of Kentucky, it was the uncertainty of playing time. Fortunately, neither his father nor Pitino shared that concern. "J.P. is going to be a big-time assist man at the next level," said John Paul Blevins. "I think Pitino sees that in him. I think he really likes a point guard who can penetrate and get inside the defense."

J.P.'s ability to penetrate came largely from confident, crafty ball-handling that made it obvious how his boyhood had been spent. When he was younger, he had dribbled so much with his left hand (he often purposely kept his right stuck in the back pocket of his cutoff jeans) that it was conceivably his best. This skill was complemented by acceleration not often seen in rural Kentucky or anywhere else. In the end, it was Pitino's evident faith in these assets that gave Blevins the faith he needed in himself to make such a momentous decision. The choice between not starting at Kentucky and starting somewhere else would have been a difficult one for him, but the director of Blevins's summer basketball camps convinced him that it was one he didn't have to make. "Pitino told me that Wayne Turner will be a senior when I'm a freshman, and I'll back him up for a year, then take over at point guard as a sophomore," said Blevins. "That's a perfect situation. He told me, 'I'm not going to recruit on top of you.'"

And so life was swell in Metcalfe County. The county attorney would see his son get the chance he never had; J.P. would have the great honor of playing basketball in the name of the flag over his bed; and Martha was just happy for the family and the town. "Around here," she said, holding open the front door of the handsome house high above the school that her son had made famous, "when something good happens to one of us, it happens to all of us."

○ ○ ○

Kentucky's "All A" tournament was not established to compete with or compromise the year-end Sweet Sixteen, for which all Kentucky high schools vied regardless of class, but was a supplemental, midseason opportunity for small schools to win a championship at the state level. Most years, it was a nice, quiet event, but with Paintsville and Metcalfe County in the field after having won their "All A" regionals, the 1997 tournament, held at Eastern Kentucky University starting in the last days of January, was transformed into another Kentucky hardcourt spectacle, the lines at the ticket windows swelling unnaturally with fans who had come to watch not only their local teams but a future Wildcat and at least two Maybecats. One gentleman, waiting patiently with his wife, had already seen Blevins play every year since the kid was in the eighth grade. Another was curious about VanHoose because, he stated convincingly, Bobby Knight had been to see him four times.

Bobby Knight had not been *to Kentucky* four times in the *decade* to see high school players, but in fact he had been at Pikeville one night in the middle of January to catch VanHoose in a tournament sponsored by a mountain television station. The General flew into Big Sandy Regional Airport with Mrs. Knight on short notice even though Runyon told him VanHoose had been sick for a few days. Knight said he didn't care; he wasn't there to see J.R. so much as for J.R. to see him. Apparently, however, VanHoose was about the only one by whom the Indiana coach wanted to be seen. He had his green coat pulled up around his ears, with only the top of his silver hair showing, and at halftime he vanished to somewhere private. The television station that sponsored the tournament never knew he was there. But Beth VanHoose, J.R.'s mother, was sitting close enough to be able to watch Knight's eyes during the game, and she could tell that they never left her son. On two occasions, when calls were made on J.R. that he was not likely to agree with, Knight raised up slightly in his seat

Top of the class: Kentucky's signing of Blevins magnified the drama surrounding its recruitment of VanHoose.

to get a close look at number forty's reaction as he came to the bench. Control was VanHoose's game; it was a test that he easily passed.

For his part, J.R., knowing already that Knight had never before made a personal appearance on behalf of a Kentucky junior, was additionally impressed that the famous visitor had taken time out in the middle of the Big Ten season. Actually, Knight's timing couldn't have been better. That very week, VanHoose had noted with chagrin that Kentucky was actively pursuing a 6-11 power forward from Massachusetts named Michael Bradley. According to their general profiles and vital statistics, Bradley and VanHoose were essentially the same prospect, the main difference being that the former was a senior. As the Bradley watch wore on, word came that he would announce his intentions sometime during the week of the "All A" tournament. VanHoose was checking every paper and newscast.

When Bradley, on cue, declared that he would join shooting guard Ryan Hogan of Illinois and Florida forward Myron Anthony in Kentucky's 1997 recruiting class, Bobby Knight started looking awfully good to J.R.

VanHoose. Kansas was climbing the chart, too—throughout the fall, Roy Williams, the head coach, wrote VanHoose and other top prospects every week for their picks in his football contest—but Knight was pushing all the right buttons at the moment. It helped that VanHoose wasn't frightened off by Knight's image as a sharp-edged disciplinarian. "J.R. has played in a program that's very disciplined," his father said. "Bill Mike is very much in control of the Paintsville program. He's been known to throw some tantrums of his own. I've seen basketballs bounce off walls, ball racks torn up, chalkboards busted, doors beaten up. J.R. has come through a system where the coach lets you know where you stand. Bill Mike is also very good at compliments. He knows when to pat you on the back. But if you have a bad game, be assured that he'll let you know you had a bad game. J.R. had a couple of bad moments in the [recent] Magoffin County game, where he dropped a pass and made another mistake. Bill Mike just grabbed him by the jersey and told him, 'You're not in this gym . . . I don't know where you're at, but get your blankety-blank in this gym!' J.R. went back out there and rebounded, threw an outlet pass, then beat everybody down the floor and shot a layup and got fouled. That kind of thing motivates him. So no, he's not afraid of Bobby Knight.

"Out of all the schools recruiting him," Bob VanHoose continued, "I think Indiana has made the strongest commitment in terms of the other players they're recruiting. Tennessee still sends him the most stuff—things like a picture of Kevin O'Neill's head pasted onto a race car driver with a caption like, 'The Vols are in the driver's seat'—but I think they know that Kentucky and Indiana are the top two. Indiana has basically said, 'We're going after you. If we don't get you, we're hurting. We don't have a backup plan, because we expect you to be there.' Not those words, but a real strong commitment to that effect." As compared to Kentucky, which signed Michael Bradley.

As events conspired to nudge VanHoose toward Indiana, Blevins became the hot item in the Kentucky community. UK followers observed him tenaciously at the "All A" tournament to see whether, as a 6-3 point guard, he could really handle the ball well enough to play that position for the Cats, or whether he shot well enough to be an off-guard. They scrutinized him for quickness, were pleasantly surprised by his spinning and crossover dribbling, and turned to each other with raised eyebrows when his first step swept him past a dazzled defender. ("The only step that matters in basketball," said the well-coached senior, court-wise beyond his years, "is the first step.") They were also enchanted by the game Blevins's Metcalfe County team played with Trigg County in the first afternoon of the tournament. Trigg County had a couple of crackerjack guards of its own, and one of them, Chris Sparks, managed to outscore Blevins 36-32. But Blevins's package included a considerable amount of playmaking, and plays were made all over the open floor in Metcalfe's 94-90 victory that entertained and impressed the Kentucky spectators in equal portions.

Paintsville's game that night was a mountain struggle that had the Tigers climbing uphill against Hazard and finally winning in overtime. VanHoose and Tackett were upstaged by Paintsville seniors Kyle Adams, who hit a game-tying jumper with two seconds to go in regulation, and Josh McKenzie, whose twenty-seven points were well within the range of his capabilities. The best junior class Kentucky had seen in a long time— and especially its concentration of talent in Paintsville—had obscured the fact that McKenzie had the brawn and the touch that plenty of college teams could put to advantage. Some of the schools interested in him were waiting to see if he would meet their academic requirements.

Paintsville and Metcalfe County both advanced through Friday night's quarterfinal round, with much of the evening crowd arriving early to catch Blevins at 6:30, but the latter had the misfortune of meeting Lexington Catholic in Saturday's semifinals. Lexington Catholic's enrollment had grown to the point that the school would not be eligible again for the "A" tournament, and the Knights' advantages entailed more than just that; as a private institution they were able to attract basketball talent from around the city of Lexington and beyond. Their top two players, like so many across the state, were juniors, and both Shawn Fields and David Graves had been contacted by major basketball colleges. Blevins battled valiantly against the waves of Lexington's pressure, but there were two Knights swiping at him every time he touched the ball. Repeatedly, he would bring Metcalfe close, only to have Lexington Catholic put in fresh troops and pull away again. "That boy's pretty darn good," said a white-haired man from Stanford, Kentucky, who had attended Eastern Kentucky University forty-five years ago and hadn't been back to the fieldhouse until Blevins and VanHoose lured him there, "but you won't see a better high school team than that Lexington Catholic. I'm just sick of these private schools winning everything. Sick of it. But you won't see a better team than that."

Paintsville's semifinal opponent was Paris, whose roster was entirely black except for one member—a fact that would have been incidental but for the contrast it represented with the large Paris cheerleading squad, which was entirely white except for three members. The contrast itself would have been incidental except for the fact that it was part of a conspicuous pattern in Kentucky. Perhaps there were simple explanations for it: maybe the white girls were more interested in and able to afford the preparatory gymnastics classes and cheerleader camps than the black girls and the disparity was accentuated by the fact that the white boys were not as aggressively inclined toward basketball as their black schoolmates. But explanations or not, in 1990 the high schools of Jefferson County—basically, Louisville—were compelled to implement a rule that required each cheerleading and dance team in the county to have at least one black member. The policy was made in reaction to formal protests by citizens who charged that the cheer and dance teams were "the last vestiges of segregation" in Louisville schools. While Louisville's action was independent of the rest of the state, its customs were not. At the "A" tournament alone, in addition to Paris, Mayfield had three black starters on its basketball team and no black cheerleaders, and Campbellsville, with four black starters out of five, had four black cheerleaders out of fifteen. Elsewhere, Washington County's team and fans were half black, but its cheerleading unit was entirely white; Marion County had three black starters and one black cheerleader on its large squad; and so on. At Eastern High School, the top-rated team in Louisville and an institution that fell under Jefferson County's quota system, the five basketball starters and top four substitutes were black, while nineteen of the twenty cheerleaders were white. If there were schools in which the ratios were reversed, they were extremely hard to find. In general, the Kentucky cheerleading scene, circa 1997, offered continuing testimony that Adolph Rupp had not invented his state's racial customs, nor had his passing had a profound effect upon them; he merely coached basketball under them.

Its sociological relevancy aside, Paris's best player was 6-3 senior guard Clinton Sims, brother of star Louisville guard Alvin Sims. Sims, more athletic than graceful, scored thirty points against Paintsville and drew his team within four with a few minutes left in the game. But Tackett was scoring every which way (35 points), VanHoose was bringing down whatever hit the backboard (18 rebounds, 24 points), and Sims missed a free throw or two that would have made the game even more interesting. "When he missed one of those free throws there at the end," said Tackett mischievously as he stuffed a pair of size-15 gym shoes into his duffel bag after the game, "I said to him, 'Your brother would have made it.'"

Paintsville's victory gave the Tigers another crack at Lexington Catholic, but they weren't yet up to it. VanHoose had twenty-two points and eleven rebounds—his fifty-nine rebounds overall were a tournament record—and the game was closely contested into the fourth quarter, but in the end the Knights had taken the Class "A" title by seventeen and advanced their record to 23-0 for the season. Paintsville could only hope that it would figure out Catholic in time for the state tournament, as it had the previous year. The pairings for the Sweet Sixteen had just been released: If Lexington Catholic and Paintsville both won their regionals, they would meet again—for the fourth time, actually—in the first round of the state tournament. In the meantime, the third meeting would take place in Paintsville on the final night of the regular season.

By then, J.R. VanHoose expected to be pledged to a major college. Originally, he thought he would have committed by *now*, the midpoint of his junior season—especially if Kentucky had offered a scholarship—but instead of straightening itself out, the situation seemed to get more complicated with every tournament, rumor, and report. While the latest signs pointed to Indiana, he wouldn't rest easy until his status with Kentucky was clarified once and for all. J.R. had been knocked for a loop when the Wildcats signed Bradley, had been dazed when Blevins and Brown committed, and in light of those things he had begun to adjust to the possibility that UK would not make him an offer; but the story seemed to change every day depending on who said what on the radio and who called whom on the phone.

On Pitino's "Big Blue Line" show one night in February, a caller from Floyd County asked the coach point-blank if he was recruiting VanHoose. Pitino said yes, then veered off into a generic discussion about native players at UK. "My concern with in-state players," he said, "is that if we recruit one or two juniors and not another one [i.e., J.P. Blevins and Jaron Brown but not J.R. VanHoose], it doesn't necessarily mean that we think one is a better player. It means that that person fits into our style. Some players, we're not sure if they do or they don't. So I need more time. Especially when they're from Kentucky. Cameron Mills, I told him he was not going to play at Kentucky. He wanted to come anyway. People say, well, what about John Pelphrey and Richie Farmer?; they were from Eastern Kentucky. Yes, and in no way do I want to take away from what those guys accomplished at the University of Kentucky. They were unbelievable for us. They did things nobody else could have done. But if they played with the guys today, neither guy would play. They'd be out there with Ron Mercer and Derek Anderson. Richie and John are not gonna want to guard those guys. Some of the top guys out there, they could play at IU or Wake, and those schools are at the same level as we are, but maybe they're not our style. It has nothing to do with where a player is from. It's all about style. With a lot of players, I just need time to be sure."

The subject was revisited that night on the *Cats' Pause* show that followed Pitino's, when the host, Oscar Combs, said unequivocally, "Kentucky will not recruit J.R. VanHoose. From people in the know, I hear that it's a question of physique and size. They don't think he's six-ten. They think he might be somewhere under six-eight. I can tell you from impeccable sources that Kentucky will not recruit him. They think he can be a star somewhere like Miami of Ohio."

Combs was known to be chummy with people in the UK athletic department, but the VanHooses were not impressed with his impeccable sources. In fact, they knew of casual inaccuracies that the editor had previously circulated: that J.R. was interested in Ohio State, for instance, and that Indiana sent him high volumes of mail. "The more I listen to Oscar, the more I get ticked off," said Bob VanHoose, who was dumbfounded that Combs would equate his son with Miami when he was being courted by many of the best basketball schools in the country. "He's never even called us. He starts going on like that and Beth and I just look at each other and shake our heads. I started to write a letter to Oscar. I never sent it, but just typing it into the computer gave me some relief.

"The fact is, after those things started getting out Pitino called the school and left a message with Bill Mike to have J.R. call him. They had a good conversation. Pitino said they were not done recruiting him. He made some comment to the effect that J.R. was an eleven-star kid on a ten-star scale, and that he had a knack for rebounding like he had never seen. He said, 'The only reason we have not recruited you hard was that you are J.R. VanHoose, and if we bring you to Kentucky and you don't play, we'll catch all kinds of heat. We need Kentucky players who can play right away. If we recruit you and you don't play right away, it's a hard situation for you and a hard situation for us.' Words to that effect. He also said, 'If I were Roy Williams or Bobby Knight or played that style of ball, I'd live on your front porch.' The last thing he said was that they were going to watch J.R. over the summer, and if he developed quicker feet, yes, they would be very interested in having him play at Kentucky. That made J.R. feel a lot better.

"Pitino even mentioned that they didn't think he was six-ten, but they weren't going to quibble over an inch. I don't know if he's six-ten, but I do know that the doctor measured him at six-ten in his tennis shoes when he went in for bronchitis and Indiana measured him themselves and had him at just over six-nine. You can list him at six-nine without any problem."

The hullabaloo over the inch or two was an indication of what the VanHooses might expect if J.R. stayed in Kentucky for his college years. As the first major mountain star in a decade, his recruitment had fast become a cause celebre in the commonwealth. More than a year before he would graduate from high school, it was already taking on the public tone of the old radio debates over Richie Farmer's playing time. To be a Kentucky fan was to have an opinion on the subject.

On Cat Chat, Frank Dudley Berry offered up his remote perspective as a native who had lived in California since the age of four:

Richie Farmer was a good, decent guard, but no one but his loyal fans would confuse him with an all-star. What happens with a genuine all-star, as VanHoose may be? The pressure to play him as a freshman, in favor of a mature Magloire and a senior Mohammed . . . The pressure in later years to give him more time at the expense of other player development . . . And, no matter what happens, someone writing that he could have broken Issel's records if he'd only been given a chance. Or something. Because there is no winning this game, as the expectations of the VanHoose fans will ALWAYS exceed the reality of his capabilities, no matter how great they may be.

My own guess (though I am nearly always wrong) is that VanHoose will probably reluctantly commit to UK in the end and Pitino will probably reluctantly give him a scholarship. A classic arranged marriage, courtesy of the people of Kentucky. May they all live happily ever after.

And H.B. Elkins, a Kentucky patriot from cradle to Internet, replied:

I still think that if there are talented Kentucky-grown kids who want to play at UK, the school should take them over higher-ranked recruits from elsewhere. The pride of a Kentucky boy playing for the Big Blue works wonders.

Facts and answers were at a premium in the case of J.R. VanHoose, but points of view were plentiful and questions greeted the family at every turn. Beth VanHoose was at a department store in Lexington, a hundred miles from home, when the clerk noticed the name on her credit card and asked, "Oh, do you know J.R. VanHoose?" Wherever the VanHooses were recognized, well-meaning Kentucky people, generous with advice and eager for information, applied a little more pressure.

After one of the "All A" tournament games, Bob VanHoose was confronted by a *Cats' Pause* reporter intent on coming away with some warm information. "Honestly," the fellow said, "tell us where he's going—Kentucky or Indiana."

"I can honestly tell you that I definitely know where J.R.'s going to school," answered VanHoose. "He's going to Paintsville. He has one more year left."

8

March

It was a Sunday morning, the second of March, when the water went over the roads and kept rising on up above the windows. Some people figured it was because church had been rescheduled for the basketball game.

The game was a big one, no doubt. In addition to being Senior Day, the last home game of the regular season—an occasion on which Kentucky hadn't lost since 1964—the opponent was South Carolina, whom the Cats trailed in the Southeastern Conference standings by one game with one to play. The circumstances were worthy of network television, which was why the game started at the ungodly hour of noon, which was why some of the Lexington churches saw fit to modify the times of their morning services or cut short the homilies (at least one of the pastors had tickets).

By the time the congregations were let out and Pitino was contorting his face on the sideline, the Licking and Ohio Rivers, among others, were way out of their banks, burying much of Falmouth and immobilizing other small towns between Lexington and Cincinnati. Falmouth resident Bob Wiggins, who embarked on another consecutive-game streak after his November heart attack, had left for Rupp Arena before the waters rushed in—his home was out of the flood plain, anyway—but what of the Falmouth grandmother who had been keeping score of Kentucky games for forty years and storing the notebooks in an old refrigerator? There was no telling all that was lost; the tragedy was immense, and that was not counting the fans who missed much of the first half because they

◀ *Cameron Mills: Couldn't guard, couldn't pass, couldn't dunk.*

had to turn back against the traffic on I-75, exit via the on ramp, and search the area for open roads to Lexington.

On most Senior Days at Kentucky, the rivers run down the cheeks of the fans who can't hold them back when the graduating Cats are out there on the floor with their parents and the band plays *My Old Kentucky Home*. In that respect, it flooded again that Sunday when Derek Anderson, Anthony Epps, and Jared Prickett took their final bows, the former two holding the hands of their little daughters. "One thing that's special about Kentucky," said Pitino over the public address system, "is that Kentucky fans never say good-bye to their players. They're part of the family for the rest of our lives."

The plan for the day was to honor the seniors and clinch another SEC championship at the same time, then celebrate with an informal ceremony for Ron Mercer. The plan did not include missing so many shots in the first half and falling behind by ten points.

South Carolina was playing unexpectedly well under conditions much more daunting than those surrounding its earlier victory over Kentucky, and doing so, Eddie Fogler's team represented an intriguing contrast to Pitino's. While the state of South Carolina was not known for producing basketball players at the rate that the commonwealth was, four of the Gamecocks' starters—including the three all-conference guards—and nine of the twelve players on the roster were home-grown. Clemson, the South Carolina school which beat UK in the first game of the season, had one more starter from the state and also one from Kentucky. In light of this Palmetto bounty, UK's difficulty in finding suitable in-state players became increasingly ironic as the visitors held the lead convincingly into the second half.

Mercer kept his side in the game with brazen shooting and the Wildcats finally went ahead when a few of their three-pointers fell, including two from the mostly untested hand of reserve Cameron Mills, but the matchups were not in their favor. The home-grown Gamecock guards— Larry Davis, Melvin Watson, and B.J. McKie—were too active for UK to contain with its press and to elude with ball movement. Clutch shooting by Epps kept the Cats within a couple of points down to the final seconds and they correctly anticipated a South Carolina inbounds play on which the outcome rested, but no call was made when Epps and McKie collided at the baseline, so enraging Pitino that he charged referee Andre Patillo and got himself ejected. Four free throws ensued for South Carolina, whose first SEC championship was well deserved.

The postgame ceremony for Mercer was delayed for an extended period of cooling off, after which Pitino summoned up some good cheer and presented his departing sophomore with a couple dozen pair of number-33 UK Spandex shorts to wear under his NBA uniform (in the tradition of Michael Jordan, who wore North Carolina colors under his Chicago Bulls shorts). To a more intimate audience in the interview room, the Kentucky coach acknowledged that two defeats to South Carolina were not flukish; that the Gamecocks, because of their mobile guards, were the better team. He also spoke again of the provincial arrogance that accompanied Kentucky's rare defeats. "Ninety-five percent of the people understand [that other teams are capable of beating the Wildcats on their own merits]," he said. "Before I leave, I want to eliminate that other five percent."

This was not mere rhetoric on Pitino's part, but a way to brace the Wildcat population for what he feared might be ahead. For him, the South Carolina setback brought home the sober realization that, without Anderson, the Wildcats were lacking in the collective quickness required to make a run in the NCAA tournament. Anderson himself, as he helplessly watched his last home game get away, had no doubt that his presence in the lineup would have made the necessary difference to win the game and consequently the conference. As it was, he was still holding out hope that he could play in the Final Four if the Cats could make it that far and was confident that if they did and he did, together they would win it.

Pitino, however, could not afford to rely on a record-breaking rehabilitation, which was what it would require for Kentucky's best player to return before the season was over. His immediate objective was to get more speed into the lineup, and his immediate solution was to start Wayne Turner at point guard for the SEC tournament in Memphis. It was a controversial move insofar as it relegated Anthony Epps, the popular Kentuckian whose leadership had helped win a national championship, to the bench, but within a couple minutes of the Cats' first tournament game against Auburn, Epps was back on the floor; not for Turner, but for shooting guard Allen Edwards, whose back was aching from a pulled muscle. When Epps or Turner needed a rest, the substitute was the unlikely Lexington native, Cameron Mills, who hit two three-pointers in the 42-point victory over Auburn and twice that many when UK easily avenged its earlier loss to Ole Miss.

Suddenly, the Cats had an entirely new look. Turner gave them the penetrating ball-handler and nimble defender they had lacked since the injury to Anderson (whose quickness and tenacity had complemented Epps's shooting and composure), and Mills provided a fresh three-point threat to go along with Turner's slashing. Mills had always been an able shooter, but the Ole Miss game—on the heels of his solid Auburn performance—raised his confidence a notch and gave him a sense of truly belonging that he'd never before enjoyed at UK. Even Epps seemed to prosper from the new alignment, embarking on his best scoring binge of the season—sixteen against Ole Miss and twenty-two against Georgia in the tournament final.

Tubby Smith's overachieving Bulldogs had reached the championship game by virtue of a 15-point upset victory over South Carolina. But that result said nothing of their chances against Kentucky; in the course of a single week, the Wildcats had amazingly, unmistakably become a superior team to the one that beat them for the regular-season conference title. The proof came in a 27-point drubbing of Georgia so thorough that Mills, of all people—whose expanding role was the very symbol of Kentucky's depth problems—outscored every player on the Bulldog roster, in the process reaching a career high (sixteen points) for the second straight game.

Ironically, Georgia had been the only major-conference school to offer Mills a scholarship out of Lexington's Paul Dunbar High School. Morehead State and a few other regional universities had places for him on their teams, and Louisville invited him for a campus visit—if Denny Crum had made an offer, Mills would have taken it—but Georgia was his big-time opportunity. The only reason he didn't go there was that it wasn't Kentucky. Mills was of a Big Blue bloodline; his father, Terry, was a mountain guard from Barbourville who played at UK with Dan Issel. Growing up in Somerset, Kentucky, and Rex Chapman's Rexington, filling up on his dad's old stories (his claim to fame, he said, was holding Pete Maravich to an average of about sixty-five), soaking up the spirit of the occasional games his father took him to, listening to Cawood in the kitchen . . . all Mills ever wanted to be was a Kentucky player. To make it happen, he took as many as five hundred shots a day in the back yard. He was not as attentive to his ball-handling, however—or his defense, or his weight. Those were the things, said Rick Pitino, that would prevent him from playing for the Wildcats.

The subject came up when Terry Mills went to see his friend, Bill Keightley, at Memorial Coliseum. The elder Mills was happy with the Georgia offer—he had been a graduate assistant under Georgia coach Hugh Durham at Florida State—but he knew what his boy wanted; that was why he asked, every evening when he got home, whether Cameron had shot the five hundred shots that day. Cameron Mills had been a good but not great high school player, making Kentucky's *academic* all-state team, and when his father laid out the scenario to Mr. Wildcat, Keightley knew immediately that it spelled walk-on. As the dad and the equipment manager talked about it, Billy Donovan, an assistant coach, happened into the room, one thing led to another, and the concept was carried upstairs to Pitino. Unable still to get a handle on the Bluegrass mentality, Pitino couldn't understand why the kid would want to walk on at Kentucky, where he would probably never play, when he could get a full ride to Georgia and shoot the ball to his heart's content. He told Cameron as much. He told him he was slow, couldn't guard, couldn't pass, and couldn't dunk. He tried his best to talk the otherwise bright young Kentuckian out of his crazy notion. Mills would have none of it. Ultimately, Pitino softened, telling the kid that if he wanted to come that badly, it could be accommodated, but he shouldn't expect to play. It was a deal.

And the deal was pretty much kept. For two years, Mills worked off his extra flesh, threw up a lot, mimicked the shooters of the upcoming opponent, and got off the bench only to high-five his teammates when they came to the sideline after another ferocious Kentucky run had forced the other side into a timeout; he considered that to be his job. Often, Pitino wouldn't even let him play in *practice*; he would become so exasperated with Mills's lack of conditioning that he would kick him out of the gym and make him run the treadmill or pedal the exercise bike for the rest of the afternoon. There were days when Cameron called home crying. But, bolstered every time by his parents' encouragement, he would not be run off—not even when, as an exercise in freshman hazing, his teammates stuffed him naked into a laundry bin and rolled him out into the coliseum halls, leaving him to somehow find a way back to his clothes.

In 1995-96, when Pitino had so much talent that he created a junior varsity team, Mills played on it with the understanding that he was not one of those for whom the team existed; it was for Nazr Mohammed and Oliver Simmons. At the end of his sophomore season, he had scored a total of sixteen varsity points, which, as a junior, he matched against Georgia in the final of the 1997 SEC tournament. Mills started to play real minutes—he had none against Clemson or Louisville, two in each of the last two regular-season road games—only when Allen Edwards became unavailable in addition to Derek Anderson and Jeff Sheppard. It was not until then that Joanne Pitino, Rick's wife, learned the name of the crewcut Kentuckian: For most of three years, she had called him "Chris"—Chris Mills being the Californian to whom the infamous Emery Express package had been sent.

Unnatural rivals: Although they lived a hundred miles apart, VanHoose and Lexington Catholic's David Graves (34) kept meeting this way.

○ ○ ○

As they rode two hours down the Mountain Parkway to Paintsville for the last game of the regular season, the Knights of Lexington Catholic High School had a chance to become the first undefeated Kentucky prep team in forty-nine years. That would require a state championship, of course, and probably two more victories over Paintsville, their likely first-round opponent in the Sweet Sixteen.

It was the second year in a row that Paintsville and Lexington Catholic had finished the regular season in the same gym. The parochial school had handily won the 1996 encounter, only to have its postseason prematurely ended by the mountain boys three weeks later. For the momentous Friday night occasion of the 1997 finale, Paintsville's gym capacity of

1,900—just less than half the town's population—was achieved during the junior varsity game, an hour and a half before the varsity tipoff. It was the biggest basketball game to hit town since John Pelphrey's team hosted Richie Farmer's in 1987.

For the local folks, round three with Lexington Catholic was an opportunity to reaffirm the precious pride they had in their basketball team. Although the Tigers had lost only three times and were on pace for the best record in school history, the season had not been entirely satisfying in light of the state championship that preceded it and the national ranking that fixed the community's expectations. The two defeats to Catholic and the Knights' perfect season added up to a hard fact—the other school had the better team—that could be dealt with here and now.

The pre-game excitement took over the town, an exception being the Fourth Street home of senior Josh McKenzie, whose grandmother had passed away earlier that day. Sensing his big forward's grief, Bill Mike Runyon knew that the Tigers would have to rely even more severely than usual on VanHoose and Tackett. He knew, also, that in the mountains—as opposed to Lexington and Richmond, the Central Kentucky cities where the teams had met earlier—the officials would not be as sympathetic toward the swiping and crowding that were accessories to Catholic's full-court, full-time press.

This was ultimately attested to by the thirty-two free throws that Paintsville ended up shooting, twelve by Tackett and another dozen by VanHoose, for whom the Knights had no other answers—especially in the fourth quarter, when Catholic was chasing the lead and Paintsville handled the press without a single turnover, thanks in large part to point guard Mike Short. VanHoose ended up with a career-high thirty-eight points to go with twelve rebounds and seven blocked shots, but it was Tackett on whom the game depended with eight seconds left to play. Paintsville was ahead by two, and his two free throws could close the deal. Uncharacteristically, he missed them both, but in a winning moment of redemption he stripped the ball from Catholic star David Graves and laid in the final two points of the Knights' first defeat.

Asserting themselves as they did against Kentucky's top-rated team permitted the Tigers to repossess the state-champs mentality that would serve them well in the district, regional, and state tournaments ahead. Another propitious sign for the Paintsville postseason was noted three days later by Bob and Beth VanHoose, who, as they pulled into their driveway, looked across the street and saw the McKenzies gathered around a trash can in the middle of their front yard. There were flames coming out of the trash can. Bob knew immediately what it was all about. Josh's mother had promised her brawny son that when he passed his college entrance exam—there had been some anxious moments despite his good record as a student—they would have a little ceremony in the yard and burn all his old results and study papers. McKenzie's preoccupation with passing the test had distracted him somewhat from his basketball tasks; now, with the ACTs behind him, he could give the Tigers the full benefit of his considerable rebounding, passing, and shooting skills.

VanHoose also got something out of the way after the Catholic game, driving with his family to Bloomington, Indiana, to visit IU and watch the Hoosiers play Northwestern. The Indiana coaches, aware of the stir over the prospect's height, measured J.R. at six-nine, and while they were sizing him up, Dan Dakich, the assistant who had spent so much time recruiting the Paintsville hero, asked him point-blank if he was a Hoosier. VanHoose smiled and said something about liking the program an awful lot.

The next weekend, Notre Dame head coach John MacLeod and South Carolina assistant Jeff Lebo, among others, found their winding way to Inez to observe VanHoose in Paintsville's two district tournament games at Sheldon Clark High School, from which the Tigers, as expected, advanced to the Region 15 spectacle in Pikeville. Their meager enrollment had not proven to be a significant handicap within the five rural counties that sent their best teams to the celebrated mountain regional; in fact, five of the eight schools that made it to Pikeville played Class "A" (small-school) football, keeping alive Eastern Kentucky's colorful underdog tradition. Many of the tiny teams that over the years made Region 15 famous in the commonwealth—Inez, Wayland, Flat Gap, Meade Memorial, Oil Springs, Van Lear, Warfield, McDowell, Wheelwright, Maytown, Feds Creek, Johns Creek, et al.—had long since consolidated into larger county high schools, but when the first week of March arrived in 1997, the spacious Pikeville gym still found room for Phelps, Prestonsburg, Elkhorn City, Paintsville, and the host team.

Pikeville, tucked into the Eastern corner of the state, near the Virginia and West Virginia lines, was a town like Paintsville in many ways—

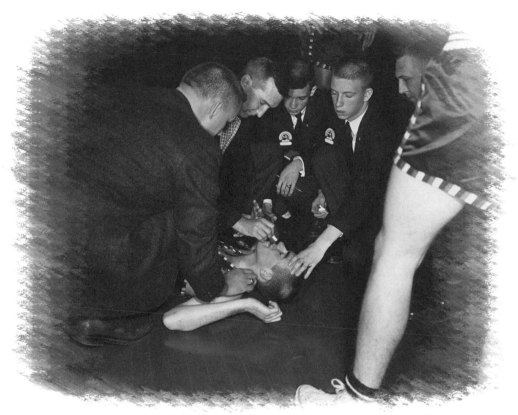

John Bill Trivette (second from left) of Pikeville: His exhausting full-court press was a forerunner of Pitino's.

a little bigger and, due to the presence of Pikeville College, perhaps more sophisticated. Its public school system, like Paintsville's, was among the best in the state, and its economy, like Paintsville's, benefited from the professional services required by the coal industry that surrounded it. The high school itself stood in the shadow of a towering monument to coal—the prodigious, six-story Pikeville National Bank.

Although it hadn't been to the Sweet Sixteen in more than twenty years, Pikeville's basketball tradition was considerably deeper than Paintsville's. This was owing almost entirely to a legendary mid-century coach named John Bill Trivette, whose fearful full-court press—a precursor to Rick Pitino's nearly fifty years later—was so effectively innovative that Joe B. Hall once quizzed him about its technical aspects.

"Let's start with the stance," said Hall, curious about the positioning of the hands and the angles of the knees.

"Oh, I don't know," replied Trivette. "I just tell 'em to hunker down and get after their butts."

In a later, longer interview, Trivette was somewhat more expansive about the defense that helped him win seven 15th Region titles and numerous Sweet Sixteen games (but never a state championship) between 1949 and 1959.

"I called it an all-court press," said the mountain icon. "What it was was a system [like Pitino's] where we would double- and triple-team, use the sideline, the middle line, and the end line as another defensive player. A system of shooting gaps between players to gain possession of the ball. My idea on this press was maybe we couldn't play [many of Pikeville's players had been smoking since they were six years old, and not one of them was taller than 6-2], but maybe we won't let the other team play, either.

"It was something I came up with from watching another team play against us. We played this little team, and they were always where they wasn't supposed to be against our set system of play. Every time we'd run something, they'd be in the way. They made us look bad without even tryin' to. I was a young coach, and like most young coaches I wanted to look good. We beat 'em, but they made us look bad. From that, I said to myself, says I, 'If they can do that and not knowing what they're doin', if I systematize that, I can make a lot of young coaches look foolish and maybe that will change the style of play a great deal in basketball today.' Of course, I've heard a lot of coaches say they were the one that came up with the press. But I don't think they were. I just have to say that they're not knowin' of what they speak. I think they're barkin' up a gum stump."

It was poignantly ironic that the system for which Rick Pitino seemed to require athletic, contemporary-style players was originated—arguably—in the Eastern Kentucky mountain town where Beth VanHoose worked five days a week and her 6-9 son hunkered down, in John Bill Trivette's terminology, to do battle in the 15th Region. Who would guess, watching Pitino's teams press and trap and fling themselves tirelessly around the floor, that what they were playing was actually mountain basketball?

John Bill Trivette had since passed away, but his son, Ken, was the director of the 1997 regional, and the old coach's wife, who once bonked a referee on the head with her handbag, was one of the honorees on Friday night, when they trotted out the fifty greatest players from fifty years of the 15th region. The Fabulous Fifty was a remarkable collection of mountain luminaries, Kentucky legends, and national scoring leaders, the likes of Grady Wallace of Betsy Layne (who led the country in collegiate scoring while at South Carolina) and Wayland's King Kelly Coleman (who, not surprisingly, declined the invitation to attend the event). The names themselves, many of them still painted onto tilting mailboxes in hollers all over the five counties, were like a mountain lyric: Couch and Castle and Conley and Adkins and Burchett and Butcher and Ratliff and Stepp . . . enough Stepps, actually, to make an entire team, including the once-famous Ervin of Phelps, who averaged more than fifty points a game over *two years*.

There were a few among the active players who might have been included in the galaxy had the guidelines permitted—VanHoose, of course, and possibly Tackett and Allen Central's Thomas Jenkins, a 6-5 all-state forward who was Paintsville's principal problem in its opening game of the tournament. Allen Central was a Floyd County school that had resulted from the consolidation of four smaller ones along the Right Fork of Beaver Creek in Floyd County—Garrett, Maytown, Martin and Kelly Coleman's Wayland. Independently, the four tiny mountain schools had been to the Sweet Sixteen nine times, but together it took them twenty-two years to get back, which Allen Central had done exactly once. When Coach Runyon found somebody who could hold down Jenkins—surprisingly, it was Paintsville's little point guard, Mike Short—it became apparent that the Runnin' Rebels would not be making another trip right away.

The Tigers' Friday night opponent was the host team, Pikeville's Panthers, who, by all appearances, must have been something special to be worthy of the gorgeous facility in which they played—there was a glassed-in weight room above and beyond one of the baskets, which served as the tournament skybox—and the award-winning, picture-perfect cheerleaders who gave them their all. But Paintsville's nine-man pep band (the electric guitar made it sound bigger) had considerably more about which to blow its horns when the state champs went up by twenty in the first half and won without a worry.

The victory earned the Tigers a spot in the regional final against Prestonsburg or Elkhorn City, which had recently lost a close game at home to national powerhouse Oak Hill Academy of Virginia. Runyon, scouting the other semifinal contest in a nicely cut gray sports jacket and spitting tobacco juice into a Long John Silver's cup, observed that the

Virginians' difficulties with the little Pike County school might have had something to do with the fact that they shot about four free throws to the home team's thirty. More impressed with Prestonsburg, he expected an opportunity to avenge Paintsville's earlier defeat to the Blackcats, when VanHoose had been unable to play. In fact, it was likely that the Tigers would consecutively encounter the only teams that had beaten them all season—Prestonsburg in the regional championship and Lexington Catholic in the first round of the Sweet Sixteen that followed.

Prestonsburg came through on its end, but when the VanHooses arrived back in Paintsville late Friday night, a neighbor phoned to tell them that Paul Dunbar had upset Lexington Catholic in Region 11. Unable to believe it, Beth called the Hazard television station to verify the news. The next morning, she and Bob were both out of bed at 6 a.m. to check the score one more time in the paper.

With Catholic out of contention for the state championship, the Knights' 6-6 junior, David Graves, showed up under the Paintsville basket Saturday night to banter with VanHoose and Tackett as they warmed up for the Prestonsburg game. The basketball lives of Graves and his classmate, Shawn Fields, ran basically parallel to those of the Paintsville pair—the four juniors were all major-college prospects—and consequently the rivalry between the two Kentucky powers had become a sociable one. This was in sharp contrast to the one between Paintsville and its Floyd County opponent in the regional final. It rested uneasily with the Paintsville players that they had never beaten Prestonsburg, having been in elementary school when the big fight broke out and suspended the series.

The regional final would prove not nearly so contentious; it was scarcely contended. VanHoose, working smartly in a high-low post with the senior who lived across the street (in Paintsville's spirited cheering section, the girlfriends of both VanHoose and McKenzie were wearing Tiger T-shirts they had bought that afternoon at Johnnie LeMaster's sporting goods store, with their boyfriends' names and numbers on the backs), scored and rebounded virtually at will in the first quarter, which ended when he put back a shot at the buzzer to make the score 22-2.

A curious second foul on VanHoose—as a Prestonsburg player drove toward him, the Paintsville center actually stepped backward to avoid contact—got him out of the game for a while and helped the Blackcats close briefly to within fourteen points, but McKenzie came up big and

Tackett hammered down a left-handed dunk to punctuate an eventual 29-point victory that sent Paintsville back, on a roll, to the Sweet Sixteen.

Its first-round opponent there would be Lexington Catholic's conqueror, Paul Dunbar, which was led by Cameron Mills's 6-foot-7 little brother, Collier. The fabled tournament would start the following Thursday at Rupp Arena, which, for as long as the Tigers lasted, would accommodate most of Paintsville's population in one of its corners.

To make it easy for the folks, school was called off Thursday and Friday.

○ ○ ○

At Dickman's Sports Cafe in Northern Kentucky, a sprawling, off-road bar and grill lit up like a juke joint in the bayou, the score on the scoreboard was still 76-67, as it had been nearly a year earlier when the final buzzer signaled the University of Kentucky's sixth national championship. It was a rainy, moonless Thursday night, and the televisions were tuned to a first-round NCAA tournament game between Fairfield and North Carolina that would not have interested the Kentucky people except for three things: it was college basketball; Dean Smith had an opportunity that night to tie Adolph Rupp's record for career victories; and North Carolina was losing. Late in the game, North Carolina was still losing.

The Tar Heels would ultimately win, of course, and Smith—who, like Rupp, played and learned the game under Phog Allen at Kansas—would surpass the old Kentucky coach the next time out against Colorado, but in the meantime it pleased the basketball patrons of Dickman's and the rest of the commonwealth to watch him squirm against the bottom-seeded team in the East Regional. ("It'll kill me in the pool," said the man in the sweater to the woman with the country-music hair, "but I don't care.") It pleased them even more to watch what the Cats did to Montana later that night in Salt Lake City.

For the second game in a row, Cameron Mills—*Cameron Mills!*—outscored everyone on the opponent's roster. This time, making good on five of seven three-point attempts (he was so deep into his zone that the shouting across the commonwealth commenced whenever he touched the ball), he outscored everyone on Kentucky's roster, also, except for Wayne

Turner, who matched him with nineteen points. It was the third straight game in which Mills had established his own career high in scoring, and he did it in twenty minutes on the floor.

The streak ended two days later—the day Rupp dropped to second in victories—when Iowa held Kentucky's newest hero to eleven points. Those eleven, however, were points that the Cats could not have done without. The game was in jeopardy until the final half-minute, when Turner and Scott Padgett stepped up to steady an otherwise wobbly 75-69 victory. It was not coincidental that most of Iowa's damage was done by a proficient guard, Andre Woolridge, whose twenty-nine points were another reminder that, as long as Derek Anderson remained on the bench, the Cats could be attacked from the backcourt.

Anderson had been working out lightly and regularly, shooting well and dunking when he felt like it. He had not been put through the rigorous paces of a Rick Pitino practice, but when the Wildcats arrived in San Jose for the West Region semifinals, the irrepressible senior could stay off the floor no longer. On Monday, March 17, he told the coach he was ready to give it a whirl. Pitino double-checked with the team physician, Dr. David Caborn, and was satisfied that Anderson's knee was up to the task. As the practice unfolded, he couldn't believe what he was seeing. "It was the biggest surprise in my twenty-two years of coaching," Pitino said that night on his "Big Blue Line" show. "I was astonished. I was taken aback. It's all the coaches have been talking about all day. We were all blown away by it."

The question that followed was inevitable. Would Anderson play again before the season was over?

"We're gonna cross that bridge when we come to it," Pitino replied. "I will say this: He practiced with us today full-out, no holds barred. And he was the best player out there. It was as if he never left, he was never injured. He dominated the practice. And we practiced harder today than we would play in a game. After all that time off, to not even favor his knee . . . to physically get in there and grind it out . . . to come in and dominate practice the way he did . . . it's astonishing to me.

"He's close to being a hundred percent. We'll see what happens come Thursday. If we need him, I'll play him . . . He could possibly play on Thursday (against St. Joseph's). I'll see after a few more practices."

If there was still doubt in Pitino's mind, there was none in Anderson's.

At one stage of the Monday workout, after Anderson had quick-stepped to the basket and beaten his startled defender, he looked up at announcer Ralph Hacker in the stands, smiled, and announced, "I'm back."

Though obviously titillated by the prospect of having his play-maker in the lineup again, Pitino checked his enthusiasm long enough to get the opinion of a few more experts. Knowing that such a quick return—two months after the ACL tear—would put

Lookin' good: Pitino was so pleased with the way the Cats played in March that he called them his favorite Kentucky team.

Anderson in uncharted territory, the coach took the extra precaution of consulting some of his medical friends in New York and, while he was in the Bay Area, the team physician for the San Francisco 49ers and Oakland Raiders, Dr. Arthur Ting.

The forthcoming opinions persuaded Pitino to come down on the conservative side. It was not an examination of Anderson's knee that ultimately swayed the Kentucky coach, but the fact that he would be playing fast and loose with a young man's career by permitting him to take a risk that no athlete had ever before taken. Two days after informally broadcasting that Anderson would probably play before the tournament was over, Pitino formally and definitively declared that he wouldn't, informing the team in a private meeting and the media in a news conference. "The doctors made the decision by giving me the research and the data," he said. "With that in mind, I decided I should treat Derek the way I would treat my son. This [playing him two months after his injury] would never get FDA approval."

It would, however, have received DA approval. For two months, Derek Anderson had been toiling and praying for the March day when the frenetic pursuit of back-to-back national championships would once again soak the blue and white shirt on his back. "When Coach said I couldn't play," he confided later, "that kind of messed me up. To be truthful, that was harder to get over than being hurt in the first place. I was confused. George [Anderson's uncle/father] was telling me, 'Go on what you feel.' He saw me work out and he said, 'You're fine. Maybe you could go ten or twelve minutes.' If it had been left up to me, I'd have gotten in. When Coach told me I wouldn't be playing, I didn't say anything. As we went along, I'd give him little hints like, 'I'm gonna get me some steals tonight.' But he wasn't going for it.

"I definitely felt I could have gone out there," Anderson said. "Every morning I'd wake up mad, but then I'd try to be Coach Pitino and put myself in his shoes. I felt bad because I felt I was able to do something for the team. If I'd been able to play, we wouldn't have lost to South Carolina twice, I'll tell you that. But for my future and for Coach's sake, the best thing was not to play. He just felt he didn't want to make that kind of mistake with somebody's career."

Pitino's decision, mostly applauded around the country for the healthy perspective it represented, was not a landslide winner in the commonwealth. One letter that arrived on his desk from Winchester, Kentucky, encouraged the New Yorker to go ahead and take the Boston Celtics' job because he wasn't needed anymore in the commonwealth. In Paintsville, a customer at the frame shop next to Cheryl's Restaurant grumbled that UK deserved a return on its investment in Anderson. And on the fervently pounded keyboards of the Cat Chat community, the Big Blue aficionados were unconvinced that Pitino's decision was as final as he said it was. Tom Baker, for one, was growing weary of the precedents in this regard:

It is becoming increasingly difficult to separate fact from fiction in Pitino's pronouncements. Who knows? While I only want what's best for DA, I must admit that if Pitino were in the office with me right now I'd probably try to choke the little Italian for putting me through this roller coaster over the past 24 hours!!!

I will respect RP's decision. He has made a remarkable journey in realizing what this team means to the people of Kentucky and surely he knows what saying DA will play, followed by saying he will not play, does to the people in the state. I just wish he would be more honest with what is going on. Show me the truth!!!

Frank Dudley Berry, on the other hand, expressed the viewpoint of those who were willing to give Pitino a wider berth.

People, we get so caught up in rumors and speculation that we take it personally if our druthers don't pan out. We know that everything Rick says in front of a microphone is a calculated strategy, never to be taken literally. And until we know for sure, we should probably save all our judgments and knee-jerks. I personally would be scared to death to put Derek in a game. It's more than a game to him, it's his dreams and his life that are at stake.

And Andy Roberts, finding a common ground for objectivity and provincial pride, tried to distance himself from the moment in order to view the bigger picture as it related to the winningest basketball program in the NCAA.

I've watched the debate rage on about Rick's decision not to play Derek Anderson, and I think everyone that has posted on this has their perspective all wrong. The decision to play DA or not is one of those that will put a mark on the University of Kentucky basketball program for years to come.

Think for a moment about UK's place in the college sports world and especially its place in NCAA history. The fallout from Rick P.'s choice to play DA or not will mark UK, its basketball program and the administration as surely as a flying chair can scratch the gym floor in Puerto Rico. If DA plays, whether or not UK wins or DA gets hurt again, the reputation of UK as the school that would potentially sacrifice someone's kids to try to win a national championship would be firmly established.

Kentucky appears to have made the choice to be the school that will do what is best for the kids involved even though it might hurt its chances to win a national championship one more time. I'm glad that win or lose, UK will be remembered as the school that cares for its players as people more than it cares about the wins.

Whatever went into his hard decision, Pitino's resolve was challenged the very afternoon he made it, when X-rays revealed that Allen Edwards had sustained a stress fracture in his ankle. In one hapless day, two versatile, slim, 6-5 Wildcats had passed across Kentucky's horizon. But the coach didn't flinch. Eschewing a last-ditch opportunity to turn Anderson loose, he instead made Epps the starting two-guard and moved up Cameron Mills in the rotation. With that, Mills was no longer a fuzzy little story: he was the first guard and best shooter off the bench for the defending national champions.

In fact, Mills was proving to be the best shooter in the NCAA tournament. Against a resourceful St. Joseph's team, he once again scored nineteen points—matching Ron Mercer—in twenty minutes and continued the most remarkable rally of three-point marksmanship anyone could remember, making five of six long ones to run his unthinkable roll (beginning with the South Carolina game) to 25 of 37.

By the time the Cats lined up against Utah—the nation's second-ranked team—in the regional final, the erstwhile high-fiver had become a marked man. While the Kentucky coaches devised an aggressive double-teaming defense to hold down the All-American forward, Keith Van Horn, Utah's Rick Majerus was busy trying to work up a scouting report on the kid whom Pitino had said couldn't run, guard, pass, dunk, or dribble.

By focusing on Mills, the Utes prevented the Lexington junior from attempting any of his specialties, but in the process lost track of Mercer, who popped off screens and found room for fifteen points in a first half ending with Kentucky ahead 34-24. The Cats had drummed Utah out of the tournament the year before, and with Mercer significantly outplaying Van Horn—whose highly rated draft prospects were similar to his—it appeared as though they had their opponent's number once again.

But Utah devised a way to circumvent Kentucky's pressure in the second half, and with more than nine minutes left to play, the score was tied at 43. Sensing that the season was slipping away prematurely, Pitino called a time-out and drew a line down the middle of his chalkboard. To the left of the line, he wrote, "Winner." To the right, he wrote, "Loser." Then he elaborated on the two options and gave the fellows their choice.

What ensued was a 72-59 Kentucky victory that sent Derek Anderson bounding onto the floor with six seconds left—unannounced and unofficial—to hug Wayne Turner (it was the point guard's twenty-first birthday) and shout in his ear, "God is good." The first Wildcat up the ladder to cut off a piece of the net, Anderson scurried down to join arms with Mills and Turner and Mercer and the rest of his teammates and the UK cheerleaders, swaying and attempting feebly to sing to the tune of *My Old Kentucky Home*. The improbable Wildcats were in the Final Four once again.

"This is my all-time favorite Kentucky basketball team," Pitino declared two nights later on the "Big Blue Line". "They're immature, they're green, and it doesn't matter. I'm kind of blown away by them. The Unforgettables, I was surprised at how well they did but I kind of knew why. Pelphrey, Farmer, and Feldhaus were all about twenty-three and Mashburn was a superstar. But I can't believe what this team has accomplished."

The Final Four would be played out three hours down the road in Indianapolis, where the Kentucky season began more than four months earlier with an overtime loss to Clemson. UK's semifinal opponent would be Minnesota, with North Carolina—Smith was adding to his new victory record—taking on Arizona in the opposite bracket. The potential matchups were compelling: Minnesota was coached by Clem Haskins, a black rural Kentuckian whom Rupp had chosen not to recruit in the mid sixties, and a championship game between UK and North Carolina—the nation's second winningest team, with whom Pitino pulled out of a contract in 1990 because he didn't think his program was ready to compete successfully at the Tar Heels' level—would give the Wildcats a chance to win one for the Baron; they couldn't get his record back, but they could avenge its capture.

Curiously, though, as the media gathered in Memorial Coliseum for one last round of interviews before the Cats headed off on the last leg of their unlikely journey, it wasn't the Clem Haskins angle that fascinated them the most, or the Dean Smith story line, or the prospect of back-to-back championships. It was the fact that Kentucky had reached this point 1) without Derek Anderson, and 2) with Cameron Mills.

Postseason hero: Kentucky basketball, said Mills, is sacred.

Up until the day that Pitino made his fateful announcement, Anderson had believed—it was his optimistic nature to believe—that this would be his time. Barring an emergency situation, he never really expected to play against St. Joseph's or Utah; the cross hairs of his ambition had been fixed all along on the Final Four. Since the end of January, his intention had been to ride into Indianapolis like the cavalry and preserve the national championship for all of Kentucky. In the back of his mind—the very back—he still harbored that hope. He continued to work out with the rest of the guys. His knee felt good. Everything said yes but the coach.

Even in his absence, Anderson was still the figure around whom the Kentucky team revolved. His injury had been its defining moment; the talent he took to the bench had represented the handicap it had to somehow surmount; the spirit he maintained had provided the inspiration it needed to persevere under difficult circumstances; and the players who stepped into the void he created on January 18—Cameron Mills being last and chief among them—had fast become the latest heroes in the perpetuating epic that was Kentucky basketball.

For Mills, the transformation began at the conference tournament and became complete at the regional in San Jose, where the national press recognized him as walking, talking folklore—the quintessential Kentucky boy living out the indigenous dream. It was no different back home. As the Cats spread themselves around the Coliseum grandstand for home-cooked questioning, even the local media engulfed Mills with warm, smiling queries about the fantasy camp that had turned into his life.

"Cameron, what were you doing this time last year, when the team was getting ready to play UMass in the Final Four?"

"I was firing up some threes in practice, pretending to be [UMass guard Carmelo] Travieso."

"Cameron, being a big part of the team, like you are now, does it make this season a lot more enjoyable for you than last year?"

"Hey, I was happy last year . . . If I had sat the bench all my years here, I'd probably have been disappointed but satisfied. Satisfied that I was part of Kentucky basketball for four years."

"Cameron, considering what you guys have achieved this year—guys like yourself and Padgett and Epps—when the team wasn't really given much of a chance after Derek got hurt, do you think there's something about Kentucky players playing harder?"

"Sure there is. You'll do anything to be a Wildcat. When you put on that uniform, there's so much tradition here, you want to live up to it. Kentucky basketball is something sacred. I think when you are raised in Kentucky and know what Kentucky basketball means to this state . . . other guys don't know what it means to this state. They don't understand what these kids growing up think about us, individually and as a team. The second you put on that jersey, you're a totally different person. You're representing something great. I think when you're from Kentucky, you're willing to go out there and throw up and run till you drop and do whatever it takes because of what's on your jersey."

"Cameron, does it seem odd to you now that, all of a sudden, there are boys in their driveways all over Kentucky who are shooting baskets and pretending to be you?"

With that one, the former walk-on looked up, tilted his head, and squinted in such a way as to suggest that the concept was one he hadn't previously contemplated.

"Really?"

9

Overtimes

The state of Kentucky needed a fellow like J.R. VanHoose to come along every so often—not just to perpetuate its tradition of schoolboy legends, mountain or otherwise, but to preserve one of its most precious natural resources.

What VanHoose had done, in concert with his consummately able teammates, was make Paintsville the latest in a celebrated succession of small schools to save the Sweet Sixteen as it is known and cherished across Kentucky. Before the big center's history-making performance led the Tigers to the 1996 state championship, there had been more than sufficient reason to doubt whether a place so tiny would ever again be able to surmount the forbidding odds against it. The days of Carr Creek, Inez, and Cuba had faded deep into folklore. Since the state tournament was integrated in 1957, only two undersized, Cinderella schools—Earlington in 1967 and Edmonson County in 1976—had managed to go all the way.

In the years leading up to Edmonson County's unexpected triumph, there had been a movement in the state's sparsely populated areas to establish separate postseason championship tournaments based on enrollment. Male High School of Louisville had won three state titles between 1970 and 1975 and the large urban schools in general had commanded the field for most of two decades. By restoring the commonwealth's faith in the underdog, Edmonson County, a near-Western Kentucky school with just five hundred students—nearly twice the size of Paintsville—bolstered the weakening timbers of the Sweet Sixteen

◀ *Valley girls: In 1956, Valley High School's cheerleaders were lifted off the floor by the spirit of the Sweet Sixteen.*

and kept it structurally sound for another generation. The faith had begun to sag again when VanHoose and his stalwart mountain confederates arrived with a fresh load of lumber and another coat of paint.

The charm and enormous popularity of the Sweet Sixteen—Kentuckians called it "The Greatest Show on Earth"—was closely tied to its David-Goliath aspects. Unlike most state tournaments, where survivors from four regions come together at one location to beget a champion, Kentucky's system accommodates an engaging diversity through four rounds of geographical matchups. The state is divided into sixteen regions, which are numbered beginning in the far Western corner of the state and snaking around contiguously to the other end. The 2nd Region, lake country that links Illinois to Tennessee, might encounter the urban 7th or the mountainous 14th at any point along the way. Such is the randomness of the pairings that Paintsville's 1996 state title was won against an Ashland team barely an hour's drive from home. The matchups could produce anything: In the late eighties, Richie Farmer and his country cohorts from Clay County represented Eastern Kentucky in consecutive finals against Louisville Ballard, splitting the series; but a Louisville team could just as easily find itself playing another Louisville team in the championship game. And it is not just the end of the tournament that proves so compelling so often: the entire spectacle is a mix-and-match collage of tobacco versus bourbon, coal versus horse, lake versus mountain, bluegrass versus street, city versus country, big versus small.

For decades, the Indiana state tournament prospered famously under similar circumstances, its symbol of the small-town underdog being Milan High School, whose state championship in 1954 inspired the movie, *Hoosiers.* But even Indiana had decided, controversially, to abandon the one-class concept in favor of separate tournaments for schools of varying sizes after 1997, surrendering to the apparent fact that there were no Milans or Paintsvilles remaining in the Hoosier state.

In Kentucky, however, the Sweet Sixteen would endure into the new century as an annual reminder of a lifestyle that had long and colorfully characterized the commonwealth. Since 1928, when Carr Creek's outlandish accomplishments reverberated in a mountain echo that was heard around the country, all of Kentucky had endorsed basketball as a grand device for the raising of the regional spirit. Consequently, the state clung dearly to the overachievers from its most inobtrusive outposts—to the

"The Greatest Show on Earth": In 1961, like every other year, Kentuckians called off school, took vacation days from work, and gathered en masse at the Sweet Sixteen.

likes of Midway, a horse-country settlement whose farm boys won the state championship in 1937 without a starter over 5-10. In 1932, the Lexington crowds took a shine to a 51-student school from the western end of Kentucky called Birmingham, whose leading guard was a 5-foot-2-inch redhead named McCoy Tarry who rode to school in a buggy. Birmingham lost in two overtimes to Louisville Male, but sixteen years later the unforgettable Tarry, by then a checkers champion at the local general store, was back with an undefeated team representing the little Western Kentucky town of Brewers, which he coached to a Sweet Sixteen title while sitting on a bag of basketballs and chewing viciously on his necktie. Hazel Green, the gymless 1940 champion whose enrollment amounted to fifty-five mountain boys, was led by a 115-pound guard named Woodrow Wilson Parker Patton whose signature shot was an underhanded heave from half-court. In time, the entire commonwealth would be apprised of Howie Crittenden's fanciful dribbling and the fact that Johnny Cox spent winter nights asleep on the floor of the Hazard gym.

Kentucky adored this resonant drama to such an extent that the Sweet Sixteen outgrew one facility after another, moving from Danville to UK's Alumni Gym to Louisville's Armory to Memorial Coliseum to Freedom Hall to Rupp Arena. In 1957, while a capacity Memorial Coliseum crowd of 11,500 watched Kentucky play Michigan State for a trip to the Final Four, more than 18,000—the largest crowd ever to see a basketball game south of the Mason-Dixon line—gathered at Freedom Hall to see Lexington Lafayette defeat Louisville Eastern for the state high school championship. In 1982, the 21,342 Kentuckians who showed up at Rupp Arena to see Virgie (near the Virginia line) take on Mason County (on the Ohio line) established a world record for a high school game. In 1987, when Richie Farmer played in his first Sweet Sixteen final, attendance for the four-day tournament topped out at more than 140,000.

After Farmer moved on to UK, the crowds gradually declined, an exception being 1993, when Anthony Epps's Marion County team defeated Cameron Mills and Dunbar in the title game. By then, the prospect of another fairy-tale finish had become so remote that tournament officials had become concerned for its well-being. Thus it was that Paintsville's remarkable run in 1996 was celebrated with front-page banner headlines in Kentucky newspapers. And thus it was that the commonwealth felt beholden to J.R. VanHoose for leading his band of Appalachian boys to one state title and bringing them back for a crack at another.

Even without Lexington Catholic in the field, however, Paintsville's defending champions did not enter the 1997 Sweet Sixteen as the forecasters' favorites. That distinction was accorded Eastern High School of Louisville, which inaugurated the tournament by taking the floor against Wayne County after the opening invocation: "We are in the building of a champion and we will crown another," said the minister to bowed heads at Rupp Arena. "But on Sunday morning, we have the opportunity to honor a true champion, Jesus Christ our savior."

Four months earlier, Eastern had begun its season with an astonishing 156-70 victory over Doss High School, Derek Anderson's alma mater. By Christmas, the stylish Eagles were averaging more points than any team in the NBA or NCAA—and were doing it largely with defense. Their scoring pace had moderated to a season's average of just over ninety a game, but in the maiden match of the Sweet Sixteen they demonstrated enough speed and dazzle to thoroughly befuddle poor Wayne County, which responded with thirty-nine turnovers.

Paintsville debuted a day later against Dunbar, which featured Collier Mills, Eric Burton—both of them brothers of big-time NCAA shooters (Burton's brother, Darnell, was a three-point artist for Cincinnati)—and sophomore George Baker, a sizable guard who had been a major player in the upset regional victory over Lexington Catholic. Early in the game, the 6-7 Mills moved away from the basket in deference to VanHoose's shot-blocking and demonstrated a shooting touch not unlike his popular older brother's, but Paintsville's three-sided attack (VanHoose, McKenzie, and Tackett) staked the Tigers to a ten-point second-quarter lead. With that, VanHoose was whistled for two swift fouls and took his sixteen points to the bench. In his absence, Mills sneaked in for a putback at the halftime buzzer to bring Dunbar within five.

VanHoose's foul trouble continued in the second half, during which McKenzie and Tackett asserted their star qualities. In the end, J.R.'s twenty-seven points (his ten field goals in eleven attempts put him near the top of another Sweet Sixteen statistical list) were more than adequately supplemented by the fifty that his two all-region teammates split evenly between them. The three of them accounted for 76 of Paintsville's first 81 points, but with a twenty-point victory, Coach Runyon showed no concern over their disproportionate share of the scoring. "I think it's good," he said. "If it were two players, that would be a problem. But the floor is so many feet wide, and it's hard to defend three. By the way, Josh and Todd are pretty good players not to make the AP all-state team, aren't they?"

As the Paintsville players finished dressing, Runyon instructed them to get to their seats as soon as possible to watch the next game, the winner of which would play the Tigers the following night. "They're big," he warned, referring to the Owensboro Apollo team that was expected to beat Harrison County, as Paintsville had done in the Lexington holiday tournament.

If Runyon preferred to see Harrison County in the next round, he had plenty of company; for what the Thorobreds had endured to arrive at the Sweet Sixteen, they had become the tournament's sentimental favorites. Harrison County High School was located in Joe B. Hall's hometown of Cynthiana, north of Lexington along the Licking River, whose banks had been overwhelmed in the early March flooding. In Cynthiana and across the county, 450 homes had been lost or damaged by the flood, including two that belonged to the families of Thorobred players. The district championship game with Bourbon County, for which Harrison County qualified by beating Paris in overtime, was being played in Cynthiana on the Saturday night that the river began to rise. It was called at halftime so that the visitors could get out of town before the bridge was under water. (Harrison County and Bourbon were declared co-champions, which had no bearing on the regional tournament; the top two teams from each Kentucky district automatically advance to the region.) At Maysville in the regional final, which the Thorobreds reached by winning another overtime struggle, they trailed Clark County by one with a few seconds remaining and pulled out the game on a three-pointer from their 6-8 center, Rob Ogden. When the team returned to its soggy village that night, it was feted with a midnight pep rally that put tired smiles on a lot of beleaguered Kentucky faces.

Arriving with much ado at the Sweet Sixteen, the Thorobreds rose to the occasion with a solid 14-point upset victory over Apollo. With that, it was apparent that Paintsville would have to find a way to defend destiny, not to mention Ogden. A soft shooter and natural rebounder who was headed for Georgetown (Kentucky) College, Ogden showed up Friday night with his game intact, battling VanHoose in a skillful, straight-up confrontation that everyone but the referees seemed to appreciate. Respecting neither Ogden's karma nor VanHoose's historical significance, they called enough unpopular fouls on both of them to make the game temporarily centerless. The frustration of the opposing pivotmen was the product of heightened motivation, Ogden because it would be his last high school game if the Thorobreds lost and the final chance to make his mark against Kentucky's best player, and VanHoose because he was a history buff and history was what he and his teammates intended to make; no small school and no Eastern Kentucky school had ever won back-to-back state championships.

With less than four minutes to play, two free throws and a drive by VanHoose gave the Tigers the apparent security of a 42-29 lead—built largely on the shooting of Kyle Adams (the sixth man who had been a starter until Runyon began hearing him getting sick in the bathroom before every game)—but soon after, the Paintsville star drew his fifth foul while standing at midcourt with his arms up to receive a pass against the Harrison County press. The Thorobreds, still believing in their destiny, closed to within five points on a lob to Ogden, but Tackett's string of free throws in the last minute accounted for a 54-42 victory that reinstalled Paintsville as the fairy-tale favorite. Even the press applauded Harrison County as it came off the court for the final time.

Paintsville was now a pair of Saturday victories away from perhaps the most remarkable accomplishment in the history of the Sweet Sixteen. At least two of its principals—the coach and the center—were eminently aware of the amazing thing that could happen. They both realized that another state championship would immortalize Paintsville as the champion of all the little Kentucky towns that had shown all the big ones; it would ensure Runyon's eternal reputation as a miracle-working mountain coach; and it would make VanHoose so very special that not even Rick Pitino was big enough to turn him away.

Eastern was still in the tournament, however, having blown away Graves County—the Western Kentucky school that consolidated Cuba— and Paintsville's semifinal opponent would be a distinguished collection of young men from Northern Kentucky. A few months earlier, Highlands had won the Kentucky big-school football championship. Several of those athletes—in addition to big-time pitching prospect Eric Glaser—played for the Bluebird basketball team that took a 27-game winning streak into the Final Four and matched Paintsville's overall record at 33-3.

Rupp Arena was packed long before Paintsville and Highlands took the floor Saturday morning. In the first semifinal game, Eastern, with its killer rotation of nine spirited black players, delighted the nearly all-white Eagle cheerleading squad with a second-half blitz that put away Warren East. It was the first time in the tournament that Eastern had been challenged for even part of a game, but junior Jermaine Taylor—one of four Taylors on the roster—explained it. "We ain't a ten o'clock team," he said. Politically incorrect to a refreshing degree, the other Taylors and the Cowards—there were two of those—didn't hesitate to note their choice of opponent for the state championship game that evening. "We'd rather play Paintsville," said senior James Coward, his gold tooth flashing in the glare of the television lights, "since they got the man that's supposedly the best, VanHoose or whatever."

Paintsville was naturally turned out for the long-awaited Saturday, its amiable high-country citizens filling both levels of the corner nearest the Tiger bench with blue, white, and nervous optimism. Beth VanHoose, with her husky toddler, Alex, always at hand, found her good-luck seat next to the friend who had accompanied her through the two previous victories. Her taller son, meanwhile, initiated the big game in good stead, blocking the first jump shot of Glaser, Highlands' silky 6-6 pitcher.

Glaser's shot was nonetheless strategic for the football champs, whose plan was to bring J.R. away from the spot where he customarily dominated the backboards. The suburban Northern Kentuckians were banking on Glaser's significant shooting ability and the rebounding prowess of 6-6 sophomore Derek Smith, autumn's tight end. Glaser's shots began to fall, Paintsville's didn't, and the challengers took a fast 7-0 lead. VanHoose had three blocked shots by halftime, but Glaser and his pals just stepped back deeper, canned whatever they took, and carried a four-point lead into the locker room.

Paintsville's inevitable rally came at the end of the third period and beginning of the fourth, when McKenzie hit some three-pointers and VanHoose's putback with five minutes remaining put the Tigers ahead by eight. Two minutes later, the lead was down to four when VanHoose was cited for traveling as he caught a ball while lying on the floor and immediately pushed it away. The call was made by a Lexington official whose whistle could scarcely get a moment's rest. "That ref is taking over the game," remarked an usher who professed no rooting interest. "His wife must be home taping it for him." His eyes evidently not leaving VanHoose, the busy official—whom the Paintsville folks remembered none too fondly from the holiday tournament in Lexington—soon thereafter nailed the big man for a touch foul that gave Glaser two important free throws. But a driving bucket and two later foul shots by Tackett made it a six-point game with a minute to play, and the Tigers were on the verge of the Sweet Sixteen championship game for the second consecutive season.

The spread was still four with twenty-one seconds to play when Glaser launched a three-point attempt from behind the top of the key. The shot bounced off the rim, and as it did the whistle blew again, courtesy of Runyon's Christmas friend. The late foul was called on VanHoose, his fifth. Curiously, Glaser was awarded two shots—a foul on the three-

All the way: Todd Tackett's basket against Highlands put Paintsville on the verge of another Sweet Sixteen championship game.

point attempt, if that was the case (the ref advised the furious Paintsville coaching staff that it was indeed a shooting foul) should have yielded three free throws—and converted them both to make the score 64-62.

Paintsville would have to hang on without the reigning tournament MVP. That was certainly not an insurmountable task, especially after Tackett made a free throw with fifteen seconds remaining. Highlands was called for traveling—by the *other* official—the next time down the floor, which gave Paintsville the ball at midcourt with a three-point lead and ten seconds on the clock. The inbounds play called for McKenzie to pass to Tackett as the latter came off a screen. The screen was set, the pass was made, but as Tackett reached for it, Glaser rushed in, a crash ensued, and the Paintsville player went to the floor holding his groin. The Lexington ref made the call. Foul on Tackett.

As Glaser went to the line for two shots, Smith whispered for his smooth teammate to make the first one and throw the second one up there hard so that, in VanHoose's absence, he could rebound it and stick it the hoop. It happened just like that. Smith's putback tied the game, and when Adams's 22-footer at the buzzer went off the rim, the two valiant teams found themselves in semifinal overtime.

Paintsville had played frequently and occasionally well without VanHoose, but with the big fellow on the bench the Tigers had never rebounded aggressively enough to suit Runyon. All season long, he had screamed at them for standing around watching J.R. rebound. By overtime of the state semifinal game, he still wasn't finished. Paintsville couldn't stop Highlands—especially the athletic, inspired Smith—on the boards, and spent the overtime trying to make up for the deficiency. The last chance was Tackett's, with two free throws that could have tied the game with eight seconds to play—he had made two a minute earlier—but, despite his fearlessness in the clutch, he was not yet Reggie Miller. The first shot bounced off, and two subsequent free throws by Highlands' Dave Schulkers put an end to Paintsville's incredible two-year run, 74-71. One of the Bluebird players heaved the ball into the air, and before it came down the Lexington official had sprinted off the playing floor, past the shouting Paintsville coaches and the bawling Paintsville cheerleaders.

As the floor and benches cleared, J.R. VanHoose remained in the sideline seat he had occupied for the last five minutes and twenty-one seconds of the game. His head was in his hands, his face hidden from the Paintsville folks who solemnly watched the scene through the glaze of their own tears. Finally, a tournament administrator touched J.R.'s elbow and led him away.

When he had dressed and composed himself, VanHoose met the lingering members of the media in the corridor off the playing floor. "I'm gonna have to work on my defense next year," he said in the thick Appalachian tongue that had become familiar around the state. "Those refs . . . I mean, the fouls I got . . . I don't know . . . I kinda figured we'd end up winning it again this year."

Without Paintsville in the championship game that night, most of the revised figuring added up to Eastern, whose cocky but close-knit starters were so moved by the position in which they found themselves that they broke down crying during the pre-game playing of *My Old Kentucky Home*. But while Eastern had the strut and the stuff, Highlands had gained title-game experience in the football season and found enough reserve strength in its weary legs to compete vigorously for what its coach, John Messmer, called "the greatest high school championship in the nation." The Bluebirds hung with their faster opponent until the fourth quarter, when Eastern's pace ultimately took its toll in a 71-59 victory that returned the state championship to the big city.

Eastern's title, coupled with Paintsville's abdication, on the surface seemed to at once restore the status quo and dismiss the folksy science of small-town basketball. The Tigers had briefly indulged the Kentucky romantic in his belief that they, along with the Cubas and Carr Creeks of Sweet Sixteen history, were not fanciful aberrations; that, instead, they were heartening manifestations of the fundamental truth that there is something essentially productive about a small community where the kids grow up with each other and play wholesome games together. Paintsville's J.R. VanHoose and Josh McKenzie lived across the street from each other; Cuba's Howie Crittenden and Doodles Floyd were playing one-on-one before either of them could get the ball up to the basket; the Carr Creek boys were cousins. By their examples and memorable others, there seemed to be an inherent, tangible value to neighborly kinship: on Indiana's famous Milan team, four of the principal players grew up next to each other in an even tinier community a few miles outside town.

While that was all very nice, contemporary reality suggested something much different: Eastern was a large city school whose impressive collection of talent could be attributed, no doubt, to urban skills and the vast number of athletes from which coach Bryce Hibbard had to choose. Eastern's enrollment, after all, was 1,650—more than five times that of Paintsville's. Hibbard acknowledged that his advantages were built-in. "First," he said after the school had become the eleventh different one from Louisville to win the state championship, "I'd like to thank God for the talent he gave these young men."

It was interesting, though, that with all the able basketball players available to him, Hibbard selected four Taylors and two Cowards to wear Eastern's blue and white. What's more, the family connections were not the only ones that bound the Eagle players together. Most of them had started playing ball with each other as little guys at Jefferson Street Baptist Church and continued as teammates at Crosby Middle School. It was their connectedness and the memories of their rich boyhoods together that had made them cry at the playing of *My Old Kentucky Home*.

For all their hip-hop, the Eastern kids were in essence a small community within the larger one—in their different way, a true and traditional Kentucky champion. Basically, they were just Carr Creek uptown.

○○○

The last time he was in Indianapolis, Rick Pitino had left wondering whether his team would win more games than it lost in the 1996-97 season.

Upon his return nineteen weeks later, he thought that the loss to Clemson was probably an appropriate way for the Wildcats to begin the defense of their national title. "What they've done best," he said, drawing perspective from the extraordinary journey he had been privileged to captain, "has been not embracing any form of success from last year. They looked in the mirror and realized who they were and what they had lost. When they watched Antoine Walker, and he's a Rookie of the Year candidate, and Tony Delk was MVP of the tournament and the conference . . .

"On the talent level, if you line them up by position [against the other three teams in the Final Four], our point guard against their point guard and so on, we're probably only going to win at Mercer's position." All things considered, it was the improbability of what the Cats had accomplished that characterized them in the view of both the commonwealth and the coach. "These guys," he concluded, "are 'The Unbelievables.'"

Pitino, in the tradition of Adolph Rupp, was fond of bestowing nicknames upon his teams. This was the fourth one that had been worthy, and the third, along with The Unforgettables and Pitino's Bombinos (the other was the 1996 national champion, The Untouchables), to which distinction had been a matter of overachievement. Historically, the only nickname team comparable to those two was Rupp's Runts, which lost the famous NCAA championship game to Texas Western. But The Unbelievables had an opportunity to accomplish what neither The Unforgettables nor the Runts had been able to; they could win it all. It was conceivable—perhaps even likely—that if they did, they would be remembered more fondly than any team in Kentucky's singular history.

As it was, they were already way up there, having exceeded even the commonwealth's expectations to such a colossal degree that they pulled into Indianapolis unencumbered by the usual Kentucky baggage. The only thing left to settle about the season was the degree of amazing, which a victory over Minnesota would certainly raise a notch. Either way, the season-long saga was past the point where it could be diminished: The Unbelievables had so captivated the Kentucky community that, in the week leading up to the Final Four, the *Herald-Leader's* basketball Internet page, *KY Hoops*, registered *two million* hits.

As rare and refreshing as it was for a Kentucky team to enter a Final Four unburdened, there was a pending story line that would restore the extracurricular pressure for which the program was so famous: a first-ever championship showdown between Kentucky and North Carolina. In spite of the intense, traditional rivalries the Wildcats carried on with Louisville, Indiana, and the familiar foes of the Southeastern Conference, the team that really boiled Kentucky's blood was North Carolina. The reasons for this were manifold. It was North Carolina that jockeyed with UK for the all-time lead in victories. It was North Carolina's coach who surpassed Adolph Rupp as the winningest in history. It was North Carolina—and only North Carolina—that Kentucky couldn't seem to beat; the Tar Heels had gotten the best of UK six times in a row and led the all-time series 16-6. It was North Carolina that knocked UK out of the NCAA tournament in 1977 and 1995. It was North Carolina that Pitino had decided not to play anymore, effectively conceding to a program that he acknowledged—he was not a *Kentuckian*, after all—was superior. And, perhaps most important in the provincial view, it was North Carolina that the national media (which, Kentuckians observed, included a disproportionate number of UNC and ACC graduates) seemed to collectively boot-lick. The thing that stuck in the commonwealth's craw was the perception that North Carolina's was the more venerated, universally respected basketball team and Kentucky's—*the winningest of all-time!*—was somehow the reprobate wannabe. In Kentucky, basketball was all about respect, and the citizens of the commonwealth didn't cotton to some other state getting that which was rightfully theirs. It was particularly hard to swallow while knowing that Carolina had their number.

The *Herald-Leader's* unbiased basketball writer, Jerry Tipton, had struck a chord in Kentucky when, foreseeing a potential March 31 matchup in Indianapolis, he wrote a column lamenting the fact that the two great teams no longer played on a regular basis. For that, he placed the blame squarely in the Kentucky camp. "Put bluntly," Tipton wrote, "the Cats are too chicken to play North Carolina. The fear of losing caused UK to pull out of a contract with North Carolina in 1990." For reporting accurately and editorializing frankly, Tipton was publicly indicted for treason. One Kentucky fan, in a letter to the editor, branded him with the most ignoble of nicknames: Tar Heel Tipton.

Even among the comparatively rational Big Blue aficionados of Cat Chat, the Tar Heels were anathema. Early in the season, the subscribers conducted an informal poll that decisively revealed North Carolina as the team whose defeats they enjoyed most. "Just the thought of that baby blue gives me the hives," submitted Mike Rosenberg, a native Eastern Kentuckian who was living in the land of the Heels. "They offend all the sensibilities of my loyalties."

"I have despised UNC ever since the first time I saw the 4-corners offense as a kid back in the 70s," added Rick Suffridge, another Kentucky loyalist who had grudgingly taken up residence in North Carolina. "Having lived in Kansas, Kentucky, Indiana, South Carolina and North Carolina, I can say that UNC fans as a group are by far the most arrogant fans that I ever have known. Dean Smith, UNC, and to a lesser extent the ACC represent all that is pure, holy, and good in the world and everyone else is just a cut below in their eyes. It is really disgusting."

David Tulloch had the final word on the subject. "Every time Dean Smith loses," he wrote, "an angel gets its wings."

If that was the case, there was a cherub who made his first flight Saturday night. Before Kentucky and Minnesota took the floor of the RCA Dome, the Tar Heels had been upset 66-58 by a young, brash Arizona team—coached by Lute Olson, who had turned down the Kentucky job before Eddie Sutton accepted it—that had already knocked top-ranked Kansas out of the tournament.

For Kentucky, North Carolina's loss ensured that the Final Four would be a basketball tournament rather than a morality play. For Minnesota, though—in particular, for Minnesota's gentleman coach, Clem Haskins, and its sixth man, Kentucky native Charles Thomas--it contained some elements of the latter.

Haskins harbored no discernible grudges toward UK—his younger brother, Merion, had played ball there—but his mid-sixties memories

Young and Wildcats: Anderson and Epps enjoyed their Kentucky days to the fullest.

remained graphic nonetheless. As a member of Taylor County High School's first integrated class, he still had a clear picture of the nasty racial graffiti that greeted him when he showed up one day for basketball practice. And he hadn't forgotten UK's indifference toward him as a scholarship candidate. Having no options in Lexington—it would be six more years before Rupp was ready enough to sign Tom Payne—Haskins had joined Dwight Smith as the first black players at Western Kentucky, where he made All-American. The recollections of those years were bittersweet; he wished he had kept the letter he received from UK star Pat Riley in 1967, acknowledging the Hilltoppers as the best team in Kentucky and wishing them well as they set out to represent the state in the NCAA tournament.

Haskins had gone on to coach at Western Kentucky, and his subsequent success in taking Minnesota to its first-ever Final Four was rewarded with a semifinal encounter against the school at which he had not been welcome. It was a feeling that he semi-shared with his top reserve, a former Mister Basketball at Harlan High School who, responding to UK's disinterest in him, had repaired to Minnesota largely because it was far from Kentucky. Harlan itself, a staunch Eastern Kentucky coal-mining town and the proud home of Fabulous Five hero Wah Wah Jones, was conflicted in its rooting interest. Its roots were Big Blue, of course, but as the Final Four was set to commence, every teacher and most of the students at Harlan Elementary School were wearing pins bearing Charles Thomas's picture.

Thomas had established himself as a clutch player in Minnesota's two Midwest Regional victories. When asked by reporters about his fearlessness in the face of postseason pressure, he answered matter-of-factly that he had gained experience in a far more grueling, nerve-racking environment: the Kentucky state tournament. Thomas's steely performances stamped him as the typical Gopher; the hallmark of Minnesota's stellar season had been its mettle under pressure, its ability to reduce a basketball game to a few minutes of will. And that was the plan against Kentucky.

Kentucky's intention, meanwhile, was to use its full-court press to break down the Gophers' composure. On their first four possessions, and six of their first nine, the Big Ten champions were so disoriented that they turned the ball over to the Wildcats, who went to the locker room at halftime leading by five points and having never trailed. The lead expanded to eight in the second half but had been pared to four, with Kentucky reeling, when Haskins became enraged at an official's call, ripped off his coat, and stormed onto the playing floor, drawing a technical foul.

As soon as the technical was assessed, necks began craning in the Kentucky corners of the dome. Around the television sets in Indianapolis taverns—packed with Kentucky fans unprepared to pay three hundred dollars for an upper-level ticket—and on crowded couches throughout the commonwealth, people wearing blue sat up a little straighter, their eyes fixed on the Kentucky bench. Pitino was motioning for a player. The player was taking off his warmup jacket. The number was twenty-three. It was him . . . Derek Anderson was getting into the game. It was only to shoot the free throws, of course. Fresh from ten weeks of rest and rehabilitation, he made them both, then sat back down to the cheers and tears of those he could see and those he couldn't.

The Wildcats were a weary, hobbling team—Edwards was still only partially available and Mercer was struggling with cramps in his calves—and Anderson's cameo appearance was at least momentarily heartening, but Minnesota's spirit was not so easily subdued. The Gophers kept coming back until they had their first lead at 52-51 on a three-pointer by the wonderful Bobby Jackson, the Big Ten's Player of the Year. From his seat in the lower level, superfan Bob Wiggins rubbed the lucky penny he had found on the street in San Jose.

Whether it was Anderson's inspiration or Wiggins's penny or something Pitino said or the lettering across their shirts, the Wildcats at that point summoned whatever it was that had gotten them this far. They answered the Gophers with a mini-run of their own, the last five points coming from Kentuckians Padgett and Mills. A later three-pointer by Padgett ensured that Minnesota would not be coming back again, and the final score was 78-69.

An hour later, in the spacious party room of the nearby Radisson Hotel that served as UK's Indianapolis headquarters, a Big Blue guy with a microphone attempted futilely to lead the tired Kentucky folks in cheers. There was no response. Hours earlier, the same Kentuckians had paid fifty dollars for a buffet supper and pep rally with the UK cheerleaders (who, with mostly in-state talent, had just claimed their third straight NCAA cheerleading championship). The fans' enthusiasm had been at a peak. Now, the victory wagon having forded another river and the NCAA finals having been attained in a year in which they seemed unattainable, they sat quiet and spent. One comment seemed to circulate from table to table: "I can't believe they've gotten this far." The national championship, the perpetual object of every Cat fan's ambition, would be played out in two days, but satisfaction had already set in deeply. It was a rare Kentucky moment.

In the lobby outside the party room, contented Kentucky partisans tried to ignore a less introspective comrade who loudly implored the ACC to kiss his ass. As the boorish fellow moved on through, a young Kentuckian named Brian Gossage—who as a boy in Campbellsville had played basketball on Clem Haskins Boulevard—was so absorbed in his serenity that he seemed not to notice. The greatest moment of his life, said Gossage, was when he had played six minutes on the Rupp Arena floor as a walk-on at Eastern Kentucky University and took a charge from Jamal Mashburn. "They called it a blocking foul, but it was a charge. Anyway,

I was there." The second greatest moment might have just happened.

He played back the fresh memory. "There was a lot of commotion," he recalled, "and when I looked down and saw number twenty-three standing at the line, I felt light in the head. If my knees would have locked, I'd have been down. Seeing Derek come out and sink those free throws—that made my season."

Priorities: Basketball ranked way up there for Jason.

○ ○ ○

At 7 a.m. on the morning that Kentucky was to play Arizona for the national championship, Jason Ryan grabbed his keys to go to work and the key chain cracked. It was, of course, his UK key chain. He couldn't believe it. His last UK key chain—the one that played the Kentucky fight song and he held up to his wife's stomach when she was pregnant—had broken the year before on the day the Wildcats lost in the SEC tournament to Mississippi State. "Surely," he said to himself Monday morning, "this couldn't happen two years in a row." All day, he couldn't shake the horrible thought.

That night, Ryan met his friends at Hometown Pizza in Williamstown, where they watched most Kentucky games together. There was nothing to keep him home; he wasn't living with Charity anymore. The divorce proceedings had begun. He figured his preoccupation with UK basketball was maybe a quarter of the reason they broke up; Charity called it "an incredible factor" that significantly affected the amount of time and money they were able to share. "If it was between me and UK," she said, "he would choose UK." They got along much better after they separated, and he was a good father to Haley, their two-year-old daughter, to whom he planned to pass along his prized Pitino taco some day. Jason had not yet developed an interest in other women, however—not during basketball season. On the night of the Montana game, he was at an unfamiliar bar when a girl asked him to dance to a country song that was starting up. As they moved onto the floor, he naturally told her about his affinity for Kentucky. When she replied that she was a Cincinnati fan, he said, "nice dancing with you," and left her standing after the first verse.

He was more comfortable at Hometown Pizza, where everybody understood how he felt. The waitresses there knew to give him a wide berth if the game was close, and his friends were sensitive enough to do the same—even Tim Webster, a big fellow who had been known as "Ax" since the day at Grant County High School when he entered a junior varsity game for the first time with forty-five seconds remaining and fouled out at :12. For the championship game, the pizza people basically shut the place down and turned it over to Jason, Ax, and the guys. They were so regular there that two of them had actually bought the remote control for the television.

While Ryan and his Williamstown buddies settled in at the pizza parlor, two hours away in Mooresville, Wayne Washburn, the rabbit man and recruiting savant, was at home on the phone, as usual, calling the pregame radio show and predicting Kentucky by twelve to fifteen. On I-65, between Louisville and Indianapolis, Indiana troopers were busy handing out speeding tickets to northbound cars with Kentucky license plates. And in the upper reaches of the RCA Dome, a couple of Chicago friends and UK graduates, Diane Massie and Jill Rappis, were finding their way to the seats they had made certain were next to each other; two years before, they had gone separate ways for the season-ending loss to North Carolina and since then, in the superstitious spirit of personal responsibility that was indigenous to serious fans everywhere, had done their best to stick together for every tournament game. (Rappis's brother had played for Arizona in the seventies, but the loyalty to her alma mater was not negotiable. Her first fight with her boyfriend had occurred when he failed to give her the sympathy she felt she had coming after the Senior Day loss to South Carolina.)

Meanwhile, in Lexington, where blue flags hung from porches and (attached by suction cups) flapped on the hoods of cars and trucks all over town, the usual taverns had been full since late afternoon and another two thousand fans, seeking more comfort and less beer, gathered in the ballroom of the Radisson Hotel, where television sets had been positioned for every vantage point. As game time approached, the most ardent of the spectators ignored the obligatory pep rally and drew closer to the screens to hear what they suspected would be the latest anti-Kentucky remark from writer and ESPN commentator John Feinstein, whom they placed in the top rank of ACC sympathizers and Big Blue antagonists. Sure enough, Feinstein's take on the Final Four was that the best championship scenario would have had Dean Smith beating Kentucky in the year that he broke Rupp's record. The UK folks, who of course viewed it the other way around, shook their heads and lamented that, even on this fine Kentucky day, the best press was going to North Carolina.

The opening tip, however, went to Kentucky, and the Radisson crowd gave it a standing ovation. The mood changed the more the whistles blew—in the desperately partisan environment, it was poignant to note how every arguable call trifled with something sacred—and the Cats moved haltingly to their accompaniment. Arizona's Miles Simon, part of a three-guard combination that made Arizona a lot like UK nemesis South Carolina, was consistently drawing fouls on his deliberate drives to the basket, too many of them being charged to Kentucky point guard Wayne Turner. On the other end, the southwestern Wildcats (it was an all-Wildcat championship) were fighting aggressively through Kentucky's screens, effectively getting to Mercer before he could shoot. As a result, Kentucky was able to establish neither the momentum nor the frenetic tempo that was essential to its game. It was only by virtue of five straight points by Cameron Mills that the Cats drew within one at halftime, 33-32.

Playing with an evident belief in the name across their shirts and getting by on the shooting of forward Scott Padgett—who had a two-goal court at his Louisville home and invited friends over every March to play out the Final Four—Pitino's dauntless athletes stayed close enough in the second half to keep everybody at the Radisson hanging onto the boyfriends, girlfriends, husbands, wives, or strangers next to them. One young woman, oblivious to those standing all around her, remained seated, her head tilted back parallel to the ceiling, her eyes closed, her lips moving crisply in prayer. A burly beer drinker in front of her turned and buried his face in the back of his chair as the game came down to its tense final minutes.

With Mercer restricted by Arizona's quickness and his lingering leg cramps, Kentucky turned to the low-post scoring out of Nazr Mohammed, who had never left the bench in the championship game against Syracuse a year earlier. Unfortunately, Mohammed's touch did not extend to the foul line, where he missed all six of his attempts. Arizona, meanwhile, was having similar problems from the field; the challengers were able to make only one field goal in the final four and a half minutes. Kentucky's defense took a blow when Turner fouled out at 1:01 with the Cats down by four, but Mercer hit a courageous three-pointer and with twelve seconds left in regulation, Anthony Epps made the umpteenth clutch play of his solid career, swishing a three that tied the game.

Kentucky obviously had the momentum going into overtime, but it was just as obvious that the defending champs were a tired team. Without Turner, it would be difficult to keep up with Arizona's three guards—particularly Simon, who had scored twenty-six points mostly on penetration. On the UK bench, Derek Anderson calculated all of this and wondered if it added up to him. "I thought for a split second that Coach might start me in the overtime for an emotional boost," he said later. "I hadn't warmed up or anything, but I could have played. The whole game, I was thinking about that. I would have been guarding Miles Simon and he would have had to guard me. He would have been on the post. It would have gotten him two fouls in the first half. We both would have had two fouls and been on the bench. I know this—he wouldn't have had his thirty."

Simon arrived at thirty with four three throws in overtime. Arizona got nothing but free throws in overtime, but there were ten of them, and they were enough to hold off Kentucky—whose season ended as it began, with an overtime loss at the RCA Dome—and win the school's first national championship by the score of 84-79. The second-place finish was Kentucky's third, and it brought silence to the Radisson ballroom. There was no discussion among the Kentuckians, no opinionated recap, no melancholy loitering. They filed out solemnly, and when they reached the sidewalk in front of the hotel, they found policemen in riot gear and broken glass on the sidewalk. Four floors above, there was a hole in a window at which a Kentucky fan had thrown a 19-inch television.

The riot police were at the ready in the event of another Kentucky championship, which the year before had resulted in more than two dozen arrests among twelve thousand revelers at the nondescript Lexington corner of Euclid and Woodland. Curiously, five thousand chins-up folks gathered there again in defeat and 30-degree weather. For them—most of them drinkers—it was a party night, win or lose.

Jason Ryan, of course, didn't see it that way. He and his friends had planned to drive to Lexington and join the fun if the Cats won, but he ended up sitting by himself at Hometown Pizza long after the others had gone home. In front of him, soap pads littered the floor. Jason and his buddies had prevailed upon the cook to bring them out so they would have something to throw at the referees.

As he sat there in the dark, waiting for the manager to finish counting the money in the other room and agonizing over why a team so special had met such an unpoetic end, Ryan couldn't silence the reasons ringing in his head. He blamed the refs, Turner's fouls, Mohammed's missed free throws, Mercer's ailments, Anderson's injury, and of course the damn key chain. When Epps hit the shot that sent the game into overtime, he had thought that he and his key chain were off the hook, but now he somehow felt as though the failure were his. He couldn't stop sobbing. About an hour after the game ended, Mary, the manager, walked over and Jason asked her if it was time to go. "Well, yeah," she said. "Are you all right?"

"I guess," Ryan said. Then he got in his truck, drove home, went to bed, couldn't sleep, got up, and walked up and down Hog Ridge Road for three and a half hours. He wasn't working the next day, anyway. He'd already told his boss he wouldn't be there, knowing that if the Cats won he'd be in no condition to work and if they lost he'd be worse off.

Sleeplessness was a condition that afflicted much of Kentucky that Monday night. In Danville, Ken Wall, a former elementary school principal, sat in front of his television for a long time, cooling off, before heading to bed, and Raymond Kirkland, a retired banker, took a sleeping pill that he knew he would need. But the next morning, they and their accomplices in caffeine arrived at The Coffee Club right on schedule—except for basketball curmudgeon Bill Kemper, who was later than usual. "I slept an extra hour and a half," Kemper explained as he poured himself a cup, "knowing what you'd be talking about when I got here."

The observations of the Old Goats were typically gracious, and they commended Pitino on the same. "Rupp would have said, 'The boys wouldn't do what I told them to do,'" remarked Maynard Van Horn, president of the local Rhododendron Society. "He would have said, 'They went native on me.'" Pitino, instead, expressed pride in what his team accomplished, and the Danville gents seconded the sentiment. "This team," said Tom Spragens, president emeritus of Centre College, "will go down in history as one that accommodated to adverse circumstances." That said, it was time to move on. Kirkland got a group together to ride over to Lawrenceburg for coconut pie.

While the coffee drinkers of Danville were going for pie, there were thousands of Big Blue zealots who wished to indulge the basketball season for one more day. Their marching orders were to report first to Keeneland Race Course, located across the road from the Lexington airport. (Having learned from experience, Lexington officials knew that if they allowed the fans to come to greet the team as it got off the plane, the airport would be paralyzed.)

The spectacle at Keeneland was another Kentucky phenomenon . . . men, women, young boys, and a conspicuous number of teenage girls, nearly all of them still wearing or painted in blue, expressing their affection and sympathy for talented young men who had the commonwealth by the tail and, in some instances, NBA fortunes in their futures. For the players who really understood Kentucky basketball—Mills, Padgett, Epps, and Anderson, the *Kentucky* players—the sympathy traveled in both directions; they recognized that the fans, having put as much emotional energy into the season as the players, also needed to be patted, thanked, and told that it was all right. Cameron Mills was particularly sensitive to this, and the Kentucky fans, in turn, were particularly sensitive to him. If the former walk-on had been taken aback by the concept that young boys were at their backyard hoops pretending to be him, he was thoroughly thrown for a loop by the screaming girls who rushed him as though he were a Beatle and swore not to wash the hands that he touched.

Most of the folks at Keeneland made a day of it, turning out that evening at Rupp Arena for a welcome-home celebration that attracted more than twelve thousand diehards. Some of them had been lined up at the ticket office by 11:30 Monday night, just minutes after overtime had broken their hearts. By the time the window opened in the morning, the line was nearly three thousand strong. Jason Ryan was in it, using the time to calculate the number of days until Big Blue Madness.

If the Cats had brought home their seventh national championship, the arena undoubtedly would have been filled the next night—attendance for The Untouchables rally was twenty thousand—but it would have been a different crowd. To Kentuckians, The Untouchables had been more heroic than dear, driving a Kentucky flag into the mountaintop after the most arduous climb in Big Blue history. Winning it all gave them national immortality, as well. If The Unbelievables had won in the end, they, too, would have taken on national implications. As it was, their legend would be Kentucky's only. The '96 champions would endure in Kentucky's history; the '97 runners-up would endure in Kentucky's heart.

Pitino himself sensed that. After entering the arena Tuesday night through the smoking mouth of a glow-in-the-dark Wildcat, to the proud introduction of athletic director C.M. Newton ("Ladies and gentlemen, this man," said the one who hired him, "continues to raise the bar for basketball coaches . . . "), and with most of the commonwealth watching on live television, he spoke like the Kentucky fan that he had apparently become over the course of eight years. "As special as that team [the '96 champion] was," he said, "this team is even more special."

One by one, the more-special players came through the Wildcat's hot breath, each wearing a new "Unbelievables" T-shirt. Ron Mercer was limping noticeably as he made his way to the center of the floor; Derek Anderson was not. Pitino's spontaneous message, however, was not about excuses, but about the spirit of Kentucky. "A year ago," he said, "Scott Padgett was mowing lawns . . . I never thought Nazr Mohammed would play a second until his second year. Now, if he lives up to the work ethic he's demonstrated, I know he'll be an NBA player . . . Cameron Mills—every practice I would make up a reason why he was doing something wrong and send him to the treadmill. Then, suddenly, he didn't know he wasn't Louie Dampier. You always talk about Kentucky dreams, incredible things that happen when you put on that Kentucky uniform. Well, this is a young man, I tried to talk him out of coming to Kentucky . . . "

It wasn't just Kentucky and Kentuckians anymore who believed in the shirt. The magic of it had evidently taken over the coach from New

York. "I said to them before the game last night, look at your jerseys, what it says and what it stands for. Never for a second," said Pitino, "did we not believe we would be in the Final Four . . .

"This is a good habit. Let's do it again next year."

Later that evening, Pitino's confidant, Jersey Red, was a radio guest on Lexington's WVLK when a caller asked him about the coach and the recurring Boston Celtics rumors.

"Over my dead body," replied Jersey Red. "He will hear from Boston, from Orlando, maybe others. But next October, he'll be back at Big Blue Madness."

10

Passages

It was Derby time again for the ponies and Pitino. The year before, as New Jersey led Kentucky's rite of spring to the wire with its thirty million dollars, it had looked as though the coach might really leave. This time, it looked as though he might *really* leave, since it was the Celtics, the most distinguished franchise in the history of professional basketball, the pride of the state where Pitino played college ball and the city where he became a head coach. On the other hand, with Pitino, who could know? By his count, he had turned down fourteen NBA jobs, the most recent being the Orlando Magic, the Golden State Warriors, and the Philadelphia 76ers.

On the day after the roses had been run for, Kentucky's biggest celebrity met with his players at Memorial Coliseum and talked about the opportunity back East. He didn't say he was going, but he made it clear he wasn't looking to be talked out of it, as he had in 1994 when he held a similar meeting to discuss a similar situation with the Los Angeles Lakers. Jamaal Magloire argued with him anyway. Cameron Mills tried to thank him for everything but ended up crying. Ron Mercer and Derek Anderson wondered if he would draft them.

Around the commonwealth, fans and media tried to read the stars in Pitino's eyes. Three years earlier, he had said he would probably return to the NBA some day. One year earlier, he had said there would be no way he would leave Kentucky, only to be tempted mightily by the Nets. A month after turning down New Jersey, he had explained that when job offers came up it was his obligation to say that he was staying at Ken-

◄ *Tubby Smith: "He's just as big a redneck as we are..."*

tucky no matter what—basically, to lie if he had to—because if he said anything different it would ruin him as a recruiter and be a disservice to the university. On and on, round and round, back and forth it went. Larry Bird called from the Celtics' office on the Friday after the 1997 Final Four, and what Pitino told him, reported the *Herald-Leader*, was that "I'm very, very happy at Kentucky. I'll be coaching at Kentucky, and I don't plan on anything other than that." A few days later, he was quoted in the same vein by the *Boston Globe*: "I can honestly say that I will be back at Kentucky. I have already told that to some of my recruits. I mean that. That's an honest answer. I have videos of Lou Holtz saying he will never leave Notre Dame, and then the next thing you know he's announcing he's stepping down. I have a video of John Calipari saying he doesn't have one ounce of interest in pro basketball and the next thing he's in New Jersey saying this is what he always wanted to do. It makes them both look like pathological liars." His intention was not to castigate Holtz and Calipari, but to discuss a college coach's dilemma when offers come in. Anyway, the words certainly indicated he was staying at Kentucky, which, like he said, was what he was telling his recruits. As the rumors proliferated, he had made a point of calling Michael Bradley in Massachusetts to assure him that the reports were ridiculous and there was nothing to worry about.

All of that had apparently changed around Derby weekend, however, and Kentuckians expected the worst when Pitino called a press conference for Tuesday afternoon at 3:30. The commonwealth optimists held out hope that it might be to announce a new contract with UK; just days before, he had said, "If I am back next year, and I intend to be, it's going to be with a long-term contract." C.M. Newton had said that he could restructure Pitino's deal with two minutes and a handshake.

Half an hour before the press conference was scheduled to begin, as the cameramen were setting up their tripods and reporters were positioning their tape recorders, Pitino picked up the phone in his office and called an old friend, Providence athletic director John Marinatto. Even though he had been to Newton's house that morning and told his boss that he was leaving, he was still waffling, as he had done for several days. But the call had gone out to someone whose answers Pitino knew ahead of time; Marinatto, after all, was a New Englander. He said the things he was supposed to say, and when they hung up, the coach signed the Boston contract on his desk, straightened his tie, and strode down to the press conference.

Around the commonwealth, everything stopped. At Ken Barth's barbershop in Newport, the proprietor lowered his scissors and held his breath as Pitino stepped up to the podium. On the message board in his shop, next to the street sign for Rick Pitino Court and the fair warning, "Not responsible for haircuts given during Kentucky games," Barth had printed in big letters: "Say It Ain't So, Rick." Never knowing for sure what Pitino was going to say—or so he told himself—the barber listened until he heard the word "leave," then resumed clipping hair. The deal was for ten years and something like seventy million.

While Pitino was ruining a lot of people's days, Newton was already busy on the next step. As soon as the erstwhile Kentucky savior had left the A.D.'s house that morning, Newton had reported straight to university president Charles Wethington, requesting permission to pursue his only candidate, Georgia coach Tubby Smith. The next day, Smith flew in a private plane to Blue Grass Airport, where he met secretly with Newton. That night, before contractual terms had been discussed, he said he wanted the job.

Newton couldn't release any news until the particulars had been worked out, but Kentucky highly suspected Smith. Minnesota's Clem Haskins, the Kentucky native, was also an obvious candidate, as were other Pitino protégés such as Florida's Billy Donovan, Pittsburgh's Ralph Willard, and North Carolina State's Herb Sendek. But Smith had the whole package. He was successful, on the rise, popular, apparently honest, a first-rate recruiter, and he utilized a playing style he had learned largely from Pitino. There were many in the Bluegrass who added to that list the fact that he was black, the reasoning being that the hiring of a black coach would open rusty-bolted doors for Kentucky and finally get the national media off its back.

Smith's race would have probably not been an issue at other schools, but this was Adolph Rupp's university and some of the people who supported it were the same ones to whom the Baron had been accountable thirty years earlier. This was the school whose traditions had begotten the unforgettable quote from then *Courier-Journal* columnist Billy Reed, who, commenting on the likelihood of UK hiring long-time assistant Leonard Hamilton after Joe Hall stepped down in 1985, wrote, "There will be a Martian in the White House before there's a black coach on the bench where Adolph Rupp once sat."

Twelve years later, at least one Kentucky journalist was still skeptical about whether the Big Blue public could apply the principles of equal opportunity to the position of UK basketball coach. As Smith's candidacy became apparent, Merlene Davis, a black columnist for the *Herald-Leader*, published an open letter imploring him, for his own sake, to stay away. "Kentucky fans aren't ready for a black head coach," wrote Davis. "In Kentucky, basketball is king. The first time you lose a game, you will not be called a stupid coach. You will be called a stupid *black* coach . . . Your mail would be hate-filled and truly evil. The things people would feel free to say to your face would be unconscionable. Criticism would be aimed at your lack of intelligence rather than your lack of coaching skills . . . I sincerely fear for your safety and the safety of your family if you agree to become head coach."

Among those with a more proactive perspective was S.T. Roach, the former coach of Dunbar High School when its student body was entirely black. It was Roach and his principal who, in the mid-fifties, had been asked by UK athletic director Bernie Shively to vacate the front-row Memorial Coliseum seats for which they had tickets. Over the course of nearly half a century, Roach's experience with the university had been rife with complexities and contradictions; whereas Shively had asked him to leave or move, Rupp—the alleged bad guy in UK's racial legacy—had frequently offered him use of the Coliseum gym and presented him with hand-me-down equipment. On the other hand, Rupp had never recruited any of Dunbar's outstanding players. But in 1974, after the Baron had retired, Roach, a visible leader in the Lexington community, had been appointed to the UK athletics board, under whose authority came the nomination of head basketball coaches.

It was for that purpose that the 81-year-old Dunbar legend reported to a board meeting late in the week of Pitino's departure. When Wethington requested a nomination for the job of men's basketball coach, the room turned instinctively to Roach, to whom the day had been generations in coming. Without hesitating, he lifted his right hand crisply into the air and submitted the name of Orlando Smith.

Smith accepted the job on Saturday. On Sunday, he and his wife went to Newton's house for a Mother's Day meal of pork roast and cooked cabbage prepared by the athletic director, and on Monday the newest basketball coach at the University of Kentucky was introduced to the state that would inevitably come to love or hate him, or both.

He was the sixth of seventeen children who grew up on a farm outside Scotland, Maryland, the product of a tireless mother and a principled father who drove a school bus and won a Purple Heart as a machine gunner in World War II. The house where Guffrie Smith tenant-farmed had no indoor plumbing until he built the family a new one in 1963; consequently, the bathtub that young Orlando so enjoyed—hence the nickname—was filled with buckets drawn from the well. The only place that the Smiths' sixth child seemed to enjoy more was the basketball floor. Tubby Smith was as good a player as St. Mary's County had ever seen, and the level head he managed to keep in spite of it went a long way toward easing the integration of Great Mills High School.

Smith's success at Great Mills led to a nice playing career at High Point College, where he married the school's first black homecoming queen. From there, his coaching track followed the traditional path to the big time—a couple high school jobs, several collegiate apprenticeships (including a significant one under Pitino), personal success as a recruiter, and conspicuously good results at his first two head coaching stops, Tulsa and Georgia. At Kentucky, he instantly became the highest-paid coach in the Southeastern Conference, football coaches included (a distinction which lasted only until Florida gave Steve Spurrier a hefty raise a few days later).

Despite the worst fears of the *Herald-Leader*'s Merlene Davis, Kentucky seemed to welcome Smith without reservation or qualification. His first radio show occasioned several invitations to dinner, indicating that the citizens of the commonwealth were awkwardly proud of their new racial incarnation. They were also, in the image of Rupp, hell-bent to win, which the tenant farmer's son was evidently well equipped to do for them. Rupp and Kentucky were always mirrors of each other, and it was consequently believable when the Baron's son, Herky, declared that his father would have shaken the new man's hand and wished him all the luck.

While Kentucky was relieved to finally achieve closure on its noisome and belabored reputation, the national media used Smith's hiring to reiterate the racist benchmarks of Big Blue history, which of course made the story. All agreed that, at least symbolically, the arrival of the gentleman from Maryland finished off a stubborn provincial tradition that had looked as though it might hang on indefinitely. On that score, a local radio station had the presence of mind to interview columnist Billy Reed, author of the "Martian in the White House" quote, who submitted that with all the rooms the Clintons had rented out to foreign contributors, he wasn't so sure he had missed the mark.

The Unbelievables: Mercer and Anderson hoped that Pitino would keep them together.

○ ○ ○

Even when he was on crutches, Derek Anderson imagined himself and Ron Mercer playing together at the next level. "Me and Ron," he said. "I thought nothing could ever separate us." But there would be some faith required to keep them on the same team; not his—goodness knows, Anderson was not lacking for faith, as he had demonstrated with the communicable smile he maintained throughout his rehabilitation—but Rick Pitino's. In order for Kentucky's synergetic superstars to take their telepathic game to the NBA, the coach needed enough faith in Mercer's potential to choose him with the third pick in the draft and enough in Anderson's recuperative powers to take him with the sixth.

It was Pitino, after all, who had said in San Jose that Anderson was the best player in practice—better, even, than Mercer, who by all accounts was projected among the top handful of draft choices. Of course, it was also Pitino who had elected not to play Anderson in the NCAA tournament, but the fact was that the former Kentucky coach, more than anybody, had reason to believe in the former Kentucky player. Curiously, Anderson had refrained from verifying himself in the NBA rookie camps, reasoning that if it hadn't been worthwhile to risk the knee for the national championship, it didn't make sense to expose it to a camp full of large young men with whom he was competing for millions of dollars. Instead, he had worked out privately for a number of teams, slashing, dunking, and hoping all the while that Pitino would believe what his eyes had told him in March.

Concluding, however, that the rebuilding of the Celtics required a fresh point guard, Pitino ultimately foiled the plan by selecting Colorado's Chauncey Billups with the third pick, then finessing Mercer with the sixth. Confidence in himself and in his fate prevented Anderson from recognizing the miracle that occurred when he was selected by the Cleveland Cavaliers with the thirteenth pick—a triumph that even his prayerful family would have had a hard time envisioning a few months earlier, when all he could do was shoot free throws. "That's done now," he said later. "I didn't get drafted that high, but God put me through that phase. Maybe He didn't want me to go to Boston."

Anderson had certainly not been forsaken. Six months after his professional career had been in utter jeopardy, he was earning over a million dollars a year in base salary and even had himself a Nike deal. Michael Jordan was starting a new line of personalized basketball shoes and had hand-picked Anderson as one of five young NBA players—the only rookie—for whom specially designed Jordan-brand sneakers would be created. Anderson intended to keep his (and Jordan's) number twenty-three with the Cavs, but neither that nor his inventive court style was the real reason the great one anointed him. "Publicly, the reason was that my game resembles his," said the charismatic Kentuckian. "But privately, there was a whole different reason. It was something that was said behind closed doors. Anyway, he wants us to start our own identity. I want to start my own identity. I want people to say, 'I want to be like D.A.,' because of my personality and my game."

It was not for the sake of gratuitous ego that Anderson longed to be liked and emulated; it was for the sake of the young people whom he wanted to like and emulate him—the young people, mainly, of the state of Kentucky and the city of Louisville. In two remarkable years, Anderson had come to realize that he and Kentucky were right for each other. All the while he was growing up, he had never fathomed such a thing; it certainly wasn't the message he had picked up from the neighborhood, where the Rupp years were not forgotten and change was treated as though it wore the wrong colors.

In the summer between his college and pro careers, Anderson had taken it upon himself to do something about all of that. An irresistible agent of harmony, he had undertaken a mission to make the city more Kentucky-friendly. The forum was a basketball camp he would run every July at Louisville's Doss High School, where as a prep star he had cultivated his wariness toward the state university. "I want the kids to be blind to the past," he explained. "If they have a chance to play basketball at Kentucky, I want them to know the facts before they make a decision. I want to inform them that no matter what you heard, this is what's going on now. Kentucky's reputation is changing. Even the older people are realizing it. I hear them say, 'Well, I don't like Kentucky, but I like the players.'"

Specifically, they liked him. Everybody liked Derek Anderson; what was not to like? He had helped win a national championship for Kentucky. He had been a superstar. He had been entertaining and gracious and brave and, most of all, disarming. He had broken down congenital prejudices that had terrorized Kentucky for half a century and he had brought together, for the first time, the two places in the commonwealth where basketball was at its best. The Big Blue and the Big City needed each other. Derek Anderson wrapped them both in his happy embrace.

○ ○ ○

In the handsome white house at the Paintsville corner of Fourth and College, the phone rang five minutes after midnight had turned over the calendar to July 1, the beginning of the period in which college coaches were allowed to directly contact high school recruits. It was John MacLeod of Notre Dame, letting J.R. VanHoose know that he was number one on the Irish list.

The next call came through in the daylight of 8:35 from assistants George Felton and Shawn Finney and head coach Tubby Smith of the

University of Kentucky. It was the first time VanHoose had heard from the Wildcats' new head coach, but he had been heartened by the hiring. While Pitino's interest in him seemed to be obligatory at best in the end, Smith had built his Georgia team primarily with in-state players and had assured the Kentucky media that Bluegrass talent would be of special interest to him. Unlike his predecessor, he seemed like the type who could relate to rural athletes. "My grandparents told me they saw Coach Smith do an interview on television and said, 'He's just as big a redneck as we are,'" laughed J.R. "I thought, 'Y'all don't say that about him. People say that about us all the time and we don't like it much.'" But when they spoke on the phone, VanHoose had a similar impression. "Coach Smith actually sounded country," he said appreciatively. The new man was not offering a scholarship, however. In fact, he made a point of telling VanHoose how few he had to offer.

At 10 a.m., the phone started ringing with a regularity that dominated the old house the VanHooses had finally finished restoring. ("I don't know how good a college player J.R. will be," his father said, "but whoever signs him will get a hell of a carpenter.") J.R. had heard that Tim Couch, the UK quarterback, kept a log of every recruiting call he received, and he decided to do the same. The ten o'clock was from Western Kentucky, followed by Marshall at 10:13, Virginia at 10:25, Auburn at 10:39, Georgia at 10:45 (he was in the shower), Wake Forest at 10:51 (still in the shower), Georgia calling back at 10:59, Wake Forest calling back at 11:10, Davidson, Villanova, Vanderbilt, LSU, Syracuse, Tennessee, Ohio State, Charleston, Michigan, Marquette, Florida, Cincinnati, Penn State . . . It was six minutes before eleven when the last call of the night came through from Bobby Knight. By the end of the first day, thirty schools had phoned, nearly every one on VanHoose's list with the exception of Kansas: Roy Williams, who had visited Paintsville in April, knew that the Fourth of July was J.R.'s birthday and was waiting until then.

Even after two years of collegiate mail and the appearing of famous coaches in the Paintsville gym, the tide of cross-country phone calls took the VanHooses by surprise. "As a freshman and sophomore, J had great years," said his father, "but I figured honestly that he was just a big ol' white boy from Eastern Kentucky and the schools he would have to choose from would be the ones from around here. Kentucky was always in our mind because, especially around Eastern Kentucky, people would say,

'He's a white boy . . . If we can just get him into UK . . . ' But I never dreamed it would be Kansas, Indiana, schools like that."

The reason for the interest in the Paintsville hero was obvious. After leading the voting in both the *Courier-Journal* and *Herald-Leader* all-state teams, J.R. had begun the summer as the fifth-ranking big man in the country, which was actually a little lower than he had been previously evaluated; the ratings changed constantly and would continue to do so until the big-time summer camps were over.

After missing the major camps the year before, VanHoose and Todd Tackett were scheduled to accompany their coach, Bill Mike Runyon, to the adidas showcase in Teaneck, New Jersey. A marketplace like adidas was considered to be a primary indicator for a prospect like VanHoose, whose skillful but physically unimposing mountain competition left college coaches wondering how he would get along in a bigger, faster environment; but J.R.'s suitors had advised him not to be concerned: A good camp would reinforce their faith in him, they said, and a bad one would be even better because it might scare the other guys away.

MacLeod, who parked under VanHoose's basket for most of the camp, had warned J.R. that he wouldn't be using many of his interior moves at adidas; in such a setting, it was common for a post player to take the ball out of bounds and not see it again until it hit the rim on the other end. And that was before MacLeod knew that VanHoose and Tackett's team included Ronald Blackshear, a shooting guard from Georgia who took the "shooting" part literally. One observer counted eight straight times down the floor in which Blackshear launched one up. When Tackett asked Runyon what he should do about Blackshear, the coach had a ready answer: "Guard him."

"But he's on my team," said Tackett.

"I know," replied Runyon. "Double-team him."

The arrangements called for players to play half of each game, and VanHoose made the most of the minutes he didn't share with Blackshear, scoring thirteen points twice in the first day. That wasn't the day Tubby Smith was there. The day Smith was there, VanHoose saw the ball very little and did even less with it. The Kentucky coach watched for about five minutes and as soon as he was out of sight, J.R. stole a pass, took it the length of the floor, and slammed it down to the whoops and hollers of the intimate crowd.

After the camps, VanHoose's national ranking dropped down into the fifties or so, depending on who was doing the ranking. Kentucky was recruiting players rated in his range, but J.R. heard nothing more from the Cats. As the silence deepened, the courteous teenager modified his ambition for the recruiting process: Growing accustomed to the fact that he would not play for Kentucky, he felt an impulse to go to a school where he would play *against* Kentucky.

That consideration nudged Vanderbilt temporarily ahead of Notre Dame in his mind, and he didn't know what to make of Indiana. The word out of Bloomington was that Knight usually went fishing in May and was out of touch until school started. Kansas, meanwhile, dropped out of the derby in mid-summer, when Roy Williams called to tell J.R. that he had received a commitment from another power forward. Florida had done the same, and Tennessee had chilled quite a bit since Kevin O'Neill moved on to Northwestern, from where he was decorating the VanHoose house with purple mail instead of orange.

When home visits were arranged for three weeks in September, John MacLeod once again lined up first. He scheduled a trip to Paintsville that would take place two days after VanHoose was in South Bend to watch the Irish play Georgia Tech in Notre Dame's newly renovated football stadium. If J.R. had been unmoved by the campus of the Golden Dome, he would have been the first. "For a Protestant boy from Eastern Kentucky, the Catholics put on a pretty good show," said Bob VanHoose, who himself had attended a Catholic college (St. Francis) in Indiana. Notwithstanding the Irish ambience and collegiate circumstance, for J.R. the most impressive thing about the visit might have been Pat Garrity, the All-American forward and 4.0 pre-med student whose position MacLeod had said he had a chance to take over as a freshman.

Notre Dame was a world removed from Paintsville, but VanHoose would not feel entirely alone if he went there. MacLeod had just landed Lexington Catholic's small forward, David Graves, with whom VanHoose enjoyed a respectful rivalry. All things considered, Notre Dame was in a position to move to the top of J.R.'s list with a good home visit, but on the appointed day, Indiana's weather took a nasty turn and fog hovered around the mountain that accommodated Big Sandy Regional Airport, persuading MacLeod not to risk the trip in his little twin-prop plane. It bummed VanHoose to sit around the house, unvisited, while every other top player in America had a head coach in his living room.

His loneliness didn't last, however. Vanderbilt's Jan Van Breda Kolff was in town at three o'clock the next afternoon to watch J.R. lift weights—the loss to Highlands in the Sweet Sixteen had sent him to the weight room with such resolve that he had increased his squat by ninety pounds in six weeks—and play pickup games with his teammates. After the workout, the Commodore coach drove the block and a half to Fourth and College, where Beth VanHoose brought snacks and soft drinks to the living room; J.R.'s brother, Alex, toddled into the den to watch Blues Clues tapes and ride his rocking horse; his seventh-grade sister, Tiffany, breezed in and out on her rounds; and Van Breda Kolff, saying little about basketball, convinced the family about the value of a Vanderbilt education.

He was gone by seven (there was no supper for the VanHooses that night), making room for Western Kentucky coach Matt Kilcullen, who was coming straight from the home of Todd Tackett. Both Western and Eastern Kentucky were hoping to keep the Paintsville pair together, but VanHoose's interest in the smaller Kentucky schools remained mostly cordial until later in the week, when he found himself surprisingly captivated sitting for three hours across from UK legend Kyle Macy, the new head coach at Morehead State. Macy and Bob VanHoose had played against each other in high school, the former being the best player the latter ever saw. In addition to his celebrity, Macy had playing time to offer and one remaining scholarship; if it went to the best player in Kentucky, he said, Morehead's grand plan would fast-forward about five years.

Night after night, the procession rolled by in a blur: Mississippi State, West Virginia, Northwestern, Penn State, Ohio State, Marshall . . . Virginia Tech made a nice presentation—J.R. had been communicating with a history professor there who was a Civil War expert—and Charleston coach John Kresse talked his school into the picture. Dan Dakich, who had recruited VanHoose hard and well as an assistant at Indiana, stopped by in his new capacity as head coach at Bowling Green. The VanHooses felt that if Dakich had remained at I.U. or been hired for the vacancy at Marshall, which was situated just over an hour away in Huntington, West Virginia (it was conceivable that J.R.'s girlfriend, Amy, could enroll there, too), the recruiting ordeal might have been over by this time.

While Tubby Smith and his assistants maintained a conspicuous absence at the VanHooses', Indiana was confirming the aloofness that had come to characterize its approach to recruiting. Knight had made it clear that he wouldn't become a beggar for the privilege of handing out scholarships to tall teenagers. His method was to extend the prospect an invitation, then get on with his life while the boy decided whether or not to accept it. The VanHooses respected this, but were nonetheless left wondering if the General's interest was a continuing one. Bob VanHoose had read on the Internet—he was peeking daily at (and occasionally submitting to) the basketball pages of several of the schools that had been represented in his home—that the Hoosiers had signed a power forward out of Alabama. If that were indeed the case, a home visit would serve no purpose. Knight's staff was sluggish about setting one up, anyway, and the boss had no intention of participating in it; he was due at a Converse clinic in California. Finally, on the second to last day of home visits, the Hoosiers' Craig Hartman made an obligatory appearance on Fourth Street.

It was a confusing time for J.R. In a way, he envied his senior teammates whose decisions were not encumbered by enigmatic coaches, attentive press, and the hopes of an entire community: Josh McKenzie and Mike Short had earned scholarships to Pikeville College, which sufficiently pleased the locals, and Kyle Adams would play at Alice Lloyd College in the nearby mountain town of Pippa Passes, Kentucky. Tackett was still undecided, but Paintsville's ambitions for him, while grand enough, could not be compared to those the town harbored for the big fellow who had put it on the map. Where VanHoose was concerned, the local sentiments were expressed by Tom Bogar, the sports editor of a Johnson County newspaper, *The Weekly Progress*:

"UK coach Tubby Smith has not made an appearance in Paintsville to watch Paintsville's J.R. VanHoose perform during an open gym," Bogar wrote on September 17. " . . . UK's recruiting seems to be centered on big men from Minnesota and Virginia rather than here in Paintsville. Smith has found the time to take part in this week's boxing fundraiser in Louisville when he should probably be visiting VanHoose's house.

"Here's hoping that recruiting efforts that ignore in-state players lead to a short tenure at UK for the new coach. How about three years? . . . Let's make it two."

Emboldened by a cachet that had not been available to him at Georgia, Smith had been devoting his considerable energy and travel budget to the very best prospects that the summer camps had produced. Among others, he was after Tayshaun Prince of California, Michael Miller of South Dakota, Souleymane Camara of Virginia (originally Senegal), Dan Gadzuric of Massachusetts (originally The Netherlands), Jaron Rush of Missouri, and two or three blue-chippers from Illinois. It appeared to be a fruitful pursuit: In the period between the home visits and Big Blue Madness, Kentucky received a verbal commitment from the 6-11 Camara, a slender, supremely athletic African native whose appeal came in the guise of potential, not performance.

Camara was projected as a power forward at Kentucky, and his announcement effectively put an end to VanHoose's protracted Kentucky affair. Without questioning Camara's merit as a player, his recruitment was the sort that bewildered Bob VanHoose, who by that time had become compelled to say things that his more circumspect son would not. "You become more candid as you go along," he stated. "It's over with Kentucky. We know that. I think I've taken the turn-down tougher than he has. He was the dad in this one. I've probably abused a phone or two over this. But the thing is, there are guys they're going after who are ranked right where J is. It's aggravating. It's frustrating.

"Mark Pope had a great career at Kentucky, he's probably going to be in the NBA, and he's not a deer; he doesn't leap out of the gym. And Prickett. And Padgett. Kentucky has had success with players like them in this system. Kids who just work hard. They said that Farmer and Pelphrey and Feldhaus were overachievers; well, I don't know if what they did was overachieving, but if that's what you call it, you overachieve when you're playing with sincerity. And Smith should realize this, because he was there when Farmer and Pelphrey and Feldhaus were there. He saw what happens when you put that jersey over your head and you've got that Kentucky across the chest."

The elder VanHoose had opened up about Kentucky only after months of observing what its indifference was doing to his son. J.R. was a well-adjusted high schooler who was eminently able to play through the pain, but the fact was, he wanted badly to be a Wildcat—despite his public understatements—and when it became apparent that his feeling for Kentucky was unrequited, the disappointment was much more severe than he would ever reveal. His parents could read his moods, though, and they understood the burden he had taken on for all of Eastern Kentucky. Theirs was a young man who was historically sensitive to a unique degree. J.R. felt, inevitably, that he had let his people down, even though he knew—he couldn't help but know—he had done all that a basketball player from Paintsville, Kentucky, could possibly do. What tore him apart was that nothing he had accomplished seemed to matter in the final analysis; the championships, the honors, the records, the history he had made . . . it was as though, on a whim, UK was invalidating all of that. There was only one standard in Kentucky, and because of it, friends and neighbors would look at him, the local hero, and conclude that he wasn't quite good enough. Some of them would look at him and somehow conclude that *they* weren't good enough. The people had been kind, certainly; his friends were of course still his friends, his fans were still his fans, and even strangers had reached out to him sympathetically; there had been letters to the editor and letters to the house telling him to hold his head high. But sympathy could hurt, too: VanHoose was about making people proud, not sorry.

"What's so disheartening to J.R.," his father continued, "is that you play to achieve. You play to win. And you do that, and then they still tell you, in a roundabout way, that they don't want you. When I talked to Coach Smith, he was saying that he wants to evaluate J.R. a little longer, maybe wait until the spring. Well, Vandy's not gonna wait until the spring; Notre Dame and Indiana are not gonna wait until the spring. In my opinion, that's a way of saying, 'If we don't find somebody better by then, we'll take him.' That's unfair to the kid.

"I've said all along that Kentucky should have taken him and Todd both. Not to take anything away from J.P. Blevins and Jaron Brown, but J.R. and Todd both have accomplished more than J.P. or Brown, either one. They've won a state championship and been to the Sweet Sixteen three times. Those other two can't accomplish that in the one year they have left. You can't teach winning. Larry Bird was a winner; he didn't know how to lose. But they recruit some of these guys—and I'm not just talking about J.P. and Jaron—they recruit some of these guys who have never really won . . . "

UK's position was not without its sympathizers. As the debate continued to engage the talk shows and the Internet boards, the VanHoose lobby was balanced—somewhat—by Kentuckians who placed a higher premium on a player's ranking than his geography. But the Paintsville point of view was particularly hard to repress: There was a nice, clean-cut kid, a student who ranked in the top ten in his class, a tangibly proud Kentuckian, six foot nine, who as a sophomore had dominated the Sweet Sixteen and led his team to the state championship and as a junior had taken it back to the Final Four (where it had been eliminated on a highly controversial call that occurred after he had controversially fouled out) and been unanimously acclaimed as the top player in the commonwealth. These were credentials that seemed to be worthy of a scholarship from the state university.

"If Kentucky had gone after him hard," Bob VanHoose said, now that he could, "that would have probably been all she wrote. The fact is, he would have been satisfied to have been no better than the sixth man on the team there. Now his attitude has changed. Now he wants to stroll into Rupp Arena his senior year and knock them out of the NCAA tournament or maybe cost them a conference championship or something. He wants to play Kentucky."

There was a day when J.R. VanHoose would have *been* Kentucky, no questions asked. Now the best player in the state was on the outside, looking in at The New Kentucky. It was Rick Pitino's Kentucky, Derek Anderson's Kentucky, Tubby Smith's Kentucky, Souleymane Camara's Kentucky, and, even still, Kentucky's Kentucky. "No longer is it the days of Pat, Dan, Jimmy Dan, Jack, Kyle, Sam, Rex, and Richie," observed Capt. Dan Armstrong on Cat Chat, effectively saying it all. "I'm cheering for Souleymane, Tayshaun, Jamaal, Heshimu, and Nazr. Times are a-changing."

For one more year, though, J.R. VanHoose would be able to hear Kentucky's cheers. In his head, he heard them all summer and fall as he lifted the weights and ran the sprints and shot the shots. A good senior season would take him to the Sweet Sixteen for the fourth time. A great season would make him Mister Basketball. A dream season would bring another state championship, which in turn would reserve him a permanent place in the upper room of Kentucky legends, in the company, perhaps, of Richie Farmer. "Wow," he said, thinking of it. "Maybe I could have a street named after me when I graduate. That'd be cool."

Entering his last winter of high school basketball, VanHoose had the sense and the perspective to know that it might not ever get better than it was at that moment. He loved playing for Paintsville High School and for Paintsville, Kentucky. The more he visited and contemplated colleges, the more he appreciated the little town in which he thrived. He loved it when Paintsville folks hung something blue on their porch before a big game. He loved the way the school and the town pulled on the same end of the rope, their community footholds deepening with each symbiotic tug. He loved being the perpetual underdog—the little guy, for a change. He loved to share his accomplishments with friends and neighbors, young and old, and make them feel a little better than they did before they met him.

He realized all of this especially on the early November weekend when he visited Marshall University, the uncelebrated Mid-American Conference school near the Kentucky border in Huntington, West Virginia. The first thing he noticed about Huntington was the color scheme; it was as purposefully green (Marshall's color) as Paintsville was blue. The second thing he noticed was that everybody talked like him. He liked that. For years, the buzzwords had been "the next level," and for a mountain kid from Paintsville, it occurred to VanHoose that this was it; Marshall University was exactly what Paintsville High School would be at the next level. Proximity no doubt had something to do with it— Huntington was the city where Paintsville people went to shop—but more than that, it was a sensation that overtook J.R. when he was there. Everything about the place made sense to him. At Vanderbilt or Notre Dame, he had a chance to be an immediate starter, but at Marshall, he had an opportunity not only to start right away but to actually *get the ball*. He was also impressed with the young Marshall coach, Greg White, who, during the home visit at the VanHooses', had pulled his chair across the room so that he could talk nose-to-nose with the recruit he coveted most. When the home visits were originally scheduled, VanHoose had rated Marshall fourteenth out of his final fifteen schools; by the time White put the chair back in its place, the Thundering Herd had jumped to fifth. J.R.'s official visit to the campus moved Marshall to second on his list behind Vanderbilt. A week or so later, that position was solidified when Notre Dame called to tell the Paintsville hero that it had waited long enough for him and was going to sign the 6-8 Kentuckian from the other end of the state, Harold Swanagan.

Vanderbilt's obvious advantages over Marshall were its academic reputation, which weighed heavily, and its membership in the Southeastern Conference. When UK's lack of interest in him had become painfully incontrovertible, VanHoose was inflamed by the urge to play and punish Kentucky; but the throbbing had since quieted and his deeper values had come to the fore. The choice was reduced to priorities: Was it more important to beat Kentucky or to get home to see Alex graduate from kindergarten? Actually, by going to Marshall he could do both: He could watch Alex grow up and he could beat UK, in his own way, by putting it effectively out of his life.

To verify his instincts, VanHoose made another short trip to Huntington the next weekend. It concluded on Sunday morning, when, before leaving to get back home, he stopped in at White's office to say goodbye. The VanHooses and the coaches were talking casually when Gregg Marshall, one of White's assistants, asked J.R. what he thought about going to school there. "Well," VanHoose replied, "I want to commit." Coach Marshall was sitting on the floor when he posed the question—rhetorically, he thought—and the young man's answer sent him straight into the air. "I swear," J.R. said later, holding his hands at about waist level, "he jumped that high from a sitting position. I don't know how he did it. But I figured, if the assistant coach can do that, they must really have some athletic ability."

The Thundering Herd also had winning persistence—it was they, remember, who had sent J.R. his first piece of recruiting mail when he was in the ninth grade, thanks to John Pelphrey, who was a Marshall assistant at the time—and, as of that memorable Sunday morning, a big man to take them into the next century. VanHoose's four-year decision became official after Paintsville's practice on November 12, 1997, the first day on which high school seniors could sign letters-of-intent to play college basketball. It was a modest, dignified occasion, with little to suggest the weight of the moment except for the words of Paintsville superintendent Paul Williams, who introduced J.R. to the intimate gathering of media. "There has always been something special about the way this young man carries himself," Williams said. "I've had administrators from other school districts call and want to visit the Paintsville schools and meet J.R. VanHoose." They most likely made the request while under the inevitable impression that the famous schoolboy would soon be a famous Wildcat.

Sensing that his long-awaited selection would be perceived as unbefitting his status, VanHoose, with the entire Paintsville team standing symbolically behind him for the big announcement, attempted to stuff the cynicism before it left the critics' throats. "I know my choice is going to be controversial," he said. "There will be people who will say that I'm afraid to play against the competition in bigger conferences. To be blunt, I don't care what the press thinks. The only thing that matters is my family. And even if my family

Bottom line: In the end, J.R. didn't want to miss seeing his little brother grow up.

doesn't like it, tough—I'm the one who's gonna be there for four years.

"Paintsville," he patiently explained, "is the kind of place where, if you're having a bad day, people will slap you on the back and tell you it's okay. It was great that I could find a place like Paintsville, a place where the university is part of the community and the community is part of the university." And then he put on the green and white cap of the Thundering Herd and signed the official letter in front of him.

As the Kentucky reporters gathered around, bending their necks to look up at his engaging, youthful face, VanHoose was ready for the question he knew was coming.

"If dreams could come true," he said, "sure, I would have been at UK. But my dad said that if dreams came true, he'd drive home from work in a Ferrari and have two eighteen-year-old blondes waiting for him at the door.

"I don't have anything against UK. I hope Kentucky wins the national championship this year." As a Kentuckian, that would make him proud. Not giddy; not overwhelmed, as he had been in 1996 . . . Given what had transpired in what was supposed to have been the greatest year of his life, Kentucky's continued success in basketball would never again give VanHoose the feeling of personal triumph that it would give other Kentuckians; but, still, it would make him happy for his neighbors and for his state, and inherently proud, as always, to be from where he was from.

Bibliography

Caudill, Harry. *Night Comes to the Cumberlands*. Boston: Little, Brown, 1976.

Chandler, Dan, and Vernon Hatton. *Rupp: From Both Ends of the Bench*. Basic Books, 1972.

Dick, David. *The Quiet Kentuckians*. Paris, Ky.: Plum Lick Publishing, 1996.

Embry, Mike. *March Madness*. South Bend, Ind.: Icarus Press, 1985.

Farmer, Richie. *Richie*. Lexington, Ky.: Antex Corporation, 1992.

Fitzgerald, Francis (Ed.). *The Legacy and The Glory*. Louisville, Ky.: AdCraft, 1995.

Hall, Joe B., with Russell Rice. *My Own Kentucky Home*. Huntsville, Ala.: Strode Publishers, 1981.

Issel, Dan, with Buddy Martin. *Parting Shots*. Chicago: Contemporary Books, 1985.

Kindred, Dave. *A Year with the Cats: From Breathitt County to the White House*. Lexington, Ky.: Jim Host & Associates, 1977.

Kindred, Dave. *Basketball: The Dream Game in Kentucky*. Louisville: Data Courier, 1976.

Lancaster, Harry, as told to Cawood Leford. *Adolph Rupp as I Knew Him*. Lexington, Ky.: Lexington Productions, 1979.

Laudeman, Tev. *The Rupp Years*. Louisville: The Courier-Journal, 1972.

Ledford, Cawood. *Heart of Blue*. Lexington, Ky.: Host Communications, 1995.

Ledford, Cawood, as told to Billy Reed. *Hello Everybody: This is Cawood Ledford*. Lexington, Ky.: Host Communications, 1992.

Macy, Kyle, as told to Cawood Ledford. *Macy*. Lexington, Ky.: Lexington Productions, 1980.

McGill, John. *Kentucky Sports*. Lexington, Ky.: Jim Host & Associates, 1978.

Miller, Don. *The Carr Creek Legacy*. New York: Vantage Press, 1995.

Pearce, John Ed. *Days of Darkness: The Feuds of Eastern Kentucky*. Lexington, Ky.: The University Press of Kentucky, 1994.

Pearce, John Ed. *Divide and Dissent*. Lexington, Ky.: The University Press of Kentucky, 1987.

Pitino, Rick, with Dick Weiss. *Full-Court Pressure: A Year in Kentucky Basketball*. New York: Hyperion, 1992.

Pitino, Rick. *Success is a Choice*. New York: Broadway Books, 1997.

Rice, Russell. *Adolph Rupp: Kentucky's Basketball Baron*. Champaign, Ill.: Sagamore Publishing, 1994.

Rice, Russell. *Big Blue Machine*. Tomball, Tex.: Strode Publishers, 1987.

Rupp, Adolph F. *Rupp's Championship Basketball*. New York: Prentice-Hall, 1948.

Smith, Mike. *When Spirit Soared*. Louisville: Concord Publishers, 1994.

Stuart, Jesse. *My World*. Lexington, Ky.: The University Press of Kentucky, 1975.

Stuart, Jesse. *The Thread That Runs So True*. New York: Charles Scribner's Sons, 1949.

Vaught, Jamie. *Crazy About the Cats*. Kuttawa, Ky.: McClanahan Publishing House, 1992.

Vaught, Jamie. *Still Crazy About the Cats*. Kuttawa, Ky.: McClanahan Publishing House, 1996.

Wolff, Alexander, and Armen Keteyian. *Raw Recruits*. New York: Pocket Books, 1991.

Wrobel, Sylvia, and George Grider. *Isaac Shelby: Kentucky's First Governor & Hero Of Three Wars*. Danville, Ky.: Cumberland Press, 1974.

Photography credits

All pictures are courtesy the Lexington Herald-Leader,
except the following:
pages 33 and 258, Kat Fahrer
pages 107,131, 197, 238, Breck Smither
pages x-xi, 145, Kenton County Public Library
page 149, courtesy Donna Cassady

Index

(Boldface indicates photograph)

Adams, Jim 40
Adams, Kyle 212,246,250,279
Addington Mining Company 192
adidas 276
Adkins, Earl 152
Adkins, Keith 137
Adolph Rupp As I Knew Him 55
Alcindor, Lew (Kareem Abdul-Jabbar)
    57
Alice Lloyd College 279
Allen, Phog 86,**87**,92,231
Allen Central High School 149,192,229
Allen County-Scottsville High School
    138
Alumni Gym 78,80,84,114,124,244
American Basketball League 147
Anderson, DeAsia 42
Anderson, Derek 9,17,24,32,36,**38**-47,
    63,65,68-71,113,120,121,161,
    167-177(**173**),184-187,215,220,
    221,232-239,**255**-258,261-264,
    267,**272**-274,282
Anthony, Myron 210
Apollo High School 245,246
Appalachian Mountains 131-134
Arlinghaus, Ted 20
Armstrong, Capt. Dan 30,169
Army 154

Arnold, Roy 114,116
Ashby, Lance 196,197
Ashland, Kentucky 82,139
Ashland High School
    124,125,139,152,242
Atlanta Hawks 62,99
Atlantic Coast Conference (ACC)
    253,254,257,160
Auburn University
    48,52,53,75,170,222,275
Audionet 30

Bailey, Darrell 183
Bailey, Jack 66
Bailey, Rex 61
Baker, Dave 20
Baker, George 245
Baker, Tom 234,235
Ballard High School 143,242
Barbourville, Kentucky 115,222
Barker, Cliff 82
Barnes, Dolly 174
Barnstable, Dale 83-86,88
Barth, Ken 269
Bartow, Gene 105
Basketball Times 30
Baxter, Kentucky 5
Baylor, Elgin 19,52,92,152
Bear Wallow, Kentucky 202
Beard, Butch 39,48,51,54-61

Beard, Ralph 44,45,82-86,88,90,142
Beattyville, Kentucky 27
Beaver Creek 229
Belfry High School 135
Bellarmine College 47
Benham, Kentucky 128,129
Bennett, Winston
    63,66,120,121,156, 160,192,207
Berry, Frank Dudley
    9,30,171,172, 216,235
Berry, Julius **49**,50,53,201
Bethel, Kentucky 31
Betsy Layne High School 155,229
Big Blue Line 21,214,232,237
Big East Conference 109,182
Big Ten Conference
    42,51,57,159,210,256,257
Billups, Chauncey 273
Bird, Jerry 152,155
Bird, Larry 268,281
Birmingham, Kentucky 243
Bishop, Darryl 62
Black Gnat, Kentucky 202
Blackburn, Tom 50
Blackshear, Ronald 276
Bleachers 5
Blevins, J.P.
    156,186,201-214 **(202,210)**,281
Blevins, John Forbes 204,205
Blevins, John Paul 202-208
Blevins, Martha 206-209
Bluegrass Coal Company 153
Bob Gibbons' All-Star Report 30
Boeheim, Jim 67,68,104
Bogar, Tom 279
Boston Celtics
    54,109,180,181,265,267-269,273
Boston Globe 268
Boston University 104
Bourbon County High School 246
Bowie, Sam 6,46,63,282
Bowling Green, Kentucky 21,207
Bowling Green State University 278
Bradds, Gary 56
Bradley, Michael 210,214,268

Bradley University 83
Brand, Elton 195,200
Branham, Terry 180
Bratcher, Bob 169
Breckinridge County High School 56
Breeding, Kentucky 202
Breslin, Jimmy 54
Brewers, Kentucky 126,243
Brooklyn Dodgers 73
Brooks, Delray 158
Brooks, Garth 33
Brown, Dale 184
Brown, Jaron 200,201,214,281
Brown, John Y., Jr. 23
Brown, John Y., Sr. 23,92,146
Brugh, Walter 135
Bruns, Charlie 67
Bryan Station High School 76,200,201
Bryant, Paul ("Bear") 82,83
Buckley, Howard and Margie 174
Burch, Dr. Jeffrey ("Dr. J") 29
Burchett, Carroll 136,155
Burkett, Tony 159
Burton, Darnell 245
Burton, Eric 245
Buser, Martin 67
Butcher, Donnis 152
Butcher, John Lee 155
Butcher Hollow 131
Byers, Walter 91,92
Byrd, Dave 169

CBS-TV 132,178,183,184
Caborn, Dr. David 170,232
Caldwell, Clemens 115,116
Calhoun, Jim **122**,153
Calipari, John 268
Camara, Souleymane 280,282
Campbellsville, Kentucky 61,257
Campbellsville High School 213
Cape Girardeau, Missouri 183
Carbon Glow, Kentucky 142
Carlisle, Ralph 166

Carr Creek, Kentucky 77,**122**-125, 130,136,139,143,144,152-155, 195,241,242,251,252
Casey, Dwane 101,102
Casey, Mike 62
Cassady, Billy Ray **149**-154
Cat Chat 7,9,29,30,171,172,180,183,185, 216,217,234-236,254
Cats' Pause, The 28-30,158,215,217
Cawood, Kentucky 155
Central City, Kentucky 153
Central High School 53
Centre College 116,117,263
Chamberlain, Wilt 52
Chandler, Albert B. ("Happy") 30,73,**80**,146
Chandler, Eck 135
Chapman, Rex 17,61,139,142,203-206 (**205**),222,282
Chapman, Wayne 61
cheerleaders
  high school 160,196,213,229, **240**,241,247,250,**293**
  University of Kentucky (see University of Kentucky)
Cheryl's Restaurant 234
Chicago Stadium 83
Chicago Tribune 125,170
Chicken Bristle, Kentucky 116
Cincinnati Enquirer 6
Cincinnati Reds 154
City College of New York 51,78,83,85
Claiborne, Jerry 29
Clark, Wally 16-**18**,20,31,34,35
Clark County High School 126,247
Clay, Cassius (Muhammad Ali) 53
Clay County High School 130,142,143,242
Clemson University 63-65,159,224
Cleveland Cavaliers 201,273
Cluggish, Marion 155
Coffee Club (The) 114-118, 171, 262,263

Coleman, "King" Kelly 136,139-149 (**141,145**),153-156,229
College of Charleston 69,275,278
Collier, Jason 70,193
Collinsworth, Cris 152
Collinsworth, Lincoln 148,152,155
Combs, Oscar 28,29,158,215
Committee of 101 67,94,179
Conner, Jimmy Dan 282
Converse 279
Co-Operative, Kentucky 142
Corbin, Kentucky 80,100,152,155
Corbin cheerleaders, **293**
Corinth, Kentucky 126
Couch, David 154
Couch, E.A. **122**,152-155,195
Couch, Joey 137,154,195
Couch, Tim 154,156,275
Cousy, Bob 84
Covington, Kentucky 50
Coward, James 247,251
Cox, Johnny 46,50,92,94,136,139,142, 152-154,185,243
Cox, Phil 155
Cox, Wesley 63,121
Cremins, Bobby 102,178
Crigler, John 77
Crittenden, Howie 126,**127**,243,251
Crook, Herb 63
Crosby Middle School 251
Crum, Denny 40,42,120,157,163,167,178,222
Crume, Jeff 29
Crummies, Kentucky 142
Cuba, Kentucky 126,127,130,241,247,251
Cumberland College 155,205
Cumberland High School 128,129
Cumberland Plateau 132,161
Cunningham, Bill 175
Curd, Ed 86,94
Cynthiana, Kentucky 24,112,246

Dakich, Dan 157,226,278
Dampier, Louie 16,46,264

Daniel, Tucker 155
Danville, Kentucky
    114-117, 171,244,262
David, Kentucky 146
Davidson College 275
Davis, Baron 186
Davis, James 140
Davis, Larry 220
Davis, Little Bill 155
Davis, Merlene 270,271
Dawahare's 153
Deford, Frank 60
Delk, Tony 4,35,43,108,252
DeMoisey, Frenchy 185
Detroit News 146
Detroit Pistons 110,136
DeYoung, Dr. Alan 129
Dice, Kentucky 142
Dickey, Frank 49,54,55
Dickman's Sports Café 231
Diddle, Ed 61
Dillard, Godfrey 56
Donovan, Billy 157,185,207,223,269
Donovan, Herman 84,85
Doss High School 40,41,171,244,274
Duke University 22,50,59,103,110,
    106,159,172,195
Dunbar High School 49,50,201,270
Dunbar (P.L.) High School (see Paul
    Laurence Dunbar High School)
Dunn, Jerry 61
Durham, Hugh 223
Dwarf, Kentucky 142

ESPN 30,106,169,181,186,188,260
Earlington High School 126,241
Eastern High School
    213,244,247,250-252
Eastern Kentucky (region) 9,24-26,
    105,125,128-126,132-141,152-155,
    160,161,212,215,226-229,
    242,246,256,275,281,286
Eastern Kentucky University
    147,151,187,201,209,257,278
Edmonson County High School 241

Edmonton, Kentucky 202-209
Edmonton Baptist Church 203
Edwards, Allen
    32,63,64,66,221,224,236
Edwards, Lisa and Virginia 203,204
Eighty Eight, Kentucky 202
Einstein, Albert 115
Elkhorn City, Kentucky 24,135
Elkhorn City High School 226,229,230
Elkins, H.B. 27,29,217
Ellis, LeRon 102
Elsmere, Kentucky 174
Emery Air Freight 101-103,224
Englisis, Nick "The Greek" 86,94
Epps, Anthony
    17,20,32,66,172,**176**,177,220-222,
    236,239,244,**255**,261-263
Erving, Julius 110
Evans, Heshimu 282
Evansville, Indiana 183

Fabulous Five, The 44-46,82-84
Fairfield University 231
Falmouth, Kentucky 18,20,25,219
Fannin, Omar **149**
Farmer, Richie 4,5,**98**,99,105-108(**107**),
    128,130,139,142,143,155,161,
    215,216,225,237,242,244,280,282
Feinstein, John 178,260
Feds Creek High School 226
Feldhaus, Deron 5,105-**107**,237
Felton, George 274
Ferguson, Boo 168
Fiddlin' Five, The 46,52,92,152,154
Fields, Shawn 201,212,230
Finney, Shawn 274
Flat Gap High School 136,155,226
Florence Mall 14,174,175
Florida State University 92,223
Floyd, Darrell 155
Floyd, Doodles 126,251
Floyd County, Kentucky
    134,143,214, 229,230
Flynn, Doug 76
Flynt, Larry 131

Fogler, Eddie 220
Ford, Ken (see Jersey Red)
Franklin County, Kentucky 3
Freedom Hall 25,55,69-71,168,244
Full-Court Pressure 108,120
Fulton, Kentucky 25
Funderburke, Lawrence 101
Furman University 155
Futurestars 30

Gadzuric, Dan 280
Garland, Jann and Sid 193-195
Garmon, David 205
Garrett High School 229
Garrity, Pat 277
Gaskin, Julia 26,27
Georgetown College 246
Georgia Tech 29,76,92,102,
    114,168, 277
Gibson, Mickey 154
Givens, Jack 46,63,142,282
Glaser, Eric 247-250
Glover, Clarence 61
Golden State Warriors 267
Goode, James 128,129
Gossage, Brian 257,258
Grant County, Kentucky 13
Grant County High School 259
Grant High School 50
Graves, David 212,**224**,225,230,277
Graves County High School 247
Greasy, Kentucky 142
Great Alaska Shootout 65-69
Great Mills High School 271
Green, Johnny 50
Green Meadow Country Club 146
Gregory, Kenny 195
Grider, George 115
Grider's Pharmacy 115
Griffith, Darrell 63,121,156
Groza, Alex 82-86,90
Guerin, Richie 148
Gumbel, Bryant 6
Guyton, A.J. 70

Hacker, Ralph 24,25,67,233
Hagan, Cliff
    46,52,76,83,88,91,102,139,
    142-144, 164
Hale, Simeon 20
Hall, Dan 155
Hall, Joe B. 6,46,62,63,79,92,100,
    105,112,113,119,164,165,174,
    191,206,227,245,269
Hamilton, Leonard 269
Hanks, Nancy 21
Hanson, Reggie 105
Hardaway, Anfernee ("Penny") 177
Hardinsburg, Kentucky 58
Harlan, Kentucky 256
Harlan County, Kentucky 5
Harlan Elementary School 256
Harlan High School 46,142,155,256
Harlem Globetrotters 90,126,147
Harrison County, Kentucky 246
Harrison County High School
    200,201,245-247
Hartman, Craig 279
Harvard University 116
Haskins, Clem
    54,61,63,237,254-257, 269
Haskins, Don 60
Haskins, Merion 63,254
Hatton, Vernon 46,50,92,142
Haynes, Marcus 126
Hazard, Kentucky
    20,24,28,61,135,136,192,230
Hazard High School
    136,153,154,214,243
Hazel Green High School 126,243
Hazelrigg, Charlie 116,117
Hazelrigg, Tab 117
Heath, Kentucky 126
Hell For Certain, Kentucky 142
Henderson, Kentucky 73,74
Henderson High School 153
Henry Clay High School 150
Henry County High School 25
Hi Hat, Kentucky 142
Hibbard, Bryce 251

Hickman, Peck 48,49
Higgins, Sean 101
High Point College 271
Highlands High School 247-251,278
high school state tournament (see Sweet
    Sixteen)
Hindman, Kentucky 126,143,153
Hirsch, Walt 83,86,88,89
Hogan, Ryan 210
Holtz, Lou 268
Hometown Pizza 258,259,262
Hopkinsville, Kentucky 20,24,156
Hopkinsville High School 143
Hosket, Bill 56
Houston, Allan 48,63
Houston, Wade 48
Hudson, Wendell 75
Huntington, West Virginia
    183,278,283-285
Hyden, Kentucky 21

Independence High School 200
Indiana high school tournament
    129,242
Indiana University 26,51,64,69,70,
    110,27,157,159,192,193,211,
    215-217,226,275-279,281
Indianapolis, Indiana (see RCA Dome)
Indianapolis Olympians 83,84
Indianapolis Pacers 99,197
Inez, Kentucky 126,130,135,136,
    149-155,226,241
Ipaye, Deen 30
Issel, Dan 25,61,92,142,174,222,282

Jackson, Bobby 257
Jackson, Chris 105
Jackson, Jimmy 41
Jamboree, Kentucky 142
Jamiel, Fast Eddie 109,170
Jaracz, Thad 60
Jefferson County, Kentucky 48,213
Jefferson Street Baptist Church 251
Jenkins, Thomas 229
Jersey Red 109-111,265

Joey C 109
John the Horse 109
Johnny Joe Idaho 109
Johns Creek High School 226
Johnson Central High School
    134-136, 155,200
Johnson County, Kentucky
    134,136,140,152,155,279
Johnson, Ellis 124
Johnson, Larry 62
Jones, Henry 50
Jones, Ken 194
Jones, Marsha 174
Jones, Wallace ("Wah Wah")
    45,46,82,83,139,142,143,155,256
Jordan, Michael 70,221,273
Judd, Ashley 186

Kavanaugh, Rhoda 166
Kavanaugh High School 166
Keightley, Bill 19,44,45,66,165-168
    (166),185,191,196,198,223
Kemp, Shawn 101,102
Kemper, Bill 116,118,262
Kennedy, John F. 16
Kentucky High School Athletic Associa-
    tion 129
Kentucky high school tournament (see
    Sweet Sixteen)
Kentucky Korner 179
Kentucky Wesleyan College 145,147
Kilcullen, Matt 207,278
Kimbro, Tony 121
Kindred, Dave 75
Kingdom Come, Kentucky 152
Kirkland, Raymond 262
Knight, Bobby
    64,69,70,157,158,178,209-211,
    216,275,277,279
Knott County, Kentucky 124,153
Knott County Central High School 130
Kresse, John 278
Kron, Tommy 77
KY Hoops 253

Laettner, Christian 22,106
Lafayette High School 76,176,244
Lancaster, Harry
   55,56,60,74,76,77,84,86,95,154
Larry the Scout 109
Lawrenceburg, Kentucky 166,263
Leach, Michelle 174
Lebanon, Ohio 27
Lebo, Jeff 226
Ledford, Cawood
   5,19,24,26,27,44,57,93,206,222
Lee, James 46,63
LeMaster, Johnnie 194,230
Leslie County, Kentucky 154,156
Lexington, Kentucky 5,7,46,50,53,
   54,59,63,85,109,259,260,262,263
Lexington Catholic High School
   138,139,195,196,200,201,212-214,
   224,225,230,244,245,277
Lexington Center 179
Lexington Herald-Leader
   4,7,24,28,29,52,100-103,108,
   139,156,203,253,268-271, 276
Lewis, Michael 70
Lickert, Billy Ray 50
Licking River 219
Life Magazine 132
Life and Death of a Rural American
   High School, The 129
Lincoln, Abraham 21,30
Line, Jim 83,86,88
Linville, Shelby 88-90(89)
London, Kentucky 66
Lone Jack High School 155
Long Island University 83
Los Angeles Clippers 99
Los Angeles Daily News 101
Los Angeles Lakers 99,267
Louisiana State University
   91,105,108,184,275
Louisville, Kentucky 25,39-42,44,56,
   57,63,113,120,121,161,168,
   213,244,251,274
Louisville Courier-Journal
   60,108,150,203,269,276

Louisville, University of (see University
   of Louisville)
Lovellette, Clyde 87
Loyall, Kentucky 5
Loyola University (Chicago)
   55,56,83, 86
Lucas, Jerry 56,61
Lunsford, Bruce 25
Lynch, Kentucky 128,129
Lynn, Loretta 131

Macklin, Rudy 63
MacLeod, John 226,274-277
Macy, Kyle 4,24,29,46,67,141,
   185,198,203,278,282
Madden, Anita 23
Madison County, Kentucky 28
Madison Square Garden 77,83,85
Madisonville, Kentucky 46
Maggard, Freddie **122**,123,144,153
Magloire, Jamaal
   17,32,64,68,168,169,216,267,282
Magoffin County, Kentucky 131,134
Magoffin County High School 192
Majerus, Rick 236
Male High School 63,241,243
Manchester, Kentucky 107,155
Manhattan College 83
Manual High School 83
Manuel, Eric 101-103
Maravich, Pete 222
Marinatto, John 268
Marion County High School 213,244
Marquette University
   14,60,157,175,193,275
Marrowbone, Kentucky 202
Marshall, Gregg 284
Marshall University 138,275,278,
   283-285
Martin High School 229
Mashburn, Jamal
   105-**107**,120,188,237,257
Masiello, Steve 71,183
Mason County High School 105,244
Massie, Diane 29,259

Matthews, John and Kathy 15,34
Mauer, John 113,123
May, Todd 155
Mayfair Bar 85,86
Mayfield High School 212
Maysville, Kentucky 155,246
Maytown High School 155,226,229
McBrayer, Paul 147
McCarty, Walter 35,43,108
McCray, Scooter 157
McDaniels, Jim 61
McDowell High School 226
McKenzie, Josh 157,212,225,226,
    230,245,248-251,279
McKie, B.J. 220
McMurtrey, Tim 203,207
Mead, Al 117
Meade Memorial High School
    136,152,155,226
Memorial Coliseum 13,17,22,**23**,25,
    31-36**(35)**,49,75,83,91,112,
    126,165,223,**243**,244,270
Mercer, Birdie 187
Mercer, Ron 17,32,36,43-47,63,64,69,
    71,113,168,169,**176**-178,180-188
    (181),215,220,221,235,236,
    252,261-264,267,**272**,273
Meshack, Kentucky 202
Messmer, John 251
Metcalfe County High School
    156,201-205,209,212
Miami (Ohio) University 215
Michigan State University 159,193,244
Mid-American Conference 283
Middle Tennessee State University 163
Middlesboro, Kentucky 155
Middletown, Ohio 88
Midway, Kentucky 126,243
Milan High School 242,251
Miller, Michael 280
Miller, Raymond 117
Miller, Reggie 197,250
Mills, Cameron 47,172,176-178,183,
    184,215,**218**-224,231,232,236-239
    (238),244,257,263,264,267

Mills, Chris 101,102,224
Mills, Collier 231,245
Mills, Terry 222,223
Minardi, Billy 109
Minniefield, Dirk 63,164
Mississippi State University
    15,52-56, 123,169,278
Mitchell, Jim 66
Mohammed, Nazr 17, 25, 64, 65, 68,
    168,169,216,224,261-264,282
Monkey's Eyebrow, Kentucky 116
Monroe County High School 204
Mooresville, Kentucky 20-22,259
Morehead State University
    49,136,151,222,278
Morgan, David 171
Morgan, Oscar 124
Morrissey, Mary Frances Snyder 34
Morton, Dwayne 121
Mullins, Jeff 50
Murray State University 127
My Old Kentucky Home
    30,33,219,237,250,251

Naismith, James 92,93
Nando 30
Nash, Cotton 15,50,53,92,142
Nashville, Tennessee 183,186,187
New Castle, Kentucky 25
New Jersey Nets
    99,108,112,118,267,268
New York Journal-American 54
New York Knicks
    48,99,104,136,147,148
New York Times 119,132
Newport, Kentucky 269
Newport High School 151
Newton, C.M.
    75,77,103,164,169,264,268-271
Nieman Marcus 111
Nike 273
Nonesuch, Kentucky 116
North Carolina State University
    159,193,269
Northern Kentucky 174,231,247,248

Northington, Nat 48
Northwestern University 226,277,278
Norton, Letcher 126
Notre Dame, University of 47,127, 137,
167,192,226,268,274,277,281,283

Oak Hill Academy 229
Oakland Raiders 233
O'Brien, Jim 196,207
Ogden, Rob 246,247
Ohio State University 40-42,51,56,
77,168,193,275,278
Ohio University 56
Oil Springs High School 136,226
Oklahoma State University 105
Olson, Lute 154
O'Neal, Shaquille 105
O'Neil, Bruce 103,104
O'Neill, Kevin 22,157,159,211,277
Orlando Magic 265,267
Osborne, Charlie 136
Osborne, Jason
39-41,49,63,113, 121,168
Oswald, John 55,56
Owensboro, Kentucky 25,46,108
Owensboro High School 138,142

Packer, Billy 178
Padgett, Scott 168,187,232,239,
257,260,263,264,280
Paducah, Kentucky 21,206
Paintsville, Kentucky 9,131-141,
155-161, 191-195, 208, 225, 234,
274,281-286
Paintsville High School 9,44,105,
130-141(131,133),155-161,
191-201,209,212-214,217,224-231,
241-251,283,284
Paintsville Yankees 135
Paris High School 213,246
Parker High School 53
Parks, Jim 185
Parsons, Dickie 77,155
Patillo, Andre 220
Patton, Woodrow Wilson Parker 243

Paul Laurence Dunbar High School
222,231,244,245
Paw Paw, Kentucky 142
Payne, Oliver 117,118
Payne, Tom 49,61-63(62),255
Peekskill High School 200
Pelphrey, Jack 135
Pelphrey, John 105-107,136-139,
154-158,161,193,214,225,237,
280,284
Penn State University 275,278
Perry County Central High School 192
Pettit, Bob 91
Phelps, Digger 178
Phelps High School 150,226,229
Philadelphia 76ers 267
Phillips Oilers 82
Pikeville, Kentucky
24,25,66,146,148,226,227
Pikeville College 152,155,227,279
Pikeville High School 226-229
Pikeville National Bank 227
Pippa Passes, Kentucky 142,279
Pitino, Daniel 108
Pitino, Joanne 99,104,109,185,224
Pitino, Mike 139
Pitino, Rick 4,14-18,25,28-36,42-48,
63-71,96-121(98,107,114),
156-161, 166-188,191-198,
203,207,208,214-216,220-223,
227,228,232-238(233),252,
253,263-265,267-269,271-273,282
Pitino's Bombinos 105,176,252
Pope, Mark 36,43,108,280
Popp, Nathan 196-198
Powers, Gary 30
Pravda 133
Prestonsburg High School
135,192,226,229-231
Prickett, Jared
17,32,64,70,179,182,220,280
Prince, Tayshaun 280,282
Princeton, Kentucky 61
Providence College 104,158,175,176
Puckett, Jason 171

Puckett, Tommy 26,27
Pulaski County High School 105
Purdue University 47,69,127
Pursiful, Larry 155

Quicksand, Kentucky 142

RCA Dome 63,64,254,259,261
Radisson Hotel (Indianapolis) 257
Radisson Hotel (Lexington) 260,261
Ramsey, Frank
    46,52,76,83,88,91,142,144
Rappis, Jill 259
Rardin, Steve 19,20,67
Redd, Mike 54
Reed, Billy 269,272
Reed, Neil 70
Rhodes, Rodrick 120
Rice University 159
Richmond, Kentucky 124
Rickey, Branch 73
Riley, Pat 16,46,56,60,255,282
Riverfront Coliseum 6,177
Roach, Sanford T. 50,270
Roberts, Andy 235
Roberts, Stanley 105
Robertson, Oscar 50,52,148
Robey, Rick 117
Robinson, Jackie 73
Rochester Royals 83
Rodgers, Guy 94
Rogers, Will 125
Rollins, Kenny 82
Rose, Gayle 77
Rose, Jim 61
Roselawn Baptist Church 88
Roselle, David 103
Rosenberg, Mike 254
Rowdy, Kentucky 142
Ruland, Jeff 94
Runyon, Bill Mike 137-140,158,
    191-193,198,209,211,215,
    225,229,245-250,276

Rupp, Adolph 8,16,**23**,25,39,40,48-63,
    72-96(**80,87,93**),105,112-115,
    119-121, 123-126,143,144,147,
    148,152,154,163,166,191,206,
    213,231,237,252,253,263,269-271
Rupp, Herky
    56,**72**,79-82,94, 95,120,271
Rupp Arena 6,13,15,20,23-26,28,
    117,118,**162**,169,174,179,263,282
Rupp's Runts 46,59,79,92,154,252
Rush, Jaron 280
Russell, Bill 52
Russell, Cazzie 59
Ryan, Charity 13-15,26,33,34,258
Ryan, Haley 13,14,33,34,259
Ryan, Jason 13-16,26,31-35(**33**),66,
    171,175,**258**,259,262,264
Ryle, Betty and Jim 15,34

St. Francis College (Indiana) 137,277
St. John's University 52
St. Joseph's University 232,235,238
St. Louis Hawks 54
St. Louis University 88,89
St. Mary's County, Maryland 271
St. Xavier High School 168
Sale, Aggie 166
Salyersville, Kentucky 152,155,159
San Francisco 49ers 233
Sanders, Colonel Harlan 80,92
Schott, Marge 74
Schulkers, Dave 250
Schultz, Danny 155
Scotland, Maryland 271
Scott, Charlie 59
Scottsville, Kentucky 61
Seattle University 19,52,92,152
Selvy, Frank 155
Sendek, Herb 269
Seneca High School 47,48
Seton Hall University 83
Shabazz, Karim 195-200
Shelby County High School 195-197
Sheldon Clark High School
    130,150,226

Shepherd, Bobby 152-155
Sheppard, Jeff 17,32,65,172,174,224
Shively, Bernie 49,88,270
Short, Mike 225,229,279
Shoulderblade, Kentucky 142
Simmons, Oliver 17,47,172,223
Simon, Miles 260,261
Sims, Alvin 213
Sims, Clinton 213,214
Sims, Lazarus 68
Slusher, Bobby 155
Smith, Adrian 46,92
Smith, Dean
    16,81,117,178,231,237,253,254,260
Smith, Derek 248-250
Smith, Dwight 54,61,255
Smith, Greg 54,61
Smith, Guffrie 271
Smith, Orlando ("Tubby")
    41,180,222,**266**,269-282
Somerset, Kentucky 20,222
Southeastern Conference (SEC)
    48-60,80,82,83,91,108,123,
    181,182,219-222,271,284
Sparkman, Ernest 77
Sparks, Chris 212
Spencer, Felton 63
Spivey, Bill 83,**87,91**
Sporting News, The 75
Sports Illustrated 44,51,60,102,104,119
Spragens, Tom 263
Spurrier, Steve 271
Stanford, Kentucky 212
Stanford University 69
Steele, Larry 62
Stephens, Elmore 62
Stepp, Ervin 229
Stewart, Terence 168
Story, Jack 126
Street & Smith 6
Streit, Judge Saul 84,85,87
Stricklin, Amy 140,230,278
Stuart, Jesse 130
Subtle, Kentucky 202
Success Is A Choice 178

Suffridge, Rick 26,29,172,183,254
Sullivan, Claude 206
Summer Shade, Kentucky 202
Sutherland, Jock 164,165,178
Sutton, Eddie 25,102,113,143,164,254
Sutton, Sean 102
Swanagan, Harold 156,200,283
Swartz, John and Mary 31
Sweet Sixteen (Kentucky state high
    school championship)
    8,9,54,126,128,130,137-139,
    142-144,150-153,194,209,214,
    229,231,**240**-252**(243)**,281,282
Syracuse University
    7,65,68,104,198,275

Tackett, Todd 138,156,157,160,
    191-193,196-201**(199)**,208,
    212-214,225,230,231,245-250
    (249),276-281
Tallent, Bob 155
Tarry, McCoy 243
Tatum, Goose 126
Taylor, Charlie 54
Taylor, Jermaine 247,251
Taylor County High School 255
Teater, Oran 140
Temple University 54,91,94
Texas A&M University 159
Texas Western University 59,60,74,80
Thacker, Tom 50,51,53-55
Thomas, Charles 254-256
Thomas, Tim 182-184
Thompson, Billy 144
Ticco, Milt 77
Time 132
Ting, Dr. Arthur 233
Tipton, Jerry 253,254
Tombstone Johnny 20
Tony & Terry's Furniture 159
Travieso, Carmelo 239
Trigg County High School 212
Trivette, John Bill **227**,228
Trivette, Ken 228
Tsioropoulos, Lou 52,76,90,91

Tulloch, David 254
Turner, Wayne 17,32,67,68,221,
    222,232,237,260-262
Turpin, Melvin 6,46,63,101

UCLA 14,57,105,159
U.S. News & World Report 79
USA Today 30,67
Ultimate Hoops 30
Unbelievables, The 252,253,264
Unforgettables, The 22,105-108(**107**),
    118,128,137,203,237,252
Unitas, Johnny 48
University Heights High School 156,200
University of Alabama
    52,57,78,103,164,186
University of Alaska-Anchorage 67,69
University of Arizona 254,259-261
University of Arkansas 159,178
University of Cincinnati
    50,55,153,159,193,207,275
University of Colorado 231
University of Connecticut 64
University of Dayton 50
University of Florida 157,159,179,
    184,185,193,269,271,275,277
University of Georgia 170,179,180,
    222-224, 271,275,279,280
University of Hawaii 103,104,159
University of Illinois 19
University of Iowa 232
University of Kansas 47,48,86,105,154,
    158,193,195,198,211,231,275-277
University of Kentucky
    Appalachian Center 128
    cheerleaders 28,180,237,257
    famous basketball teams (see Fabulous
        Five, Fiddlin' Five, Pitino's
        Bombinos, Rupp's Runts,
        The Unbelievables, The
        Unforgettables, The Untouchables)
    scandals 4,7,24,39,45,52,82-91,
        100-104

University of Louisville 25,28,34,39-42,
    48,49,56,61,63,69,106,111,120,
    121,157,163-169,172,193,224
University of Massachusetts 32,109-111
University of Michigan 59,108,159,275
University of Minnesota 237,253-257
University of Mississippi 75,169,222
University of Montana 231,259
University of North Carolina 28,42,
    108,159,172,186,221,231,237,
    253,254,259
University of North Carolina-Asheville
    168
University of Notre Dame (see Notre
    Dame)
University of Oklahoma 83
University of Pittsburgh 269
University of South Carolina 155,168,
    181,182,219-221,226,234,259,260
University of Southern California 159
University of Tennessee
    25,48,51,57,58,155-159,169,187,
    192,193,207,211,275,277
University of Texas 159
University of Tulsa 180,271
University of Utah 59,236-238
University of Virginia 275
Unseld, George 47,48
Unseld, Westley
    39,40,44,47,48,51,54,56-58
    (**57**),60,120,139,141,143
Untouchables, The
    35,36,43,108,178,231,252,264

Vallandingham, Robert 16
Valley High School **240**,241
Van Breda Kolff, Jan 278
Vanderbilt University 48,51,56,78,
    155,159,173,176,177,186,187,
    275-278,281-284
VanHoose, Alex 248,278,284,285
VanHoose, Beth 194,209,215,217,
    226,228,230,248,278

VanHoose, Bob 137,138,156,
192-194,198,200,211,215,226,
230,277-282,285
VanHoose, J.R. 9,44,130,134,137-140,
155-161,186,**190**-200**(197)**,203,
205,208-217**(210)**,**224**-230,241,
244-251,274-286**(285)**
VanHoose, Tiffany 278
Van Horn, Keith 236
Van Horn, Maynard 263
Van Lear High School 136,226
Villanova University
61,182,183,186,275
Virgie High School 155,244
Virginia Tech 278
Vitale, Dick 71

WHAS Radio 165
WLW Radio 175
WVLK Radio 165,265
Wake Forest University
159,207,215,275
Walker, Antoine
35,43,71,108,109,188,252
Walker, Kenny 6,63
Walker, Solly 52
Wall, Ken 262
Wallace, Grady 155,229
Wallace, John 68
Wallace, Perry 56
Warfield High School 151,226
Warford, Reggie 63
Warren Central High School 204,207
Warren East High School 247
Washburn, Wayne 20-22,259
Washington, Bobby 54,201
Washington Bullets 120
Washington County, Kentucky 21,22
Washington County High School 213
Washington Generals 90
Watson, Melvin 220
Wax, Kentucky 142
Wayland, Kentucky
136,143-148,155, 226,229

Wayne County High School 244,245
Webster, Tim 259
Weekly Progress, The 279
West, Jerry 50,144,148
West Liberty, Kentucky 140
West Virginia University 144-146,278
Western Kentucky (region) 25,40,
62,92,126,142,202-209,242,243
Western Kentucky University 28,48,54,
61,136,187,202,205,207,255,275,278
Wethington, Charles 269,270
Wheat, DeJuan 63,168
Wheelwright High School 226
White, Greg 283,284
White, Junior 136
White, Leon 204
Wiggins, Bob 18-20,66-69,219,257
Will, George 51,95
Willard, Ralph 269
Williams, George 40,41,234
Williams, Paul 284
Williams, Roy
105,158,210,216,275,277
Williamson, Russell 150,151
Williamstown, Kentucky 13,171,258
Wilson, George 54
Winchester, Kentucky 234
Wisdom, Kentucky 202
Wooden, John 57,105
Woodmere Academy 196,199,200
Woods, Sean 105-**107**
Woolridge, Andre 232
Wright State University 167

Yale University 204-206
Yates, Tony 6
Young, W.T. 25

Zimbabwe 73